PLAGUE

ALSO BY MICHAEL BLISS

Canadian History in Documents (1966)
A Living Profit: Studies in the Social History of Canadian Business,
    1883-1911 (1974)
A Canadian Millionaire: The Life and Business Times of Sir Joseph
    Flavelle, Bart., 1858-1939 (1978)
°Confederation: A New Nationality (1981)
The Discovery of Insulin (1982)
Banting: A Biography (1984)
°Years of Change: 1967-1985 (1986)
Northern Enterprise: Five Centuries of Canadian Business (1987)

°for young adults

MICHAEL BLISS

·

PLAGUE

A STORY OF SMALLPOX IN MONTREAL

HarperCollins*PublishersLtd*

First Edition

Canadian Cataloguing in Publication Data

Bliss, Michael, 1941—
Plague

ISBN 0-00-215693-8

1. Smallpox — Québec (Province) — Montréal — History — 19th
century. 2. Plague — Québec (Province) — Montréal — History —
19th century. I. Title.

RC183.55.C3B5 1991   614.5'21'097142809034
C91-094593-4
91 92 93 94 95 AG 5 4 3 2 1

ACKNOWLEDGMENTS

The idea for this book, another study of health and the human condition, came to me after a chance remark, probably about AIDS, by Joe or Valerie Schatzker. In addition to the works cited in the bibliography, my writing was influenced by the concepts of historical re-creation in the novels of Penelope Lively as well as the notion of the "non-fiction novel" popularized by Truman Capote's *In Cold Blood*. Nothing in this book is invented.

Thanks to James and Laura Bliss, Joanne Stiles, Nelson MacPherson, and Laurie Chambers for spot research help, Fernando Montserrat and the staff of the Fraser-Hickson Institute in Montreal, and Glenn Wright at the National Archives of Canada. Thanks to Arthur Silver, Dennis Duffy, and Katherine Ridout for reading earlier versions of the manuscript and giving me many good ideas. The bad ideas are mine.

Thanks to Diane Mew, a Shackleton among editors, for the usual resolute, good-humoured leadership on this our fifth expedition. Special thanks to my wife, Elizabeth, who endured a desk-bound husband chattering about smallpox during those beautiful summers in Leaside.

Michael Bliss

CONTENTS

FOREWORD

Today's Montreal is a sprawling modern metropolis. The city and its suburbs cover the whole of Montreal Island, a 250-square-mile land mass in the St. Lawrence River below its junction with the Ottawa River. Former villages on the south shore of the St. Lawrence have become dense bedroom suburbs, and to the north on Île Jésus the city of Laval is part of Montreal in all but name. There are upwards of three million Montrealers. The city dominates the Canadian province of Quebec.

No amount of paving and building will ever obliterate the dominant features of the city's landscape. Montreal is defined by its river, one of North America's greatest, whose last major stretch of rapids ends just above the old city, and by the 770-foot-high Mount Royal/Mont Réal, an extinct volcano. In the sixteenth century a band of Laurentian Iroquois lived at the mountain's foot in a village they called Hochelaga. In 1642 a party of French missionaries and adventurers established an outpost on that site which they named Ville Marie. It was meant to be a beacon of French and

Christian culture in the New World. The name of the mountain gradually became the name of the settlement.

New France was conquered by Great Britain during the Seven Years' War (1756-63), but the French inhabitants of Canada managed to retain their faith and language and they steadily increased in numbers. Montreal is about 60 per cent French Canadian, and is one of the largest francophone cities outside of France. Until it was surpassed by Toronto in the 1960s, Montreal enjoyed more than a century as the largest and wealthiest city in Canada, guardian of the great St. Lawrence entrance to the heart of the continent. French Canadians have often seen control of Montreal—demographic, political, cultural—as part of their struggle to maintain a distinct identity in the ocean of English-speaking North America. But waves of immigrants, the first beginning with the Conquest, the latest still in progress, have also given the city a cosmopolitan tone throughout its history.

In ways other than language, Montreal is not easily distinguishable from many other large North American cities. It has its share of poverty and late-twentieth century slums, but by older standards the affluence and technological sophistication of the modern city is simply dazzling. Even in its poorest quarters Montreal is a far healthier city than it was in the era before water purification, antibiotics, and the development of other weapons in society's defences against sickness. While this book was being written it happened that Montreal and the province of Quebec did suffer a major epidemic of measles. Lack of vaccination was a major cause of the outbreak; there were three deaths. Some months later whooping cough became a serious problem, again because of lack of immunization. As well, of course, the people of Montreal join the rest of the world in being menaced by a new plague, unknown to the nineteenth century, AIDS.

o   o   o

In the 1880s Montreal and its suburban villages contained upwards of 200,000 people. They clustered on flat land by the river and on streets and avenues that climbed the southern terraces of the mountain. The City of Montreal was bounded by Sherbrooke Street in the north, its port facilities on the river in the south, the industrial town of Hochelaga in the east end and the poor working-class villages of Ste-Cunégonde and St-Henri in the west end just north of the Lachine Canal.

Westmount, which became the heart of English Montreal in the twentieth century, did not yet exist. But almost the whole of Montreal west of St. Lawrence Main (the main north-south street) was an English-speaking city. Since the Conquest, the city's commanding heights had literally been occupied by the English. By the 1850s, after a major influx of Irish immigrants—who tended to cluster in the south-western quarter, on both sides of the Canal—Montreal was about 60 per cent Anglo-Saxon and Celtic. The high birthrate of the French Canadians, combined with a steady influx from rural Quebec, gradually changed the balance. In 1867, the year that the Dominion of Canada was born as a consolidation of the provinces of British North America, Montreal was about equally divided between English- and French-speakers. Francophone Montreal lay east of St. Lawrence. The French were flowing north of Sherbrooke onto the gentle southeastern slopes of the mountain as newcomers transformed the old village of St-Jean Baptiste into a dense, dreary suburb of tenements and humble cottages.

By the 1880s the French had become a clear majority in Montreal: approximately 56 per cent of a population of 167,500 in the city, a much greater majority in most of the suburbs. French voters dominated municipal politics. But commerce, the press, and high culture were still remarkably dominated by the English. To many outsiders it was at least as English a city as it was French. You could live in Montreal for years without speaking a word of French. The language normally used at City Council meetings was English.

The mountain was inescapable, immovable, not yet hidden from most streets. God's temples dominated the man-made landscape. "This is the first time I was ever in a city where you couldn't throw a brick without breaking a church window," Mark Twain quipped during an 1881 visit. The spires reached for heaven from different sanctuaries: most of Montreal's French and Irish were Roman

Catholics while its English adhered to several Protestant denominations. Religion determined the schools the living would attend and the resting places, separate Catholic and Protestant cemeteries behind the mountain, of the dead.

Montreal was an imposing commercial city, its harbour and downtown crammed with fine stone warehouses and offices, its English suburbs adorned by the well-spaced mansions of its merchant princes. By today's standards, though, it was a dirty and smelly place. The city was not well drained. Animals and animal excrement were everywhere. So was human waste. While some streets were paved or cobblestoned, many were still dirt lanes or alleys. Butchers dumped animal offal in vacant lots. Soapworks, tanneries, and factories poured noxious fumes into the air. The river was a convenient receptable for all kinds of trash. Montreal seemed to be an unhealthy city, particularly in summertime, and there was much complaining about the odours that wafted from the harbour and industrial areas and working-class quarters all the way up to the grounds of the grand residences on Dorchester, Sherbrooke, and the higher terraces.

Still, it was an enlightened progressive time, in Montreal as in the rest of North America, Great Britain, and Europe. Throughout the nineteenth century there had been immense material and, it seemed, moral advances towards higher standards of civilization. This was the heyday of Victorian progress. Montreal was the commercial and industrial giant of Canada, its tentacles stretching literally from sea to sea as the Canadian Pacific Railway, Canada's first transcontinental, neared completion. There were nine daily newspapers in Montreal, four in English, five in French. It was the age of the railroad and telegraph, the dawning of the age of telephones and electricity. Universities flourished—Montreal's McGill University was one of Canada's best—in an era of wonderful advances in science, learning, and culture.

If there was a "primitive" or backwards part of Canada, it was surely out on the far western frontier, where aboriginal people were only beginning to give way before the forces of settlement. That transition was not easy. The year 1885 is best known in Canadian history for the half-breed or Métis rebellion in western Canada led by Louis Riel. Canadian troops had to be rushed to the west, several battles were fought, and Riel's fate became a burning national issue.

This book is a non-fictional history of "violent" events raging in Montreal at the same time—a conflagration in the city far worse than the prairie fires of the North-West Rebellion. What happened in Victorian Montreal in the mid-1880s was, in a way, a relic of barbarism more primitive than any of the events on the Western frontier. It was a visitation of plague, and it opens a window on the life of a community caught between tradition and modernity, rent by fear and ignorance, forced to reckon with human frailty and disease. This is an amazing, sad story of life and death and the search for salvation.

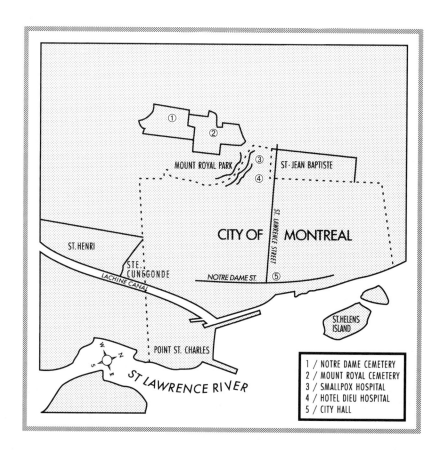

PART I

> Oh, happy posterity, who will not experience such abysmal woe and will look upon our testimony as a fable.
>
> — Petrarch on the Black Death in Florence

CHAPTER 1

THE ICE SEASON

THERE WERE NO FOUL ODOURS. ON *clear winter days the air was as clean and pure as the north country itself. The earth lay under blankets of snow; the river and the canal were ice. Animals hibernated or shivered in stables and sheds; plant and animal matter froze and was still. In their stone houses and brick tenements and wooden cottages, the people of Montreal kept warm by their fires. Pillows of smoke from thousands of chimneys vanished into thin blue air. Puffs of warm breath froze for an instant and disappeared.*

The moon and snow and ice lit a winter's night. Gas flames flickered along black, steep thoroughfares. Primitive electric lights shone in a few offices and homes and at some of the outdoor skating rinks. Strings of Chinese lanterns ran the length of the "glissoires" or toboggan slides on the lower slopes of the mountain. Snowshoers carried torches on tramps and rambles up and around the mountain. Bonfires crackled and their flames danced and warmed. On festive nights—at carnival time or when the Prime Minister came for his seventieth birthday—the sky burned with

Roman candles, shooting stars, aerial bombs, pyrotechnic rockets. Beams from locomotive lamps cut the darkness as trains slid through the city, vanished into the tube of Victoria Bridge, and broke night's curtain on the south shore.

The trains wailed, chugged, clattered, and clanked. Sleighs swished on snow and ice, bells jingling. Toboggans rumbled down the thousand-foot ice slides. Skaters waltzed and twirled to band music, notes drifting into the night. Streets heard bass drumbeats, tinkling tambourines, snatches of Salvation Army hymns. Whinnies of horses, hooves ringing on cobblestones and ice, turds plopping gently to steam and freeze on the snow.

During the week factory whistles and striking clocks called Montrealers to work. On Sundays the bells from a hundred churches called them to sing, chant, murmur the words of worship and prayer. At midnight on December 31, the church bells and the electric fire alarms rang the numbers of the new year, "1 ... 8 ... 8 ... 5."

      ❖   ❖   ❖

Tuesday evening, January 27

The second day of Winter Carnival week. Clear and very cold, about -10 F (-24 C). Streets blaze with torchlight, electricity, bonfires, lanterns. The toboggan slides are crowded. Montreal is packed with American tourists. Crowds throng Dominion Square, the Champ de Mars, and Place d'Armes to see the ice palace, the ice condora, the ice lion.

CARNIVAL ODE

To all a Canadian welcome,
And the grasp of a hearty hand,
Tho' our clime be rude it serves us well
In our hardy Northern land.
Our sons are brave and stalwart
Our daughters blooming and fair

And more than wealth is the glow of health
Which they draw from the wintry air.

There is a grand procession of snowshoers over a tree-lined ice boulevard to St. Helen's Island in front of the city. Torches and fireworks light the island park like a volcano. This event has been organized by the East End carnival committee, working with Le Trappeur Snowshoe Club. In its first two years the Winter Carnival was effectively a festival of English Montreal. Now the French have joined enthusiastically. There is some discouragement tonight when it is observed that hardly anyone joins the procession wearing the *tuque bleue* of the Montreal Snowshoe Club, the city's oldest and largest—and, like most of the other athletic associations, very English.

Warmth and nourishment are taken at the old-time hunter's camp which has been reconstructed on the island, the Johnson Fluid Beef stands in the squares, and Chase & Sanborn's "Standard Java Grotto" in the ice palace. The java receipts will be donated to the Montreal General Hospital. The intense cold is said to be bracing, invigorating, blood-warming. This is Jack Frost's hardy kingdom. Proper carnival dress is a blanket suit for tobogganing, buffalo robes for the sleighs, and other traditionally Canadian furs and skins.

The absent English snowshoers are said to be conserving their energies for tomorrow's massed assault on the ice palace. More likely, many have passed up the St. Helen's fête to attend a special masqued ball at the Victoria Skating Rink. The Victoria Rink is the world's largest enclosed sheet of ice, located just off Dominion Square behind the Windsor Hotel in the heart of English Montreal.

Sharp at nine the band of the Victoria Rifles strikes up "God Save the Queen." His Excellency the Marquis of Lansdowne, Governor General of Canada, unveils a bust of Queen Victoria, flanked by images of a Canadian snowshoer on her right and a fair Canadienne, in snowshoe costume, on her left. The procession of costumed skaters, bathed in coloured light, is led by Father Time. There are angels and tramps, dudes, darkies, and kaffirs, fair maidens, Caesars, Napoleons, and several Miss Canadas. Most are English-speaking Montrealers. "Jockeys, soldiers, drummers, cavaliers, distinguished generals, negro minstrels," the *Gazette*'s reporter notes. "Around the course this kaleidoscopic gathering revolved, imbued with the spirit of Puck, flashing with smiles, glittering with tinsel, grotesque with all manners and shapes of absurdities, charming with varied types of grace and beauty...."

The band played and the revel went whirlingly on. Every so often amid the swirl, and music, and the laughter, there appeared the figure of Death, the grim reaper, carrying his scythe.

o   o   o

Wednesday, January 28

Very cold, windy, heavy snow. Early in the morning on Bleury Street near Lagauchetière, police constable McIntyre comes upon a mother and two children "in a frozen condition." One child is five years old, the other nine months. McIntyre takes them to the station and then to the Protestant House of Refuge.

At the Victoria Rink Lord Lansdowne attends the fancy skating competition for the championship of America. The winner is Louis Rubenstein, a Montrealer, soon to be hailed as North America's "King of the Ice." The day's program includes curling matches and exhibitions of the newest ice sport, hockey. The weather is too severe for His Excellency to visit the toboggan slides. Les Trappeurs are disappointed again, for today is the grand opening of their Glissoire Russe (a slide with several hills) at St-Denis and Sherbrooke in the East End. The East End committee holds a Mardi Gras to open the slide, but the storm keeps people away and observers who do come are not impressed with the masque. The carnival committee announces that the siege of the ice palace will proceed tonight whatever the weather.

At City Hall/Hôtel de Ville, five members of the Health Committee of City Council sit down to discuss human excrement. They are about to let a contract for the removal of Montrealers' "night soil." It has been conservatively estimated that 150,000 people in the city produce an average of forty ounces of faeces per person per day. This amounts to 170 tons every twenty-four hours, 215,350 tons during a year.

Human waste disposal in the city is chaotic and unhealthy. (Animal waste disposal is little better, but in winter is a problem that can wait: Montrealers pile animal manure outside along with much of the rest of their garbage, where it freezes.) Some of the shit is flushed with water in water closets, drains into city sewers, and, if the connections have not rotted or broken (many drains are made of wood) or frozen, empties into the St. Lawrence. Some water closets empty into private cesspools or old privy pits; some of these are drained or emptied from time to time. Other Montrealers use earth closets, sprinkling dirt over their deposits and putting them out for the scavengers (garbage collectors) to collect with the other trash. In the poor areas of the city, most people still defecate into the holes of outdoor privvies. These pits gradually fill up and are emptied or are abandoned. They saturate the soil and often overflow, particularly during heavy spring rains or floods.

The city's medical health officer, Dr. A.-B. Larocque, estimates that there are ten thousand privy pits and cesspools in Montreal. They cause many of the foul odours that blanket the city in warm weather, and are thought to be primary sources of the zymotic diseases—typhoid, scarlet fever, diphtheria—which carry off so many Montrealers and give the city its unhealthy reputation.

Civic-minded Montrealers are determined to improve their city's health in this age of affluence and progress. Winter has given them a break to discuss the issue in the newspapers, at meetings of the Medico-Chirurgical Society, and in the all-important Health Committee. Some sanitary experts believe that water closet/sewer disposal is ideal for a city with the fine natural drainage of Montreal and such a large fast-moving river to wash the excrement away. Others worry about polluting the St. Lawrence, know the city's sewers are a mess right now, and believe it would take decades to install plumbing and water closets in every tenement and cottage. The alternative, drawn from British and American cities with similar problems, is to replace privvies with earth closets and regularly collect the faecal matter.

Once collected, it can no longer be simply dumped. The city's waste disposal habits are already a great aggravation in the suburban east end villages—St-Jean Baptiste, St-Louis du Mile End, and Côteau St-Louis—which have grown up near dump sites that were once farmers' fields. Some European cities lime human excrement and sell it as fertilizer, but Quebec farmers seem to have enough animal manure to meet these needs. The experts concur this year that the best thing to do is burn human waste. Fire does a better job than water or earth in destroying fever-causing toxins and protecting the purity of Montreal's air.

The Health Committee have decided to proceed with an experiment in carbonization. Aldermen Mooney (in the chair), Tansey, Beauchamp, Gray, and Beausoleil open tenders for removal of night soil. Mr. William Mann is the lowest bidder, offering to collect and dispose of it for $2.50 per load or seven cents per cubic foot. For a further $8,000 he will undertake its cremation. The Health Committee decides to support Mann's tenders, and adjourns.

The snow has ended. The air is cold, crisp, and pure. Huge crowds gather in the evening as 2,300 snowshoers, the cream of Montreal's sports-minded young men (well, not many from Les Trappeurs), lay siege to the glittering ice palace in Dominion Square. The attackers are armed with Roman candles. From inside the walls a troop of defenders shoot back. Fire screams across the sky. The resistance falters, King Winter's frozen fortress is surrendered, and the triumphant snowshoers parade by torchlight up the mountain.

Montreal has again proven itself the greatest city in the world for winter sports and spectacles. Lord Lansdowne's vice-regal party returns to Ottawa. Some of the members of Montreal's fire department, who occupied the centre tower of the palace during the siege, nurse serious burns from the fireworks.

The boosters pronounced Carnival a brilliant success. A few critics thought standards had slipped from previous years, and wondered if it was not time to have a year off. With or without Carnival Montrealers would always enjoy their winter sports. These special festivities were designed mainly to attract American visitors and counter the image of Canada as a frozen tomb of a place in winter. Some of Montreal's Roman Catholic clergy thought Carnival and most other forms of winter celebrating were excessively materialistic and hedonistic. Thoughts of young women whirling around on skates, or tumbling wildly down toboggan slides, skirts swirling, ankles and lower limbs flashing, were disturbing to the black-robed mind.

✿   ✿   ✿

Saturday, February 28

Overcast in the morning, sunny in the afternoon. High 33 F (1 C). Montrealers had to watch for falling snow and ice, loosened by the sun. It was a perfect day for snowshoeing; the Emerald Club's races were some of the best ever; new records were set in the two mile open, two mile club, and quarter-mile open.

The Hackman's Union held its annual charity drive. At two o'clock more than one hundred sleighs mustered in Victoria Square to pick up passengers who had bought fifty-cent tickets for a special ride round the mountain. Proceeds to Montreal General and Hôtel-Dieu hospitals, where injured hackmen received free treatment.

An embarrassing incident was narrowly averted at the beginning of the parade when one Mr. Brown, a gentleman who happened to be coloured, got into an empty sleigh. No one else could be persuaded to ride with Brown. The cabman asked him to get out. He refused, showed his ticket and said he had as much right to a ride as anyone. "Well, then I will stay here," said the driver. Just then two young ladies got in the seat in front of Brown, then two young boys sat down with him. The party went off as happily as could be.

Led by the four-in-hand of Messrs. Dumaine and Halpin, undertakers, the procession glided east on St. James Street, along Notre Dame (the city's main east-west business street), up Papineau Road, across on Craig and up St. Lawrence. The sleighs took the toll road behind the mountain, passed the Protestant and Catholic cemeteries, and then came down the Côte des Neiges road through the English city, stopped briefly at the Windsor Hotel, and returned to Victoria Square promptly at five. A splendid winter's outing.

If you talked politics with your hackman during the drive you probably got an earful. On Monday Montrealers would elect a mayor for the next year. Would it be the colourful incumbent, old Jean-Louis Beaudry, who had been in and out of the job since 1862, and was now offering himself for a fifth consecutive term? The one promise Beaudry made every year was that the next term would be his last. Or would the voters replace the old man with the handsome young editor of *La Patrie*, M. Honoré Beaugrand?

It was widely thought that the English would decide the contest. They no longer had the numbers to be certain of electing one of their own as mayor, but if enough of them were fed up with Beaudry's shameless use of patronage and jobbery on behalf of the French faction, they could probably sweep Beaugrand into office. As well as being a friend of all races, Beaugrand was presenting himself as a special friend of sanitary reform. Virtually his only concrete promise was to support the Health Committee in its efforts to clean up Montreal. Old Beaudry, by contrast, had a record of neglecting health issues, begrudging money for public health, and stacking the committee with incompetents. Many Montrealers felt it was time for a change.

The hackmen would likely tell you to vote for Beaudry. They were still angry about their humiliation when the Carnival committee issued a special proclamation warning visitors about extortionate cab fares. Beaugrand, a prominent member of the committee, had signed the insulting document. The Hackman's Union officially endorsed Beaudry for mayor. On the other hand Beaugrand's keen interest in the Carnival and winter sports was winning him much support from Montreal's young men, the boys of winter. More cerebral voters discussed Beaugrand's suitability for such high office so soon in life, and his somewhat checkered past. Was Montreal really ready for a mayor who had publicly proclaimed himself an advanced liberal, and, worse yet, a Freemason?

Another masque was held at the Victoria Rink that night. Dr. Thomas Rodger, one of the city's younger medical men, was not able to attend. Early in the evening he received a telephone call from Bonaventure Station. The Grand Trunk Railway's western train, due from Toronto at nine, had telegraphed ahead that a conductor on one of their Pullman sleeping cars was sick. Rodger, retained by the Grand Trunk as railroad doctor, was asked to meet the train and attend to the sick man.

The train pulled in on time. Dr. Rodger boarded the Pullman and examined the conductor, one George Longley. He was mildly feverish, suffering from chills and a cough. What most worried him were some red eruptions on his hands and face that had appeared two days earlier and were not going away. Longley had recently been stranded in Chicago during a snowstorm. There was known to be smallpox in that city. Could this be his trouble?

Rodger asked Longley to undress. The conductor's arms, legs, and chest were also marked with the red spots. Rodger told the conductor he had smallpox.

It did not seem to be a particularly serious case. Longley was not very ill and did not have very many or very angry papules. But smallpox was highly contagious, and the patient would have to be somehow isolated and cared for. It would be impractical to try to isolate him in the boarding house where he usually stayed on Montreal layovers. Montreal did have a civic smallpox hospital of sorts, but there had been no cases in the city for four years and it was closed. Doctor and patient would have to try the city's regular hospitals. Longley was a Protestant, so Rodger decided to take him to the Montreal General Hospital.

They arrived a few minutes before ten o'clock. The resident physician, Dr. James Gray, confirmed Rodger's diagnosis—and then refused to admit the sick man! The reason was that the governors of the hospital did not authorize the admission of smallpox patients. The disease was too contagious. That was why there was a special smallpox hospital. It was not the General's fault that it was closed.

Rodger persuaded Gray to let Longley stay at the General while Rodger looked for other accommodation. The conductor was placed by himself in an isolated room in the contagious diseases wing. Rodger phoned the company to tell them what had happened, ordered that Longley's Pullman be placed in quarantine, and went looking for somewhere else to place Longley.

William Hales Hingston was at home that Saturday night, probably still pondering the weather. The evening before he had given a talk to the Montreal Natural History Society on the impact of the Canadian climate on health. He knew whereof he spoke, for the fifty-five-year-old Hingston was one of Montreal's most distinguished and scholarly physicians. He had made a special study of the influence of climate and was about to publish a book on the subject. The cool Canadian climate made people healthier than in the United States, Hingston had told his audience. Canadians were also more mentally balanced and less scrofulous than Europeans. About the only climate-induced Canadian disease he had been able to discover, Hingston said, was *mal de raquette*, chronic leg-muscle soreness caused by excessive snowshoeing.

Just before midnight Hingston was roused by knocking at his front door. Young Dr. Rodger stood there asking for help. He had a railroad man who had been exposed to smallpox and seemed to have it, though in a very mild form. Hingston, an Irish-Canadian, was the surgeon to the Roman Catholic hospital, Hôtel-Dieu. Would Hingston authorize this patient's admission to Hôtel-Dieu?

Hingston knew as much as anyone in Montreal about contagious disease and how to handle it. Back in the 1870s he had served as a reforming mayor of the city, dedicated to public health and particularly the eradication of smallpox. He had been a strong champion of creating the special civic smallpox hospital. Now in 1885 he was a little out of touch. Not knowing the smallpox hospital was closed, he advised Rodger to take his patient there. The railroad doctor explained the situation and again begged Hingston to admit the case to Hôtel-Dieu. Poor Longley obviously could not be taken back to the railroad station, to any hotel or lodging house, or to the police station. The doctors could not turn him out on the streets. What was to be done?

Hingston was worried about admitting a smallpox case without notice, but knew that Montreal hospitals had taken smallpox patients in the past when there was no alternative. He knew that whatever the General said, the hospitals were still in law obliged to take such patients. In an acrimonious rehashing of these events a year later, Hingston claimed that he never knew Rodger had tried the General first—where at least there were special quarters for contagious patients—and had left the patient there. Hingston thought the wretched Longley was waiting out in the cold in Rodger's sleigh.

Dr. Hingston agreed to write out an order to admit Longley to Hôtel-Dieu. Rodger picked up his patient at the General (where as soon as they left, Longley's room was disinfected). Doctor and patient presented themselves at the gates of the old Hôtel-Dieu, a multi-winged grey stone building which still stands, at Pine Avenue and St. Urbain Street. Rodger showed Hingston's letter, and the sister hospitaller admitted Longley. Each doctor thought the other was responsible for describing the case to the hospital authorities. The sister was not told that it was probably smallpox.

*   *   *

"Why, sir, you have smallpox!" exclaimed the nun who came to take Longley's name, address, and religion for the register the next morning. Embarrassed at having one of the most loathed diseases known to man, Longley said nothing.

"Why did you not take your disease to the English Hospital?" she added, when she learned he was English and Protestant.

"I went there, but was refused," Longley said.

"Then we are very happy to have you here," the sister said, noticing his embarrassment. "I am glad to say your case is a light one, and you are not likely to be marked."

In truth it was such a mild case that Hingston and Rodger, when they examined Longley that day, thought it might actually be chicken-pox. To be safe, they did warn the sisters to keep the patient isolated—no easy job in a building bursting with patients and with no special isolation rooms. Both Rodger and Hingston saw the patient from time to time, but no one quite sorted out who was responsible for Longley. Each doctor thought the other was in charge.

Dr. Rodger did know his responsibility to the City of Montreal and to the Grand Trunk Railway. After seeing Longley for a second time on Monday, March 2, he went to City Hall to the Health Department's offices and reported the case of smallpox to

I.C. Radford, the sanitary inspector. Rodger borrowed the city's disinfecting apparatus, hired an assistant, and went out to the Grand Trunk yard in Point St. Charles. The contaminated Pullman stood alone at the far end of the yard by the river. Roger boarded it and set up the brazier-like disinfecting stand. He lit coal in it, which ignited pieces of sulphur whose fumes gradually saturated the car. The process would take at least twenty-four hours. The assistant was left to stand guard.

On Tuesday, March 3, Rodger again boarded the Pullman. He decided that simple fumigation was not enough. "I gathered together the sheets, pillow cases, cushions, blankets, carpets, mattresses, curtains, in fact everything which, according to my judgment, had been exposed to contagion. I carried the whole into the yard, and made a heap of it. I then sent my assistant for two gallons of coal oil, which he poured over the effects; then we set fire to it." Rodger tended the dancing flames.

In houses where you mind to make your dwelling,
That neere the same there be no evill sents
Of puddle-waters, or of excrements,
Let aire be cleere and light, and free from faults,
That come of secret passages and vaults.

Though all ill savours do not breed infection,
Yet sure infection commeth most by smelling.

— Mediaeval poem

CHAPTER 2

THE DREAD DISEASE

HONORÉ BEAUGRAND, THE thirty-six-year-old reform candidate for mayor of Montreal, had seen more of the world than most of his countrymen. Born in a small town near Montreal, apparently destined to become a priest, he left the novitiate at age fifteen, took rudimentary military training in Montreal, then left Canada and went adventuring.

At age seventeen Beaugrand was a sergeant of the "contre-guérillas" fighting in Mexico in the service of the French emperor Napoleon III and his puppet, the Archduke Maximilian. Wounded and taken prisoner in that campaign, Beaugrand drifted to France, where he worked as a journalist, housepainter, bookkeeper, longshoreman, signpainter, and violinist. In the 1870s he was a Franco-American, editing newspapers in Fall River, St. Louis, and Boston. Some were English journals, most were French, aimed at the many thousands of French Canadians who had emigrated to the United States from thickly populated rural Quebec. In 1878 Beaugrand published a novel about French-Canadian emigrants, *Jeanne la fileuse.*

15

Beaugrand married an Anglo-Protestant. He cut more of his cultural roots as he drifted away from the Catholic Church and in politics adopted republican beliefs that to conservative Canadians were distinctly radical. For a time he changed his name to "Honorius Champagne." When Beaugrand settled back in Montreal his political opponents described him as "déraciné" and a "wandering jew."

To his more doctrinaire enemies Beaugrand was positively menacing. The extremely conservative wing of the Roman Catholic Church in Quebec was profoundly opposed to everyone who advocated the ideas unleashed in the world by the French Revolution of 1789. "Ultramontane" Catholics (Catholics "in the Italian style," loyal to the Church beyond the mountains, rather than the more liberal Catholicism of France) distrusted ideas of liberty, tolerance, the separation of church and state, and progress. They had turned their backs on the nineteenth century, lashing out against liberals, republicans, revolutionaries, Protestants, secularism, progress, and all the other works of Satan. They championed the authority of the Church, papal infallibility, social stability, and the European social order that had been destroyed in 1789 and afterwards. The flag of Bourbon France flew proudly over the offices of Montreal's ultramontane daily newspaper, *L'Etendard*.

Ultramontanes were a powerful force in Quebec Conservative politics, where they energetically combated anyone supporting liberal ideas or the Liberal party. Honoré Beaugrand and the newspaper he founded in Montreal in 1879, *La Patrie*, did both. *La Patrie* tended to be irreverently, sometimes brilliantly liberal in the stuffy world of French-Canadian political journalism. Beaugrand's voltairean columnist, Louis Fréchette, loved to poke fun at the vanities and superstitions of the extreme clerics, mocking the odour of sanctity they gave off as they prayed for miracles to cure their constipation. You struck the cruellest blows at Quebec's beavering "Castors," as the ultramontanes were nicknamed, by laughing at them.

To Senator F.-X. Trudel, editor of *L'Etendard*, and to conservative ultramontanes of his ilk, Honoré Beaugrand was a man of shocking irreverence, lack of principle, and unbelief. Here was a candidate for mayor who seemed to believe in the same anti-clerical liberal fanaticism that had brought revolution, anarchy, and rivers of blood to France and now in the nineteenth century was warring everywhere against the Holy Catholic Church and its servants. Why, Beaugrand was even a Freemason, a member of the dreaded secret society that ultramontanes believed had spawned anti-Catholicism in the French Revolution. Had not Beaugrand confessed his apostasy in his own words? Day after day before the election *L'Etendard* reprinted an angry editorial Beaugrand had written in an American paper seven years before stating that he was not only a Freemason but a "franc-maçon très avancé," not only a liberal but a "libèral très avancé," and to boot a believer in the principles of the French Revolution and the Declaration of the Rights of Man. Could this happen in Christian, civilized Montreal, ultramontanes asked: the election of "Honoré Champagne," an unbeliever, a Freemason, a liberal, a man who would probably hoist the red flag of anarchy over City Hall?

English-speaking Montrealers knew that Beaugrand was young, handsome, civic-spirited—a good worker for the Carnival—and an eloquent and perfectly bilingual orator. Who cared about the abstract philosophical quarrels of long-winded journalists and priests? This was municipal politics. Beaugrand said he believed in better drains and sewers for Montreal. He said he would be a mayor of all the people who would serve all nationalities and religious groups without fear or favour. He would be honest and hard-working and save the city from what his campaign manager, an anglophone merchant, called "the thraldom of Beaudryism." The boys of winter worked hard to elect one of their own.

On election day, March 2, Beaudry carried the heavily French wards in the East End, St-Jacques and Ste-Marie, but by less than his usual majorities. Beaugrand swept English Montreal and won the election by 3,322 votes to 2,923, inaugurating what everyone hoped would be an age of reform and progress at City Hall. Supporters brandished brand new brooms at the victory celebration. Opponents faded away. Only one stubborn Beaudryite spoke his mind. Alderman Hormidas Jeannotte from Ste-Marie ward, a leading Castor and staunch supporter of the old regime, announced that he would resign rather than serve under Beaugrand.

Beaugrand delivered his inaugural address to City Council on March 9. He told the aldermen he was not interested in the theoretical debates of ultramontanes and conservatives. Fights about great European social questions, he proclaimed, were "largely the work of utopian or over-excited intellects" and had no reason for existing on the banks of the St. Lawrence. "This year ... the great question of the day is that of the public health."

Beaugrand's speech was mostly about the sanitary condition of the city. He was going to serve in the tradition of Montreal's last health-conscious mayor, Dr. Hingston, he said, who had worked so hard in the 1870s to clean up the city, but whose achievements seemed to have been undone by successors such as Beaudry. The city's high death rate had hardly changed since Hingston's day, and it was time for action. "Montreal, by its geographical and topographical situation, by its splendid position on the banks of the St. Lawrence, and its high elevation above that noble river's banks, ought to be one of the healthiest cities on the continent of America.... Our streets can never be too clean nor our public health too well protected.... I promise you that all my efforts will tend towards making the work connected with the health office more and more effective."

The inaugural reception at City Hall that night dazzled those Montrealers who fought their way through blinding snow to attend. It was a gathering of youth and beauty, laughter and music, the advent of a new era of brightness, good humour, and grace in the sombre civic chambers. The torch was being passed, change was in the air. The new broom of reform and public health.

o   o   o

Alderman Mooney was the first to be swept aside. As chairman of City Council's Health Committee, J.H. Mooney was a genial Irishman without any special aptitude or vigour, a kind of fossil from the Beaudry years. The problem was how to get rid of him. Despite the reform rhetoric of the mayoralty campaign, the personnel of City Council had barely changed in the election. Even Alderman Jeannotte reconsidered his decision to resign. Most aldermen had little desire to upset the status quo. Beaugrand had neither a loyal following nor more than his own vote at Council. Mooney told his fellow aldermen that he wanted to stay on as chairman of the Health Committee and they agreed to defer to his seniority.

But the city's English newspapers learned of the backroom deal and condemned it, demanding change. Amidst rumours that dissident aldermen would challenge his reappointment, Mooney told the first meeting of Council that English sentiment, as voiced in the press, had persuaded him to resign. He supported as his successor Henry Gray, a forty-seven-year-old English Catholic dispensing chemist (pharmacist) serving his second term on Council. Everyone knew that Gray was the best-qualified health man on Council—"the right man in the right place" according to the *Witness*. On Mooney's withdrawal, Gray was unanimously elected chairman of the Health Committee. With Beaugrand's active support, Gray set out to reorganize the Health Department and prepare Montreal to face the disease everyone worried about that spring—the dreaded cholera.

∗ ∗ ∗

The spectre of cholera haunted nineteenth-century cities. In 1817 cholera had broken out of its home on the Indian subcontinent and begun to move along global shipping routes. In 1831-32 Europe and North America suffered their first major "visitations." The disease reappeared every few years, exacting a horrible toll.

When the cholera struck a community, nightmarish events occurred. Apparently normal and healthy people would start vomiting and defecating uncontrollably, sometimes at work or in the street. Putrid liquids poured from bodies racked by spasms and cramps. Dehydration caused eyes to sink into their sockets, skin to wrinkle and wizen, the voice to become low and husky. The body turned black and blue as capillaries ruptured. For more than half the victims death came in one or two days, sometimes in only a few hours. Sometimes bodies spurted poisons, aged, withered, and died, seemingly in minutes, the way they do in horror movies today. Not since the bubonic plague itself, which had disappeared from

Christendom centuries ago, had there been a disease whose imma-
nence—whose very name—inspired such terror. It was always "the
dreaded cholera."

Cholera came to North America from Europe on immigrant
ships. Communities along the St. Lawrence–Great Lakes waterway
suffered major cholera epidemics in 1832, 1834, 1849, 1851, and
1854. The disease usually appeared at the first port of entry, Quebec
City, then moved with the newcomers up the river to Montreal and
on to the Lake Ontario towns before dissipating in the interior.
American cholera epidemics usually began in New York and other
Atlantic ports, but sometimes the disease crossed the border along
north-south routes.

Statistics from the cholera epidemics are fragmentary and unreliable; the death toll was probably exaggerated. The year 1832 saw
the worst epidemic everywhere. In Montreal that year there were
about two thousand cholera deaths in twenty-two weeks, an astonishingly high 6 per cent of a population of about 32,000. It was said
that bodies went unburied for days in the city that summer. In the
1854 epidemic Montreal's population of about 75,000 suffered 1,200
cholera deaths. The port city of Saint John, New Brunswick, saw
1,500 souls taken by cholera that year, almost 5 per cent of its population. This is the equivalent of a modern city of 100,000 losing
5,000 people to a single disease in a few months. The memory and
fear of cholera epidemics lasted for decades.

◦   ◦   ◦

Doctors could not treat cholera effectively. The only way to fight the
disease was to prevent people from getting it. The trouble was that
except for clergymen who preached that cholera was God's punishment of sinners, no one knew its exact cause. Yes, the way it was
introduced from the immigrant ships showed that humans somehow
carried and transmitted the cholera. So it was contagious and one
way to fight it was to isolate its victims. From the beginning ports
tried to quarantine cholera ships. The chief Laurentian quarantine
station was Grosse Isle, just below Quebec City.

Quarantine did not seem to work very well. Cholera would sometimes break out among people who had not been anywhere near a sick person. Somehow the poison became part of the environment, ready to strike at random. Perhaps it flew into the air from the victims, or was exuded from their bodies, their excrement, even their clothes. Perhaps it was exuded in a kind of miasma—a cloud of poisonous gas which might contain the seedlings or "germs" of the disease. Maybe you could smell cholera. Certainly you could smell a lot of bad things in the air that were cast off as organic matter putrified or fermented. Perhaps the cholera and other diseases multiplied through such pollution; perhaps the poison could be generated everywhere in a town where there was decay, stagnation, rotting, stench.

Cholera epidemics sparked an important nineteenth-century debate on the causes of infectious disease. Contagionists said humans spread the germs. Miasmatists said the particles permeated the air as miasma. Miasmatists had everyone's sense of smell on their side. The identification of bad odour with disease was deeply imbedded in folk wisdom and in our animal instinct for sensing danger. As with chlorine or other poisonous gases, the miasmatists thought that sensing the foul smell meant you were inhaling the toxin of the disease. Odours could kill.

Contagionists and miasmatists could agree on the need to keep clean. Cleanliness helped prevent both contagion and the formation of mephitic vapours. Sick people's soiled and dirty clothing should be shunned. So should the air that was polluted by their breath, their excrement, or any other bad smell around them. In fact all bad smells should be avoided and, if possible, destroyed.

Foul water was another source of sickness, people realized, particularly after the studies of certain English doctors, notably John Snow, who in 1854 traced a series of cholera deaths to a single polluted source of drinking water. Montrealers' concern about the safety of their water in that cholera year led to a major effort to supply the city with fresh water, piped from the river above the city's effluvia.

Fear of cholera was the most important factor in the development of nineteenth-century sanitary regulations in North America. The prospect of a visitation caused governments to establish their first boards of health and confer on them the power to begin cleaning up communities. Their work was usually too little, too late, and too transitory. In time, and with increasing standards of living and expectations, sanitary reforms became more substantial. When cholera again threatened in 1865-66, for example, Montreal sanitarians were able to overcome the opposition of young mayor Beaudry and obtain the appointment of the city's first paid health officers.

Cholera did not come again after all, but the health officials found much else to do. Montreal was plagued with other infectious diseases—including diphtheria, typhoid fever, scarlet fever, and measles—and there was more than enough dirt and stench around the city to spark enthusiasm for better sanitation. It was a major challenge just to find out the truth about Montreal's health. How many died? Who died? Of what cause? In what part of town? Where were the unsafe places? What caused unhealthy conditions? What could be done about them?

What powers should health officers have? There would have to be sanitary inspectors, certainly. Should they inspect private homes? Should they have the right to inspect goods sold in public markets? What powers of enforcement would the sanitary police, as they came to be called, exercise? Could anyone force merchants, homeowners, a whole city, to be clean?

City Council repeatedly debated the powers and composition of its Health Committee, and the amount of money Montreal should spend on cleanliness. The 1870s saw rising concern about public health across North America and Europe. English-speaking Montreal, led by a distinguished medical community centring on McGill University, wanted to be in the forefront of progress towards healthier urban living. Dr. Hingston's mayoralty from 1875 to 1877 was an early high point in public health crusading. Beaudry, his quasi-permanent successor, seemed more interested in saving public money than expanding Hingston's good works. As early as 1878 the editor of the *Canada Medical Record* urged Beaudry's defeat on health grounds: "It is utterly impossible to compute the grave injury he has done to our city. We care not to estimate the valuable lives which have been sacrificed for the want of an active Sanitary Board, the non-existence of which is largely due to him...."

The health office survived budget cuts, reorganizations of its supervising body, and waves of official indifference. Even reactionary civic administrations never totally abandoned public health, for everyone wanted a livable, better Montreal. And gradually the city became healthier—not always because of the work of the Health Department, but because of improvements in the water supply, drains and sewers, the paving of streets, and, perhaps most important, the decision in the 1870s to make the heights of Mount Royal a splendid public park. Slow progress. Better than none.

Many Montrealers' expectations outran the effects of a few paved streets and parks. Why was the city's death rate so high, well above 30 per thousand per annum, in an age when most North American and European cities were in the 20s or lower? Why was there so much infectious disease in Montreal, claiming a fearful harvest of poor little boys and girls every year? "Le massacre des innocents," Dr. Larocque called it. Why did smallpox, which plagued many big cities during the early 1870s, linger endemically in Montreal through the whole decade, striking down innocent children by the hundreds? What was wrong with Montreal? Was it the climate or some other peculiarity of the city or its people? Or were the deaths caused by apathy, ignorance, and neglect? By politicians? Stingy taxpayers? The masses? The rich and powerful?

The climate hardly seemed at fault. Montreal did not have any particularly unhealthy or miasmic winds, such as those blowing fever out of swamps in tropical climes. Perhaps the heat and humidity of Canadian summers weakened people somewhat, especially the fragile young, predisposing them to infection. The winter cold, on the other hand, seemed to be bracing and exhilarating, making this a healthy city for people with respiratory problems, such as consumptives. Dr. Hingston's trail-breaking studies in climate and health certainly did not show Montreal at a disadvantage. Add to the salubrious Canadian air the fact that Montreal was a sloping, well-drained city on the shores a rushing river, and it did not seem that the community had any natural reasons for being unhealthy.

Hingston and every other expert on Montreal's health believed that French Canadians' remarkably high birthrate—a natural or unnatural phenomenon depending on your point of view—distorted the statistics. Babies were always the weakest, most vulnerable of the species. Montreal had huge numbers of them, including many newborns brought in from outside to be cared for by nuns in the city's convents. Infant mortality skewed all the death tables. Break the raw statistics down in certain ways relating to nationality and age and maybe the Canadian metropolis was not that bad. For all people beyond age ten, for Protestants, for those of English or Irish nationality, Montreal was as healthy as Boston or Philadelphia, almost as healthy as upstart Toronto.

The one certainty was that all of the numbers were unreliable. Nobody knew how many infants there were in Montreal, for example, because neither Canada nor Quebec required registration of births.° Death statistics were taken from cemetery returns. In one of their early victories, the Montreal health officials helped bring in a rule that interment could not take place without a medical certificate showing cause of death. No one believed that these certificates, which did not require medical verification, were very accurate. It was not clear how many of the newborn or newly deceased were real Montrealers: the living poured into the city looking for work; some of their corpses were taken out, for burial in the old parish. No one knew how many Montrealers there were except in decennial census years.

Newcomers to the city carried their diseases with them. Immigrants had brought the cholera (and probably had supplied most of its victims). Primitive boards of health had been powerless to stop the movement of germs and the infected across the invisible lines of municipal borders. Increasingly in the 1870s and 1880s the health authorities in Montreal blamed their city's problems on other people's poor health and poor sanitation. The neighbouring suburban villages did next to nothing about water supplies, drainage, and

---

° Civic authorities relied on church baptismal records. These were apparently well kept and reliable for the Roman Catholic Church (which for that reason argued that civil registration was unnecessary), but were difficult to assemble. The returns from Protestant denominations, where infant baptism was not uniform, were fragmentary. As well, in an age before legalized abortion, it was not uncommon for civic authorities to find dead babies in the river, in parks, back alleys, and on doorsteps.

garbage. The Quebec countryside seemed to be feeding the city with an endless stream of poor, not-very-healthy rural people with large families. Pestilence was not a parochial problem.

The Montreal sanitarians, led by Dr. Alphonse-Barnabé Larocque, the city's first and continuing health officer, tried to encourage provincial and national initiatives in public health. Somebody should improve the keeping of vital statistics. Some government should require all municipalities to create boards of health. Some politicians should pay as much attention to the problems of human health as federal and provincial departments of agriculture did to animal disease.

Nobody knew if any levels of government above the municipalities were responsible for public health. It was not a function of government that the Fathers of Confederation had thought important enough to list in their division of powers between Ottawa and the provincial governments. Medical men and sanitarians lobbied all governments indiscriminately. Politicians waffled carefully, not sure whether they wanted to get involved. The government of Canada certainly was responsible for the quarantining of immigrants, and also began tentative initiatives in the area of vital statistics. The provinces seemed to be responsible for most other areas of public health, certainly for the actions of their municipalities. In 1881 Ontario led the way in Canada by creating a permanent provincial board of health.

Montrealers hoped that Quebec City would soon follow suit for their province. In their lobbying they could justly argue that Quebec's largest city was a national leader in many areas of public health work. Progress was starting to show. By 1881, for example, smallpox had been driven out of Montreal, leading to a sharp drop in the death rate. Despite the city's ongoing problems, many of its physicians were wholeheartedly behind the great nineteenth-century gospel of sanitation. The English had led the way in the 1870s, but now French-Canadian sanitarians had their own Société d'Hygiène de la Province de Québec, with its new (1884) *Journal d'Hygiène Populaire.*

But now in this winter of 1885, as the *Witness* put it, "the gaunt spectre of cholera is on its westward march." Cholera was raging in

Egypt and other Mediterranean countries, killing tens of thousands, alarming the whole civilized world. Enjoy the Carnival, the *Journal d'Hygiène* urged its readers in January, the celebration before the trial, because cholera was already lurking, "comme un ours [bear] dans un tronc d'arbre." As soon as the ice left the St. Lawrence, ships would come up to Quebec and Montreal bringing immigrants. Would they bring the scourge with them, causing another ghastly epidemic? In his inaugural address Honoré Beaugrand referred to the "dreaded cholera" as the main reason for his desire to rejuvenate the Health Committee. As the new chairman, Henry Gray, readied the Health Department for the spring clean-up of Montreal, the insidious menace of cholera posed the overwhelming question.

❖   ❖   ❖

One of the more astonishing developments of the age had just occurred in the fight against cholera. In February 1884 the famous German doctor and researcher, Robert Koch, announced that he had discovered the exact nature of cholera germs. With their increasingly powerful microscopes, scientists could at last see the little micro-organisms or microbes that many had thought might cause disease. Louis Pasteur in France and Koch in Germany were racing to correlate the presence and absence of tiny organic rods, known as bacteria, with the symptoms of various diseases. In 1877 they identified the bacillus that caused anthrax. In 1882 Koch announced his discovery of the tubercule bacillus, the cause of consumption. Later Pasteur worked on the bubonic plague bacillus. Now Koch could see and isolate the source of cholera, a minute organism shaped like a comma: he named the cholera bacillus *vibrio comma.*

Montrealers could see it too. At the Natural History Society early in April, Dr. J.B. McConnell gave a learned lecture on the history of epidemics and the prospects of a new assault on Montreal. And then, one of the wonders of the age, he actually exhibited specimens of *vibrio comma* taken from a German cholera sufferer. He set up a microscope that enlarged them eight hundred times. Practically the whole audience, the largest of the season, lined up to see "the nasty little animal that causes so much trouble."

There it was, and the observers were in on the dawning of the golden age of bacteriology, one of the landmark eras in the struggle against disease. But what could you do about these damned things? Koch's discovery did not yet involve new methods of attacking the bugs. As in the past, it was vital to stop the nasty little animals from getting a foothold, as it were, in Montreal. More delegations were on their way that spring to Ottawa and Quebec City urging national and provincial action on health issues. The quarantine station at Grosse Isle would be the frontline in the struggle to keep cholera from Canada. If it broke through, it might still be possible to forestall an epidemic by denying the bacillus a medium, such as bad water or decaying faecal matter, in which to grow and multiply. Individuals were urged to strengthen themselves to resist cholera by adopting temperate personal habits (the *Journal d'Hygiène* counselled abstinence from "des *cock-tail*, des *hot-scotch* et autre douceurs alcooliques"). And everyone agreed that Montreal should gird itself for anti-cholera warfare by cleaning up.

At the first meeting of the new Health Committee, on March 17, Henry Gray spelled out the department's plans. The annual post-winter, post-breakup cleansing of the city would be particularly thorough. Last year's committee had already let new contracts for scavenging (garbage-collecting). The scavengers, who had started on March 1, seemed to be doing well—though their real test would not come until the snow and ice were gone at the end of April or the beginning of May. William Mann had the contract for collecting night soil and was erecting his incinerator. The contract for the removal of dead animals from city streets—a major problem in nineteenth-century cities—would soon be let. New staff would be hired in the summer to handle citizen complaints about unsanitary conditions. Improved plumbing and drains would be a high priority.

The committee would take a stronger stand this year against bad food and water. Ice cut from polluted areas of the harbour and canal would not be allowed to find its way into ice houses (some of the bad ice had been used in the Condora at Carnival; it had not sparkled the way ice palaces should). Sanitary Inspector Radford and his squad of sanitary police would stop the sale of rotten fruit in the markets and try to enforce the law against butchers' selling diseased meat. The Grand Trunk Railway would be written to about the unfit hogs it shipped into the city.

But there would be was no easy way to stop Montreal's butchers from driving cattle through city streets, slaughtering them at their private abattoirs—often a fancy word for a shed or stable in the backyard—selling uninspected meat, and dumping their offal on some vacant lot. For six years the Health Committee and Council had been trying to require butchers to do all their slaughtering at designated public abattoirs. The issue had become unbelievably tangled in a thicket of public versus private interests. Henry Gray promised to cut through the matter and bring the butchers to heel.

Honoré Beaugrand attended a meeting of the Health Committee a few days later to offer visible support for the work. It was the first time in six years that the mayor of Montreal had appeared at the Health Committee. He came because reformers were determined to get results, and everyone was anxious about cholera.

❉   ❉   ❉

The smallpox patient, George Longley, had a comfortable stay in Hôtel-Dieu. He never became very sick and developed only a few repulsive pustules on his face and hands. Drs. Hingston and Rodger looked in on him from time to time, as did a house physician. No one had to do very much for Longley in the way of treatment. He might only have chicken-pox, they still speculated. But of course if it was smallpox, you couldn't be too careful, so normal precautions were taken. Longley's room was well-separated from the wards, it was kept thoroughly ventilated, apparently to prevent the formation of miasmic exudations, and a special servant and sister attended the sick man. No one vulnerable to smallpox was allowed into the room. One day Rodger found Longley writing a letter to his sister and forbade him to send it because of the danger of passing on the infection. The hospital probably did not follow Dr. Rodger's extreme methods with the Pullman linen. Longley's bedclothes were cleaned, not burned.

In some respects it was important not to go too far with fright about smallpox. Dr. Hingston thought it wise, for example, to advise the staff not to talk too freely about smallpox being in the hospital, lest the story cause undue alarm.

Dr. Larocque at the Health Department knew about Longley in Hôtel-Dieu. Within a day or two, Larocque learned about a second case of smallpox in the city when Dr. W.A. Molson (a relative of the brewing Molsons) came in to report that another Pullman conductor, recently arrived on the Grand Trunk from Chicago, had smallpox. One H. Shattuck had not felt well for several days before arriving in the city on February 25. On the 27th he broke out in a rash. Two weeks earlier, on a trip to Chicago, Shattuck had sat near a woman passenger; later he learned she had smallpox.* Now he had it. Longley probably got his smallpox from Shattuck.

Shattuck was confined to his home on Mayor Street. Larocque thought it would be better to admit him to Hôtel-Dieu, but the sister hospitaller firmly refused. One case in the hospital was danger and trouble enough. It would be up to the Health Department to keep Shattuck and his household quarantined from contact with the outside world. Larocque sent a sanitary policeman to stand guard at the house. Then Dr. Molson insisted that the department also supply a nurse, a washerwoman, and disinfectants for the stricken home.

The quarantine failed. Two young ladies got out of Shattuck's house before it was sealed off. Both came down with smallpox. One took sick in the village of St. Andrews, Quebec. She had good medical care, was securely isolated, convalesced, and recovered without infecting anyone else. The other girl lived on St. Catherine Street West in Montreal. Dr. Molson had kept an eye on her and as soon as she took sick he insisted that she be moved back to Shattuck's house. Larocque thoroughly disinfected her own quarters.

---

* The woman who infected Shattuck was reported to have caught the disease in Europe while on her honeymoon. She took sick in her Pullman at Syracuse on her way back to Chicago. Her car was fumigated in Chicago, but three people who worked in it later came down with the disease, causing a small outbreak of smallpox in Boston that spring. There was no smallpox in Chicago. Eventually all the upholstery in the car was burned, and the vehicle was repainted, revarnished, refitted, and rechristened.

The two patients on Mayor Street were well looked after and enjoyed a comfortable convalescence. When they had recovered, the house was thoroughly cleaned and disinfected. On March 21, George Longley was released from Hôtel-Dieu, somewhat surprised at being asked to pay for his care at the astonishingly high rate of $2.50 a day. The normal rate for private patients was $1.00. The sisters were perhaps charging for the extra costs of isolation, perhaps getting a little extra out of the Grand Trunk Railway Company of Canada, perhaps a little of both. Longley later said he found Hôtel-Dieu "a poor place for pleasure but middling good for relaxation." It seemed that the little spark of smallpox in the city had been stamped out.

* * *

Pélagie Robichaud was an Acadian girl who worked as a servant at Hôtel-Dieu. She had no contact with George Longley. On March 23, two days after Longley left the hospital, Pélagie took sick with smallpox. The fever came upon her while she was working on one of the wards. She was immediately isolated in a small room off the corridor leading to the hospital's mortuary chapel. No one could understand how she had contracted a disease of which she was known to be terrified. The sisters wondered if her fear of smallpox had not led her to make a point of questioning the servant who did go into Longley's room. Or she may have handled some of Longley's bed linens. Somehow the spark had jumped.

The hospital reported the Robichaud case to Larocque at City Hall. He came and examined Pélagie, told the sisters that the Health Department would have a great deal of trouble opening the civic smallpox hospital because it did not have any staff on hand, and advised Hôtel-Dieu to carry on with isolation and ready use of disinfectants.

Pélagie Robichaud died of smallpox on April 1. This was the first death. It was not reported in the newspapers. In Quebec City that day a large delegation of mayors and sanitarians from several Quebec cities urged the government to create a provincial board of health as part of the preparations for the war against cholera.

Pélagie's body was quickly removed from the hospital, put into a double coffin, and taken away for burial. Her room was disinfected, the nurses bathed and changed their clothes, and life went on. Pélagie's sister, Marie, who had been kept away from the girl since she had first become feverish—and who certainly would not have been allowed to see the body, which was highly contagious—was grief-stricken. Her own health became suspect. On April 6 she developed a violent fever. On April 7 it was realized that she also had the smallpox. Marie's was a case of haemorrhagic smallpox, the "black pox" or, as the French Canadians called it "la picotte noir." The worst kind.

The frightened staff of Hôtel-Dieu urged Larocque to reopen the smallpox hospital. The Health Committee met that afternoon and authorized action. Larocque hired some of the convalescents from Hôtel-Dieu to make ready the old hospital. It was the old Hill house, a stone farmhouse that stood in an orchard above Fletcher's Field, a wooded area on the lower slope of the mountain just behind the main hospital. Marie Robichaud was taken there immediately. By Thursday, April 9, Larocque's staff had the smallpox hospital officially ready to receive patients. Marie Robichaud died there on April 11.

       ❂   ❂   ❂

On March 23, the day Pélagie Robichaud took sick, word reached Montreal of an outbreak of violence in the Canadian North-West. The first reports were sketchy—somebody had cut the telegraph lines out there—but it soon became evident that Louis Riel was leading another rebellion.

Fifteen years earlier in the Red River country west of Lake Superior, the French-speaking half-breeds or métis, the offspring of fur trader liaisons with native women, had taken up arms to negotiate better terms with the expanding Dominion of Canada. Their leader was their best-educated, most articulate young man, a sometime candidate for the priesthood, Louis Riel. Riel's provisional government succeeded in 1870 in making a deal with Canada. The Red River colony entered Confederation as a new province, Manitoba, in which there was protection for the special schools and language usages of French Catholics. Louis Riel became a heroic leader to many of his followers, the founding father of Manitoba. To many other Canadians he was a trouble-maker and rebel, who had used excessive force during the uprising. Riel fled the country, a price on his head for murder. He eventually received an amnesty, but by then was an embittered exile in the United States.

Now Riel was back and seemed to be doing it again. No one in the east knew much about the situation in the Saskatchewan district of the North-West Territories, several hundred miles west of Manitoba, where many of the métis had resettled in recent years. It appeared that Riel and his supporters had taken up arms against the Canadian government and were urging the plains Indians to join them. It would probably not amount to much. "The rising of a few hundreds of half-breeds and Indians does not seem a very serious matter here," the *Gazette*'s Ottawa correspondent wrote on the 25th, but strong measures would certainly have to be taken. "Riel is a nuisance that ought to be supressed."

Then word came of real fighting, a battle on March 26 at Duck Lake in the Saskatchewan country between Riel's forces and a group of North-West Mounted Police reinforced by local volunteers. The rebels drove the Mounties away, killing twelve policemen and civilians. Some of the western forts were being evacuated, some communities were cut off and at the mercy of hostile Indians. Bloody rebellion threatened to engulf the whole of Canada's great plains.

Sir John A. Macdonald's government determined to bring massive force against the rebels. Ottawa ordered the mobilization of regiments of volunteer militia across Canada. The eastern units would travel to the prairies on the new Canadian Pacific Railway, the transcontinental line that, fortunately, was nearly finished. There were a few short gaps north of Lake Superior; otherwise a ribbon of steel connected eastern Canada with its western empire.

The CPR was Montreal's transcontinental railway, the creation of a syndicate of the city's merchant princes backed by the Bank of Montreal and the Dominion government. But most Montrealers probably knew less about the North-West than they did about the landscape of the Sudan in Africa, which had been in the news because some four hundred voyageurs, mostly French Canadians and Mohawk Indians from reservations near Montreal, had helped transport British troops up the Nile in an attempt to relieve General Gordon in Khartoum. Within forty-eight hours Montreal was full of experts on the situation on the Saskatchewan frontier, "Riel" was on everyone's lips, soldiers mustered and marched, and war fever was in the streets.

Groups gathered outside newspaper offices for the latest poster-bulletins. Crowds packed the streets in front of the armouries as militiamen gathered to see if they would be called to fight. All the regiments began sharpening their parade skills. It was the largely French-Canadian 65th Regiment, Les Carabiniers Mont-Royal (Mount Royal Rifles to the English) that was called to active duty and would leave for the front as soon as possible. Crowds followed the disappointed Victoria Rifles as they paraded to City Hall to salute their Canadien brothers-in-arms. Bands played "Vive La Canadienne," "The British Grenadiers," "La Marseillaise," and "Rule Britannia." The people cheered. Mayor Beaugrand exhorted everyone to submerge race or nationality in the common cause. On the 29th, Palm Sunday, Protestants and Catholics alike prayed for the well-being of the soldiers and an early end to the violence. The national anthem, "God Save the Queen," was sung as a hymn.

Huge crowds offered deafening cheers on Thursday, April 2 when 250 men of the 65th marched to the station to the strains of "The Girl I Left behind Me." Their commanding officers, Lieutenant-Colonels Ouimet and Hughes, had several times addressed the men on the need to be a credit to their uniform and their country. Needy families at home would be looked after by a special Citizens Fund, organized by the mayor. Donald Smith and George Stephen, the two wealthy merchants heading the CPR syndicate, had already pledged donations of $5,000 each. No one in Montreal seriously quarrelled with the view that armed rebellion in the North-West had to be suppressed; hardly anyone objected to the calling out of French-Canadian soldiers, even though they might have to fight men who spoke their language and had common racial ancestors. A few sympathizers with Riel's cause were said to be holding meetings in Montreal, but even they agreed that the government was acting constitutionally. The men of the 65th got on their way just in time, as one of the worst spring snowstorms in memory paralysed the city over Easter weekend.

*　*　*

Wednesday, April 8

The city is buried in snow and ice and slush. It has already spent $16,000 on snow removal this winter and may have to spend $16,000 more. Council is considering charging people who fail to clear their sidewalks. A distinguished lawyer has fallen on the ice and broken his leg. The Recorder, French Montreal's equivalent of a police magistrate, fines James Enright and Joseph Julian $5 or fifteen days in jail for throwing snowballs. The Salvation Army marches through the slush as though the streets are clear. The drummers and preachers are pelted with snowballs. Habitant farmers are carting loads of hay into the city before the ice bridges go out. Flooding is likely.

In the North-West last week Cree Indians from Big Bear's band massacred nine innocent people, including two priests, at Frog Lake. The armed forces of Canada are still trekking west, sometimes literally as they march through snow-covered wilderness in 20-degree below weather across the gaps in the CPR line. By the time the men of the Mount Royal Rifles reach Winnipeg a fair number of them suffer from exposure and snow-blindness; others have come down with diarrhoea. "What Is This Disease That Is Coming Upon Us?" asks the column-head back home in the Montreal papers, day after day. The answer is dyspepsia, and it can be invariably cured by Seigal's Curative Syrup. Indistinguishable from a news report, the Seigal column is just the usual paid puffery. Patent medicine purveyors are newspapers' most ubiquitous advertisers.

Most of Montreal's nine dailies devote an inch or two to reporting yesterday's meeting of the Health Committee. The English papers (*Gazette, Star, Witness, Herald*), which are thicker and more prosperous than the French (*La Minerve, Le Monde, La Presse, La*

Patrie, L'Etendard), have the most detailed reports on municipal politics and other local matters. They do not report the decision to reopen the civic smallpox hospital because the Health Committee excluded reporters while the subject was being discussed. Nobody let it be known that there had been cases of smallpox in Montreal. Chairman Gray did go out of his way to stress the importance of the decision to appoint new public vaccinators. Listeners might have thought Gray had smallpox on his mind as he worried aloud about the need to protect the city from an epidemic. Only "by God's mercy" had Montreal escaped the smallpox outbreak that had recently beset nearby Hastings County in Ontario, Gray claimed. The city might not go scathless much longer, he warned.

Perhaps suspecting something, a sharp-eyed reporter for the *Witness* studies the weekly death returns from Côte des Neiges Cemetery. Two deaths are listed as being due to "variole." The journalist calls on Henry Gray, who readily admits that smallpox has come to Montreal from Chicago. The disease has been "completely stamped out" in the case of the one Grand Trunk conductor, Gray says, and the contagion from the other is now limited to one case in the civic hospital. As a precaution, Dr. Larocque is vaccinating all the patients in the Hôtel-Dieu.

Gray does not know that Larocque is too late. Smallpox has broken into the wards of Hôtel-Dieu. Before the day is over two new cases will be diagnosed. There are more to come.

* * *

The *Witness*'s little news item about smallpox was picked up by some of next morning's papers, but was not of great interest. Warnings about the need to prepare for cholera got much more attention. Montrealers felt no alarm about smallpox. War news, the weather, politics ... the usual topics of conversation. Why was Canada's House of Commons sitting day and night in Ottawa to argue about a franchise bill? What about the clause in the bill giving some women the vote? Surely it would never survive. Was juvenile crime increasing in Montreal? Why were the scavengers doing such a bad job of cleaning the streets and lanes? Would his ultramontane enemies succeed in unseating Mayor Beaugrand? Apparently a few years ago he had become an American citizen! Why was the mayor spending money from the Citizens' Fund on champagne and cigars for the officers of a regiment passing through Montreal from Halifax? Honoré "Champagne" again?

At Hôtel-Dieu two more cases of smallpox appeared on the 10th. Aside from shipping the victims to the smallpox hospital, what could be done? Should the sisters isolate everyone who had had close contact with the victims and who might now be carrying the disease? The trouble was that Hôtel-Dieu was overflowing with some 240 patients, its nursing and servant staff, and a steady stream of visitors. On Saturday the 11th, with still more cases breaking out, the hospital finally set aside a small ward in which to isolate suspected sufferers. It was too late. More cases appeared every day.

Smallpox was loose in the hospital and could not be contained. The medical staff advised the Sister Superior that it would be necessary to cleanse the whole building. All patients who were not too sick to move and who did not seem infected with smallpox would have to go home. On April 14 Hôtel-Dieu began discharging four-fifths of its patients.

On April 15 a case was reported outside the hospital, a servant girl in a convent who had been a patient. The health officers admitted that they feared an epidemic. Another case in a home on St. Catherine Street. A patient in the General who had been transferred from Hôtel-Dieu. Send them all to the smallpox hospital and disinfect furiously. By April 18 the old Hill house in Fletcher's Field had sixteen inmates. On that day the nearly-empty Hôtel-Dieu sent over the last of its smallpox sufferers. The Health Department kept reporters informed of developments and of their unhappiness with the negligence of Hôtel-Dieu in letting the disease get started. Little notes of alarm sounded in some of the accounts in the English newspapers.

On the 18th Dr. Hingston responded to the *Gazette*'s inquiries with a lengthy defence of his and Hôtel-Dieu's procedures in the Longley case and since. The staff did not appreciate criticism of this great and beneficent institution, he wrote. Nor was Hingston happy with press coverage generally. "It may be questioned whether drawing constant attention to the unwelcome visitor is productive of the good which is no doubt intended." In any case, the hospital was being completely purged of the contamination and there need be no future worries about Hôtel-Dieu. "If the disease again occurs," Hingston wrote, "it will be brought from without."

He was right, in the worst kind of way. This was a terrible, disastrous mistake. In sending home so many patients, some of whom were in the incubation stage of smallpox, Hôtel-Dieu guaranteed that the disease would now stalk the streets of Montreal. On April 18, the day of Hingston's comments, the day that Hôtel-Dieu declared itself smallpox-free, Henry Gray told the Health Committee that there was "a serious epidemic of smallpox in the city."

And Behold a pale horse, and he that sat upon him his name
was Death.

— *Revelation, 6:8*

CHAPTER 3

TWO WARS

Smallpox epidemics could be stopped in their tracks by 1885. The disease was one of the most loathsome, contagious, and lethal scourges menacing humanity. But it was also one of the most containable, thanks mainly to the discovery of vaccination.

Victims of smallpox suffered from what was later identified as a viral infection. Most of the orthopox viruses, such as camelpox, horsepox, cowpox, raccoonpox, and monkeypox, are confined to the lower animals. Thousands of years ago one of the strains of the virus managed to cross species, as the AIDS virus has in our time, and adapted itself as a parasite on the human body. Viruses are the most minute specks of living matter, nothing but bits of genetic material with an outer casing. When they get into the right kind of host cell they are able to reprogram it to replicate themselves. The viruses multiply and spread in the infected organism until they either destroy it or are destroyed by its immuno-defence system.

Victims had no inkling that they had been invaded. The smallpox virus usually entered the body through the mouth or nose and began quietly to incubate and multiply. After ten to fourteen days, millions of infected cells in the lymphatic and reticuloendothelial systems were literally bursting with viruses, showering them into the blood stream and around the body. These triggered the first symptoms: chills, fever, headache, backache, vomiting, sometimes convulsion and delirium. In another three to five days, as the virus attacked the epidermis, the skin began to erupt in red spots.

A sixth-century bishop gave the disease its Latin name, *variola*, from *varus*, a pimple, or *varius*, spotted. In English the word "pox" descends from a family of northern European words—pocks, pocce, pokke, pocque—which refer to swelling or containers (like the pockets in clothes). In French "la variole" was also known as "la poquote," and eventually in French Canada "la picote" or "picotte," a word that may also have been derived from "pic," for smarting or stinging. After syphilis appeared in the Europe in the early sixteenth century it became common to distinguish between the larger marks or "great pocks" its rash made on patients and the "small pocks" of *variola*.

Smallpox was also called "the red death" and was the disease most associated with images of fire. Even in a relatively mild case the skin turned hot and red, sometimes bright scarlet, and began to blister as the spots became pimples and then fluid-filled pustules like boils. The worse the attack, the more scorched the body appeared as the red spots ran together and became confluent. In malign cases the skin seemed burned and in places scorched to a purplish blackness. Sometimes the whole body began to haemorrhage, as collapsing tissues leaked blood internally and externally. Hardly anyone survived this fulminating or "black pox," with death coming within five days of the onset of symptoms. The deeper the fire burned—eruptions could appear on the tongue, mouth, larynx, stomach, even the rectum—the more likely the sufferer was to die. But victims who were spotted with the most repugnant pus-filled boils might only be suffering from a relatively benign, superficial attack—unless, as often happened before antisepsis, the suppurating boils became soaked with bacteria, causing major secondary infections.

Mirrors were not allowed in smallpox hospitals. Almost all patients became hideous. The pocks were usually most dense on the face and hands. As they burst or bled, the pustules gave off one of the most disgusting odours associated with any disease—sweet, sickly, and nauseating—so foul that the only adjective most physicians could find to describe it was "unforgettable." The masque of smallpox was a reeking, suppurating, swollen mass of seared flesh. "The patient presents a terrible picture, unequalled in any other disease; one which fully justifies the horror and fright with which smallpox is associated in the public mind," William Osler wrote of confluent smallpox in his classic medical text, *The Principles and Practice of Medicine*. Osler had extensive experience with smallpox. While teaching at McGill during the mid-1870s he had worked in the old smallpox ward of the Montreal General, and had published several studies of aspects of the disease.

By the eleventh or twelfth day, the pustules had burst or softened, forming crusts and scabs. During convalescence these gradually wore away, survivors regained strength, and by the end of three weeks were able to go on with their lives. Some, whose corneas had erupted in pocks, were blind. Most, not all, were marked by the stigmata of smallpox for life, bearing scores of pock-marks from the virus's destruction of the sebaceous glands, which are particularly numerous on the face.

Once the victim was infected, doctors were unable to stop smallpox from taking its course. Before the nineteenth century they had often helped it along, deliberately bleeding or purging patients to try to get the seeds or germs out of the system. Heat and astringent substances were applied as counter-irritants. Folk healers and physicians alike turned to the sympathetic magic of flames, cloaking sufferers and their chambers in scarlet, bathing them in red light, none of which did any harm. By the latter half of the nineteenth century the well-trained healer simply kept the patients as comfortable as possible, applying ice and cool-packs, giving as much nourishment as could be tolerated. Eggnogs loaded with whiskey offered a kind of relief, for example.

There was nothing else to do but try to stop the disease from spreading. Smallpox patients literally poisoned their surroundings with their germs. They were a menace from just before the onset of the rash to the disappearance of the last crusts some three weeks

41

later. An invisible halo of contagion, a kind of smallpox miasma, enveloped them as they exhaled and coughed virus-soaked droplets. They dripped virus-laden pus that impregnated their clothes and linen. Dried scabs that crumbled into dust by their beds teemed with active virus.

Anyone in the same room with a smallpox patient, even for a few minutes, might come into contact with the virus. You might carry it away on your clothes, send it down to the washerwomen, give it to a loved one in a letter. You could catch it or spread it from handling the corpse of a victim. Anyone who strayed near the flames or the embers could be burned; anyone could carry sparks to new tinder. The corpses of smallpox victims were thought to be particularly contagious, throwing off clouds of the poison as they decayed. Well into the nineteenth century many physicians and common folk assumed that the smallpox germs, like those of cholera and other zymotic or "fermenting" diseases, could nest and grow in filth, maybe even be generated during putrefaction, and then be carried in foul-smelling, miasmic air. Many thought that certain climatic conditions might predispose individuals to be vulnerable to the invasion—as dry wood is to fire.

So smallpox did more than its share to make history a sad tale of sickness and suffering and death. Smallpox had stricken pharaohs of Egypt (the marks are thought to be on the mummy of Ramses v) a thousand years before the birth of Christ, and it was incubating in the body of Abraham Lincoln the day he gave his Gettysburg address (he took sick that night with a mild case which left few marks; he infected his valet, who died). Smallpox was probably the plague that devastated Athens during the Peloponnesian wars, and smallpox laid waste Montgomery's American army that besieged Quebec in the winter of 1775-76, thus helping save Canada for the British Empire.

The disease burned on every continent, but nowhere more brightly than in a New World whose native peoples were helpless fodder for the virus. The "Indian plague" was the white man's hidden helper in the conquest of the Aztecs, the Incas, and the rest of the Americas, slaying Amerindians by the millions, fire after fire, clearing the land. Some soldiers apparently tried to spread smallpox among natives by giving them infected blankets. Picture, too, the Jesuit priests of New France in the 1630s going from one Huron lodge to another, sprinkling their holy water on the dying sick. The virus travelled in their black robes. Baptism, infection, and death, thanks to the white sorcerers. Indians sometimes drowned themselves in lakes and rivers trying to escape "the burning fever."

Like fire, the smallpox could die out. Unless frozen, the virus could not live for more than a few days outside a human body. The sparks might not reappear in a population for years, decades, centuries. Smallpox did not seem to plague Israel during biblical times, for example. Unless Job's "sore boils" were smallpox, the disease is not mentioned in the Bible.

The more densely people lived together and the more they multiplied, the more likely the virus could find fuel and survive. At the end of the Middle Ages in Europe smallpox began to replace the bubonic plague as the most dread harvester of souls. It burned endemically throughout the continent, particularly in its great cities, often marched with kings' armies, sometimes raged in devastating pandemics. "From love and smallpox but few remain free" ran the German proverb. Palaces were no haven, as British queens, Hapsburg emperors, Russian czars, and everyone's little princes and princesses were taken or scarred. "My liege, thou shalt have the pox," Queen Elizabeth I's German physician told her as she shivered with fever in October 1562. "Have away the knave out of my sight," she ordered—only to become delirious and near death within hours. Her knavish doctor was recalled, presided over her treatment (which included wrapping the virgin queen in scarlet cloth) and was handsomely rewarded when she survived with hardly any facial scars.

England's next reigning queen, Mary II, wife of William of Orange, was killed by smallpox in 1694. In 1774 Louis XV of France caught smallpox at Versailles, and fourteen medical attendants could do nothing for him. The king was in a state of "living putrescence," an historian has written, when death ended his suffering. He was buried immediately, without ceremony, in a double-lead coffin, his body covered with lime, vinegar, spices, and wine. It was said that one of the workers who helped put the body in the royal crypt died of vomiting—or worse—caused by the stench. Smallpox took as many as sixty million lives in the eighteenth century. The English historian T.B. Macaulay called it "the most terrible of ministers of death."

o   o   o

The new king of France in 1774, twenty-nine-year-old Louis XVI, was deliberately infected—inoculated—with smallpox by his physicians. He suffered a very mild bout of the disease and was not troubled by it again. He died prematurely, but of other causes.

The practice of inoculation, which became popular in Europe during the eighteenth century, was the first important step forward in the amelioration of the scourge. It was based on the age-old observation that survivors of a dose of the pox were usually never troubled by it again. In much of Europe it was evident that most people would sooner or later be afflicted (thus a pock-marked woman was not always unattractive as a marriage partner; she would not be carried off in the next visitation). If you could not hide from the flames or pray them away, perhaps the safest course in the long run was to expose yourself to them and through exposure become fireproof. We now know that antibodies formed in reaction to the original infection confer the long-term immunity.

Peasants in many countries had learned to expose their children and themselves to mild cases of smallpox in the hope of contracting a gentle case from a "kindly pock" and then being safe. "Buying the pox" it was sometimes called, for you could literally buy patients' scabs and then rub your body with them or put them in your nostrils. Physicians began to gather information on ways of transmitting smallpox; needles and lancets worked best to convey "virus" (the word was first coined to refer to poisonous matter) from subject to subject. During a London epidemic in 1721 Lady Mary Wortley Montagu, wife of the British ambassador to Turkey, ordered her daughter's "ingrafting" with smallpox, according to the Turkish custom. Others were experimenting with similar techniques. The British government supported organized experiments on prisoners and orphans. When these succeeded, aristocrats and physicians enthusiastically supported the idea of inoculation or variolation (inoculation with variola) to stave off serious cases of smallpox. Across the Atlantic in Boston, Massachusetts, the Reverend Cotton Mather also convinced physicians to begin inoculating in 1721. One of his sources for the idea was an African slave.

The inoculator simply scratched the skin with a needle that had been rubbed in crusts or dipped into a vesicle on the arm of someone with a mild case. A pustule would form at the site of the inoculation. After nine days there would be a mild fever, then a mild rash on the body, with few other pustules and little or no marking. Variolation worked, most of the time, because the virus multiplied just under the surface of the skin, rather than in the circulatory system or internal organs. Antibodies were created while the invasion was still fairly localized. The best infections were epidermal, those closest to the surface of the skin. (Inoculators who tried to make a medical art out of deep scarification, cutting well into the tissue or opening blood vessels to make sure the germs "took" and/or to justify high fees, caused the most serious cases, sometimes killing the patient.) Good inoculators bragged about never losing a case. The death rate from the operation was seldom more than 1 per cent. Without such defences, smallpox normally killed 15 to 25 per cent of its victims. So inoculation was positively a lesser evil.

The preventive operation spread rapidly through England and its American colonies and most European countries. Some conservative critics were horrified at the thought of deliberately infecting a healthy person with the seeds of a dread disease. A frightening prospect, particularly if your city or region was smallpox-free. Why take a 1 per cent risk when there might be no risk at all? Why take the real and serious risk of causing a generalized outbreak of smallpox as a result of introducing it by inoculation? Inoculated people were contagious. The most benign case could set off a major conflagration. The inoculator as arsonist. There were intense, sometimes violent arguments about the efficacy and desirability of inoculation, a foretaste of worse disputes to come. Historians still disagree about the impact of inoculation in reducing the death rate from smallpox. Later experiments in inoculation against plague and syphilis were fatal disasters.

Bourbon France lagged behind England and most continental countries in accepting inoculation. *Ancien régime* physicians, centred in the Paris Faculté de Médecine, offered a host of medical, social, and theological objections to this daring, almost Promethean, approach to conquering a disease. It was left to the radical *philosophes*, children of Enlightenment ideas about many things, to popularize this English preventative. Voltaire, for example, urged his countrymen to inoculate "for the sake of staying alive and keeping their women beautiful." When inoculation first came to Paris in the 1750s, women celebrated by wearing *bonnets à l'inoculation*—their ribbons were dotted with pock-spots. When Louis XVI was inoculated, the queen's milliner was said to have invented a hairstyle, *pouf à l'inoculation*, to commemorate the occasion. The Bourbons were the last European royal family to begin being inoculated. For at least the well-to-do it had become common procedure. By 1800 their faces were starting to become free from the ash-marks of smallpox. As the upper classes became immune, a pitted face was ugly and sad.

◦　◦　◦

Some women seemed immune from smallpox without inoculation. Milkmaids in certain rural areas of England occasionally caught a disease from the udders of the cows they handled—it was often called cowpox—that caused a few pustules on their hands and then went away. Girls who had cowpox never seemed to get smallpox. Whether the immunity was noticed because of their attractive complexions, their resistance to variolation, or as a result of peasant gossip, can never be determined. It is not known, either, who first had the idea of trying to protect a person from smallpox by inoculating them with cowpox.

It is known that Edward Jenner, a forty-seven-year-old physician in the village of Berkeley, Gloucestershire, who was inclined to scholarly activities (his paper on the "Natural History of the Cuckoo" won him election to the Royal Society) decided in 1796 to inoculate James Phipps with cowpox taken from the hand of Sara Nelmes, a milkmaid. After the boy had reacted positively to cowpox, Jenner tested his resistance to smallpox by inoculating him with its germs. There was no reaction. "I shall now pursue my Experiments with redoubled ardor," Jenner wrote. In 1798, after more experiments, he published a pamphlet, *An Inquiry into the Causes and Effects of Variolae Vaccinae, a Disease, Discovered in some of the Western Counties of England, particularly Gloucestershire, and known by the Name of Cow Pox,* which became a landmark in the history of the betterment of the human condition.

Jenner named cowpox *variolae vaccinae,* smallpox of the cow. If inoculating with smallpox was to variolate, then inoculating with cowpox was to vaccinate. Vaccination worked, worked wonderfully (virtually no mortality, no risk at all of causing a smallpox outbreak), and was immediately put into practice by Jenner and other enthusiasts. By 1801 Jenner claimed that one hundred thousand vaccinations had been carried out in England alone. The method had already spread to most of Europe and to North America, where in that year President Thomas Jefferson vaccinated his family and neighbours. "Yours is the comfortable reflection that Mankind can never forget that you have lived," Jefferson wrote Jenner. "Future generations will know by history only that the loathsome smallpox has existed, and by you had been extirpated." The first child vaccinated in Russia, an orphan, was renamed "Vaccinoff" and given a state pension by order of the royal family. In 1798 John Clinch, a clergyman in Trinity, Newfoundland, received vaccine from Jenner, with whom he had studied. When Clinch could not persuade anyone to volunteer, he vaccinated a reluctant teenage nephew and put the unhappy boy in the same bed with one of the worst cases of smallpox in the community. When nothing happened, everyone was amazed and wanted to be vaccinated.

Within two decades of Jenner's discovery millions had been vaccinated around the world. Governments in the German states and Scandinavia were beginning to pass laws making vaccination compulsory. A Spanish expedition of "vaccine conquistadores" had taken the discovery to Latin America to help undo the ravages brought by their ancestors. During an epidemic in Rome in 1814 the pope endorsed vaccination as "a precious discovery which ought to be a new motive for human gratitude to Omnipotence." Gratitude to Dr. Jenner for one of the greatest discoveries in history was nearly universal, though not quite as rewarding as he had hoped. Parliament only granted him

£30,000, and he was never knighted. In 1807 the Five Nations of the Iroquois Confederacy sent him a fulsome address ("We shall not fail to teach our children to speak the name of Jenner and to thank the Great Spirit for the bestowing upon him so much wisdom and so much benevolence") as well as a string of wampum.

Smallpox was virtually extinguished wherever there was massive vaccination. Variolation/inoculation fell into disuse and was eventually outlawed, mainly because of the risk of spreading the disease.

Then a strange and fearful irony developed. As raging epidemics became a thing of the past—that is as vaccination worked—there seemed to be less urgency to be vaccinated. Resistance to the operation, which had always been present to harass vaccinators, became stronger. Some of the opposition was simple conservatism, inertia, or apathy. Some, such as the fear that vaccination would lead to "minotaurization"—the development of cattle-like features in humans—was rooted in nervous ignorance. The most serious opposition was based on concern about side-effects. In rare cases the cowpox induced by vaccination could be fatal. More commonly, bacterial contamination of vaccine or vaccinators' equipment could lead to serious infections.

Vaccinationists insisted that the operation, properly carried out, was never harmful. Puffed up with enthusiasm and arrogance (some had claimed that vaccination could cure all sorts of other maladies, ranging from rheumatism to pimples), they had a tendency to over-state their case, always blaming the victim, never the vaccine. Cases of infection after vaccination, they said, must have been brought on by a subject's weak constitution, or perhaps by unpropitious climatic conditions. They gradually realized that it was vital to use good vaccine. Vaccine lymph taken from humans in arm-to-arm vaccination fell out of fashion as being too often contaminated. By the 1870s the best vaccinators used lymph taken from otherwise healthy calves infected with cowpox.[*]

---

[*] Jenner's original cowpox virus was probably lost. Medical historians and virologists have argued vigorously about the exact nature and origin of the virus used in vaccination. Sometime in the nineteenth or early twentieth centuries the cowpox virus was accidently replaced in vaccination by another orthopox virus, now known as vaccinia virus. Its exact origins, whether in nature or as a hybrid of cowpox and smallpox, are obscure.

Proper vaccination always conferred lifetime immunity to small-pox, Jenner and his followers claimed. They were wrong. It took many years, many cases, some deaths, and some tragically missed diagnoses, before the need to re-vaccinate every few years was widely accepted. Conductor Longley appears to have had a classic case of post-vaccination smallpox, or "varioloid" as it was called. These were often mistaken for chicken-pox or measles. For reasons we will see later, the Montreal health authorities never mentioned that Longley had once been vaccinated. Every case like this was so much fodder for critics who said that vaccination was not a preventa-tive. Other anti-vaccinationists reasoned that there was no point vac-cinating at all if (thanks to vaccination) the smallpox was nowhere near your community.

⁰ ⁰ ⁰

So smallpox continued to simmer and flare, sweeping across cities every few years until stopped by vaccination or, occasionally, quaran-tine. Death counts were much lower now, and the cholera, which had a higher mortality rate and for which there was no preventative, was the more dreaded plague. But this was still the "loathsome smallpox" and sometimes it crackled fearfully. For most of the first half of the nineteenth century it was endemic in great cities such as London. In 1824-29 and 1837-40 the whole European continent was swept by pandemics. England recorded more than thirty thousand deaths in the latter outburst, causing a bitter epidemiologist to sug-gest the carnage was like throwing children to their death from London Bridge, day after day. British laws of 1840, 1853, and 1867 made vaccination universally available without charge and compul-sory. They were not easy to enforce. As the upper classes willingly embraced vaccination, the disease found its main fuel among the poor and ignorant and reckless—groups the state always has trouble reaching.

The Franco-Prussian War of 1870 sparked Europe's worst and last serious nineteenth-century outbreak of the disease. It centred in France, where vaccination had been sporadic, was then spread by troops and travellers all over Europe, and came to North America on immigrant ships. There it settled in large cities, including Montreal. In five years the smallpox killed an estimated five hundred thousand Europeans. The good news was the lesson that vaccination, revaccination, and tough isolation and quarantine measures could defeat the red death. Country after country expanded its public health activities and tightened its vaccination and control laws. Smallpox would never again rage out of control in Europe. The states and provinces of the United States and Canada, where death tolls of from five hundred to fifteen hundred during epidemics in major cities in the early 1870s seemed appallingly unnecessary, followed suit.

Most jurisdictions had driven out the disease by 1875. Montreal took longer. The municipality did not keep statistics for deaths in 1870-71. After that year the official, not very reliable, smallpox death toll was:

Year	Deaths	Deaths per thousand
1872	896	7.41
1873	228	1.83
1874	647	5.10
1875	590	4.54
1876	704	5.29
1877	506	3.76
1878	728	5.48
1879	472	3.49
1880	140	1.03

The unvaccinated were the most vulnerable to smallpox. Francophone Montrealers were less likely to be vaccinated than other nationalities and therefore suffered more than the English or the Irish. French-Canadian children who were neither vaccinated nor survivors of smallpox had the highest death rate.

French Canadians had not been enthusiastic about either inoculation (which apparently came to Canada with British army surgeons at the Conquest) or vaccination. Vaccination had been practised only intermittently in Lower Canada, never as a concerted public health policy. An 1861 statute of the old Province of Canada made vaccination compulsory, but it was never enforced. Some private citizens in Quebec had themselves vaccinated as a matter of course. Many did not. Smallpox waxed and waned in cities, towns, and the countryside. Certain physicians vigorously opposed vaccination.

During the 1870s Montreal's health officials gradually learned how to contain and destroy the disease. During Hingston's mayoralty, campaigns of public vaccination were organized and reorganized, better vaccine was procured, serious public education was encouraged (Hingston himself wrote a well-distributed pamphlet on vaccination, endorsed by most of the city's medical community), and the ranks of the vaccinated mounted into the thousands, then the tens of thousands. The opening of a separate smallpox hospital in the Hill farmhouse in 1876 was a major step forward, as it put an end to the old smallpox wards at the General and Hôtel-Dieu hospitals which had leaked contagion. A young doctor, William Bessey, developed a local supply of excellent calf vaccine. Techniques of quarantine and isolation became more sophisticated and forceful; physicians cooperated more freely in reporting cases (though some expressed serious professional doubts, based on the confidentiality of the doctor-patient relationship); the sanitary police learned to disinfect and fumigate religiously. In the spring of 1880 the last ember of smallpox in Montreal expired.

Travellers reintroduced the disease within months. It happened all the time in this age of easy transportation by rail and mass population movements. In the summer of 1881 a young girl from Terrebonne, Quebec, came to live in the city with her parents. Soon after arriving, she broke out in smallpox. The germs infected fifty people in the neighbourhood around her, causing five deaths. But the Health Department had a great triumph. By systematic vaccination and isolation, they contained the outbreak, and stamped out the smallpox. The catastrophes of years past were not repeated. There was no smallpox in Montreal from July 1881 to February 1885.

In the spring of 1885 Henry Gray of the Health Committee referred to the city's good fortune in having not been touched by the serious smallpox epidemic just over the provincial border in eastern

Ontario. In September 1884 a British immigrant boy brought smallpox—a mild case, apparently varioloid—from Liverpool to the backwoods villages of Hungerford Township in Hastings County. A local boy who slept in the same bed as the newcomer came down with the disease. An itinerant thresher who had slept in the same bed as the local boy spread it widely among the poor farm families of the district. He died, and his body infected a few more who came to his funeral. The fire was well set in the township before its doctor realized he was dealing with smallpox.

There was no time to build defences. Some people fled; others huddled in their homes, barring the doors to anyone, including medical officers. The one country doctor was impossibly overworked. The township's reeve, who became chairman of the hastily established Board of Health, found he had smallpox in his own family and had to isolate himself. In some hamlets there was no one to care for the sick, hardly anyone to bury the dead. Finally the residents of nearby towns, terrified that their rural neighbours would infect them, petitioned the province to intervene. Early in December the Ontario Board of Health moved into a community that was disintegrating under the impact of sickness and fear.

Dr. Peter Bryce, secretary of the Ontario board, organized a frontal, authoritarian assault on the smallpox. The board ordered the closing of schools and churches in Hungerford Township, banned all other public gatherings, and suspended stagecoach service into the community. Constables were stationed on roadways and at railway stations to control the movement of anyone who might carry the germs. Fines and imprisonment were threatened for anyone disobeying board orders regarding quarantine. Medical students were brought in from outside to conduct house-to-house vaccination. A special pamphlet was distributed attacking a local practitioner of "empiric" medicine who questioned the efficacy of vaccination. All infected houses were disinfected and fumigated, and their residents "carbolized" (required to bathe in a solution of water and carbolic acid) before returning home. Clean clothes were brought in from outside.

By the end of January 1885 Bryce's men had put out the smallpox in Hungerford Township, and it did not spread. There had been 202 cases and forty-five deaths. That month the Ontario Board of Health arranged that municipal elections in the township would be uncontested. Democracy might attract crowds and re-ignite the disease.

*   *   *

There was not much concern in Montreal when the Health Department admitted in mid-April, 1885, that smallpox was "epidemic" in the city. Chairman Gray, medical health officer Larocque, sanitary inspector Radford, and their staff knew what to do. The smallpox hospital was open and receiving. After a patient was in hospital, his or her residence was thoroughly sealed and then disinfected with fumes from sulphur. The sulphur was burned for six hours, three pounds of it for every thousand cubic feet to be cleansed. In rare instances where removal to hospital could not take place, strict isolation was practised. Disinfection followed as soon as the patient had recovered. Most important, vaccinators went to work. Private physicians vaccinated their own patients; two public vaccinators offered the protection free of charge to anyone who needed it.

On April 18 Henry Gray reported that the public vaccinators— Dr. J.E. Nolin in the East End and Dr. William Bessey, the vaccine supplier, in the West End—had already treated 240 people, mostly in the neighbourhood of infected residences. Everyone who had been in contact with sufferers had been vaccinated, as had all the children in the immediate vicinity. An "immense number" of Montrealers had been privately vaccinated, Gray said. Several institutions, including the convent in which a case had developed, were having all their inmates vaccinated. At Montreal General Hospital, where one case had found its way from Hôtel-Dieu, extremely thorough disinfection was being carried out. The Health Department arranged for notices to appear in the newspapers reminding doctors of their legal obligation to report cases of smallpox.

Thanks to the vaccination and with proper reporting, Henry Gray thought, there should not be much risk of further spread of the disease. By April 24 he felt the department had the smallpox under control. On the 28th the newspapers published small notes to the effect that the epidemic was over. A longer article that day, "An Alarming Disease Afflicting a Numerous Class," was another ad for the sure-fire dyspepsia remedy, Seigel's Curative Syrup.

❖ ❖ ❖

Many Montrealers were having their stomachs turned by the stink of spring. As the huge snowdrifts melted, the ice rotted and thawed, and life returned to the St. Lawrence, the refuse of the winter began to assault eyes and nose. In some of the poor sections of the city, such as the lower west end suburban village of Ste-Cunégonde, the slush and mud of the streets was mixed with garbage tossed from the balconies of tenements. Further up the mountain, the well-to-do classes would never foul their streets this way. Instead they used their back lanes as winter dumps, and tried to avoid seeing or sniffing out back until the spring clean-up was over. An offended citizen described the lanes of fashionable Montreal in mid-April:

> Mountains of ashes, coal, lobster tins, decaying vegetable matter, manure heaps, and every imaginable kind of filth is [sic] deposited in many of these passage ways so as to make them well nigh impassable. The rapidly melting snow is revealing the refuse of six long months from thousands of human beings. Let any interested citizen take an afternoon among these winter accumulations and he will not wonder at the prevalence of diphtheria, typhoid, small-pox, etc.... He will see for himself the most glaring illustration of the absolute incapacity of the Board of Health and Sanitary Inspectors. He will see the by-laws of the city violated by ninety per cent of the entire population.

It was unrealistic to expect Inspector Radford and his sanitary police to look into every dirty lane in Montreal. This was really just the normal seasonal mess and it would get looked after. The city always required its scavengers to do a special spring cleaning of the lanes in addition to normal refuse collection. Their contract required everything to be done by June 1. True, Messrs. Dumaine & Larin, the new scavengers, seemed to be having some problems with their normal pick-ups, but these would surely ease. If the city really wanted to avoid the dreaded cholera, Radford reported to the Health Committee, it would pay to put some of its own properties in order. At Montreal's central market, Bonsecours, for example, there were neither water-closets nor privvies. People urinated and defecated in the cellars underneath the produce stalls. The sewers draining the market were clogged with garbage. Streets around it were unpaved, except with diseased fish and other refuse tossed out by stallkeepers.

Aldermen were too busy handling a flood of complaints about the scavengers to take action on the market. Every spring day, each warmer and more odoriferous than the last, revealed more problems and caused more citizens to hold their noses. Barrels of garbage were not being picked up, empty containers were littered around the streets, loads of garbage were being dumped by the scavengers on vacant lots inside city limits, and the lanes were not being cleaned. To health-conscious Montrealers, the bad smells indicated that the miasmas and poisons of disease were polluting the city. Germs were breeding, gases were escaping. Efficient scavenging was essential to public health. Messrs. Dumaine & Larin explained to Gray that they had been held up by impassable conditions on the streets and would soon do better.

On April 24 the St. Lawrence River itself began to cleanse the lower portions of Montreal. Ice jams below the city caused the waters to rise and flood the communities of Point St. Charles and St. Gabriel and many lower city streets. Thousands who lived south of the Lachine Canal, mostly anglophone working-class families, were stranded for several days in the upper stories of their dwellings. To get bread and meat they let down baskets to tradesmen hawking goods from boats and rafts. Sewers backed up in unflooded areas of the city. Privy pits overflowed. Gas pipes burst. Chickens and pigs were drowned by the score. A hackman drowned in Centre Street in Point St. Charles. The sanitary police tried to stop people taking ice from the dirty piles of it on the wharves, but were not sure of their legal authority.

The receding waters left more filth than ever—mud, dead animals, clogged sewers, a frightful stench of putrefaction and sewer gas. Not particularly unusual for a Montreal spring—ice jams after the harsh winters of the 1880s led to flooding practically every year—but not good news for a city worrying about cholera and suffering a scavenging problem.

The war news from the North-West frontier was more encouraging. Throughout April the government of Canada mobilized its forces against the Métis and Louis Riel. By the end of the month some fifty-five hundred Canadian troops were closing in on the rebels from three directions. It would be only a matter of time before their uprising was stamped out. The cost in casualties would not be nearly as high as originally feared. Only a handful of Plains Indians had gone on the warpath along with the half-breeds. The violence had been contained in the Saskatchewan country.

Montrealers waited and worried, prayed and offered special penance in time of war. Sentiment about events in the far-off North-West was not undivided. The 65th Regiment was not going to be in the thick of the fighting, for it had been sent to Fort Calgary, well west of the rebel stronghold. Perhaps it was just as well that French Canadians would not be required to attack French-speaking Métis. Some English-Canadian journalists' despatches contained disparaging, malicious references to the fighting qualities of the 65th. And there was matter of the sudden, unexplained return to eastern Canada of its commanding officer, Lieutenant-Colonel J.-A. Ouimet. On the home front, some French Canadians were less than whole-heartedly behind the war effort. A group of political activists centring on the Liberal-oriented Club National began holding open-air meetings in late April to discuss the Métis cause sympathetically. Should this incipient sedition be tolerated, some anglophone ultra-patriots wondered? Squads of police were delegated to keep order at the demonstrations. Except for a little inflammatory oratory nothing happened. The whole North-West affair would soon come to its inevitable end.

o   o   o

The smallpox epidemic had not ended. Early in May new cases were being reported at the rate of two or three a day. Some were fatal.

Some of the patients were not being removed to the smallpox hospital either. Parents at 39 Napoleon Street would not allow their sick child to be taken away. Neither would the mother of a little girl who died in Hypolite Street. And that family posed a special problem: they were not technically Montrealers, for although they lived only six blocks from Hôtel-Dieu, they were actually outside the city limits in the village of St-Jean Baptiste. It would be up to the village to look after these people. Naturally Montreal would confer with St-Jean Baptiste about the proper precautionary steps, including disinfection. Patients who were not taken to hospital would have to be isolated, wherever they lived. Placards would have to be fixed to the doors of residences with smallpox, warning others away. It was decided to do this just after May 1, Montreal's traditional moving day, when tens of thousands of families changed their dwellings.

Suddenly there were alarming complaints about vaccination. Some doctors reported serious side-effects in children vaccinated by the Health Department. Arms turned red, swelled, developed rashes and sores. The medical attendant at St. Joseph's orphanage, Dr. E.J. Bourque, claimed that twenty-one vaccinations had caused twenty-one cases of erysipelas, a disease characterized by fever and nausea, angry inflammations and rashes. Parents claimed their children were desperately ill, even dying, as a result of vaccination.

The Health Department did not credit the complaints. It knew of only three bad reactions from 1,814 public vaccinations in April. Dr. Bessey, vaccinator and vaccine supplier, who probably knew more about inoculation with cowpox than anyone in Montreal, was particularly sceptical. He thought the complainers were exaggerating the natural reaction to vaccination (localized pustules, some redness, a day or two of fever). Perhaps a few recipients were constitutionally debilitated and prone to inflammations like erysipelas or scarlet fever. Dr. Bourque had habitually opposed vaccination, Bessey charged. He, Bessey, knew how prone the anti-vaccinationists were to exaggerating side-effects. As for himself, he had been supplying vaccine lymph for eight years. By now, he said, "I ought to know good lymph when I see it."

The doctors responded by supplying names and addresses of people harmed by the vaccine. At least one infant, the Blaie child in Rolland Street, had died from erysipelas after vaccination, Bourque claimed. He wrote to the French newspapers "pour mettre le public en garde contre un nouveau fléau qui nous menace" —the "fléau" or plague being the vaccine, not the smallpox. Other doctors supported his charges. At the Asile Bethléhem, for example, nine orphans had erysipelas or serious ulceration. Bourque and his colleagues, including the president of the Socièté d'Hygiène de la Province de Québec, Dr. N. Fafard, believed the vaccine was contaminated. They had no confidence in the vaccination offered by the Health Department and they would not recommend that anyone subject themselves to the ordeal.

The Health Department's medical officer, A.-B. Larocque, was not available to sort out the charges and counter-charges. He was not coming to work, apparently because he was sick himself. Some wondered if his "head sickness" was caused by disputes with Bessey or Chairman Gray. Others blamed it on drink. In Larocque's absence, Gray asked a group of outside physicians, headed by the prestigious Dr. Hingston, to look into the charges about the orphanage.

They found that Bourque was exaggerating, but had a case. There were six or seven cases of erysipelas following vaccination at St. Joseph's, and several of the vaccinations had been defective in other respects. We now know that poor sanitation, by either vaccinator or vaccinated, caused the sores to be contaminated with bacteria. In that year, still in the foggy dawn of bacteriology, Hingston's predilection was to think about the climate. He blamed the atmosphere. Its "crude and unsettled condition" helped cause trifling irritations to erupt into erysipelas, he suggested. Hingston recommended that until the atmosphere improved only perfectly healthy individuals should be vaccinated, or there should be no vaccinations at all. On May 11 Dr. Bessey announced the suspension of public vaccinations.

o   o   o

"Doctor" Alexander Milton Ross was determined that his voice be heard on the vaccination question. There was hardly a man in Canada who had worked harder for enlightenment, progress, reform, and liberty, as he understood it, than A.M. Ross.

He would be the first to tell you. As a young Canadian *errant* in New York in the early 1850s, this native of Belleville, Ontario, had frequented the haunts of the most advanced radical circles. He came to know exiled Upper Canadian rebels, French republicans, English Chartists, Italian Carbonari (he named his son after Garibaldi, whom he met on Staten Island), German Communists, and American reformers of every stripe. The great American reform cause of the century was the struggle against slavery, and Ross threw himself into it with a passion. He became, in Lincoln's words, "a red-hot abolitionist from Canada," who toured the South urging slaves to flee to Canada and having his own hair-raising escapes from slave-owners chasing after the northern "nigger thief." During the Civil War he visited the White House several times to inform Lincoln of the activities of Confederate agents in Canada. Afterwards he settled down to the practice of medicine in Toronto and Montreal, along with studies of the flora and fauna of Canada which made him one of the Dominion's pioneering naturalists. For his time he was also an "advanced" religious thinker, rejecting the dogmas of man-made creeds in favour of what he called "Spiritism," a quest for higher things.

Ross's medical training, such as it was, had been in New York at the feet of R.T. Trall, one of the better-known American practitioners of hydrotherapy, the principles of the water cure. Trall and the hydrotherapists were at the forefront of radical medicine in their era. They led an intense reaction against old-fashioned therapies, the medical establishment, and unhealthy ways of living. Doctors' techniques of bleeding and blistering their patients, or doping them with mercury compounds, the reformers argued, did more harm than good. Most drugs were harmful. The way to be healthy was to adopt a healthy lifestyle and, when sick, to trust in natural cures. Drink only water, eat no meat, stay away from tobacco, whiskey, and women, think good thoughts, exercise and breathe fresh air, and you would have a long and fruitful life.

You should also avoid self-abuse, or masturbation, the reformers taught. It was an unnatural draining away of vital life fluids and often led to insanity or worse. To a man who had dodged gun-toting legrees in Alabama and Mississippi, it didn't take a lot of courage to shock Canadian Victorian pruderies by distributing anti-masturbation tracts to young men. Just more good work in the great cause of reform. Alexander Milton Ross was nothing if he was not a reformer. Proud of it, too. Very proud. At fifty-two a very self-satisfied man whose flesh had thrived on its natural food and drink.

Now it was time to take up the smallpox challenge. Ross was an anti-vaccinationist. He believed that vaccination, like the administration of most other drugs, was an injection of vile poison into the body. "Vaccination and revaccination, whether from smallpox inoculation, cow-pox, horsegrease or human corruption has proved impotent to prevent or mitigate small-pox," he wrote to the *Herald* on May 19. "Vaccination has spread scrofula, syphilis, consumption and many other disgusting diseases." Yes, he knew that the majority of the medical profession supported vaccination. "Majorities have no monopoly of truth. The majority of the medical profession for 40 years opposed Harvey's discovery of the circulation of the blood. The majority bled the people for a century.... The majority mercuralized the people till they became walking barometers. In short, the majority has usually been in error."

Dr. Ross was used to being out of step with conventional wisdom. He never hid the road he was taking, and he was going to have more to say on the matter. He also knew that he was not alone among Montreal physicians in being prepared to speak out. Hadn't Bessey's spoiled vaccine proven them right?

o   o   o

On May 12 in the valley of the Saskatchewan, General Frederick Middleton's troops crushed Métis resistance at Batoche. Louis Riel and a few of his followers fled, some of the Indians were still at large (the 65th Regiment finally saw action in several skirmishes as they helped hunt down Big Bear and his band of Cree), but the rebellion was effectively over. Total deaths on both sides, civilian and soldier, have been estimated at about one hundred.

Back in Montreal the air continued to be fouled by the stench of spring. The scavengers were making no progress. Aldermen and health officers were deluged with complaints. It seemed as though Montreal had no scavenging service at all. Gray and some of the other aldermen realized that they had made a serious mistake in giving the 1885 contract to the low bidders, Dumaine & Larin. William Mann, who currently had only the night soil removal contract, had done the scavenging for years. He had been expensive but competent. Dumaine & Larin were cheap and incompetent. They were failing utterly to clean up a city infested with smallpox, ravaged by floods, naked to the menace of cholera. Immigrant ships were already heading for the ports of Canada. Now that the ground was soft, the winter's dead were being buried in Montreal's cemeteries. How many would join them before the next freeze-up?

Montreal's Health Committee had a stormy post-mortem that day about vaccination and the generally unhealthy condition of the city. Bessey admitted that there had been real cases of erysipelas following vaccination. He still blamed these on either the atmosphere or on sickly constitutions, but felt obliged to submit his resignation as supplier of vaccine and a public vaccinator. The Health Committee accepted it. Alderman Beausoleil made the motion to endorse Bessey's decision to suspend free public vaccination. It was unopposed.

The man who had bungled vaccination did not leave the scene in disgrace. Dr. Larocque was still absent from work. Montreal needed a medical officer. The aldermen thought Dr. Bessey, for all his faults, was the person best qualified to act in Larocque's absence. So they promoted him to acting chief of the Health Department.

Gray wanted to suspend the scavenging contract and call in William Mann to do the job properly. He could not persuade his committee. Dumaine & Larin hadn't been doing that badly before the bad weather and the floods, some said. Why not give them a second chance, say until June 1? They had had one chance after another, Gray replied. He would have raised the matter much earlier had the contractors not been friends of some members of the Health

Committee. Unless something was done, the chairman argued, citizens would descend on city hall to demand all their resignations.

The Health Committee decided to stick with its friends and give the sinking scavengers one last chance. Gray thought about the situation for a day, decided he had had enough, and announced his resignation as chairman of the Health Committee and as an alderman. He said he was quitting because of the demands of his business. Everyone knew he was fed up with the Health Committee, the scavengers, Larocque's absenteeism.

Henry Gray was qualified, knowledgeable, popular, bilingual, a member of the English minority and the Roman Catholic majority. In health matters Gray was not just on the side of the angels, he was one. He could not be allowed to go now. "It will not be accepted," said the most senior alderman, Jacques Grenier, of Gray's resignation, "Alderman Gray must stick to the ship now." "With smallpox in the city, and the possibility of a cholera visitation," the *Star* editorialized, "public opinion will not allow this ... question to be trifled with." According to the *Herald*, "the acceptance of Alderman Gray's resignation will mean that the City Council do not want sanitary reform, that its members prefer dirt and disease to cleanliness, health and comfort."

On May 16 Montrealers learned that Louis Riel had surrendered to Canadian soldiers. The Riel story was scooped that day by the *Herald's* feat of pioneering investigative journalism. It had sent reporters into lanes and alleys all over the city. They literally sniffed out an appalling story of filth, foulness, garbage, rot, and reek:

> The lane back of No. 305 St. Antoine Street is filled with a mass of half melted snow, broken bricks, potatoes, parings, and every conceivable kind of filth and nastiness. Three weeks have elapsed since the scavengers have paid this section an official visit.... The lane and yards in the area of the residences from Nos. 386 to 418 St. Antoine Street are half choked with ashes and decaying vegetable matter. The stench arising from this mess of filth is something horrible.... The lane in rear of Nos. 33 to 39 St. Denis Street was found to be in a disgraceful condition.... Vegetable and other refuse lay around in various

stages of decomposition, the bodies of several dead rats were seen, evidently having lain for months.... Outside a stable window a large receptacle, intended for manure, was nearly filled with all manner of domestic refuse, rotting vegetables, etc., the manure having overflowed on the ground in a large heap, and being crowned with the dead bodies of a cat and a rat, enemies in life but tail to tail in death.

In the slums the reporters saw women dumping their garbage from balconies, and urchins playing in yards ankle-deep in filth. "On St. Elizabeth ... the usual accompaniment of muddy street, dirty children and slovenly women was noticed. In a court behind 560-562 Mignonne Street ... were several large tenements apparently inhabited by the poorest classes. The reporter penetrated as far as he could but at the last was compelled to retreat by the smell. This spot would prove a fine breeding place for the cholera or any other infectious diseases...." Not just the slums, either. Sanitary policemen showed reporters the lane behind the fashionable St. Hubert Street residences of Honoré Beaugrand, alderman Beausoleil, and other prominent citizens:

The English language is hardly rich enough in adjectives to adequately describe its condition. If a fouler spot exists in our fair (?) city, it must be terrible indeed.... Barrels of decaying refuse stood in dirty water on every hand; every door had its ash-heap covered with all manner of waste, constantly added to and increasing in death-dealing power day by day. Decaying vegetables, fish, eggs, bones and other organic matter, broken bottles, pots and pans, old iron, straw, manure, ashes, sweepings and fragments of domestic utensils encumbered every inch of space, and it is not too much to say that the quantity of refuse contained in this lane is sufficient to raise its surface at least two feet.... With aristocratic exclusiveness, the back doors of the St. Hubert street houses were tightly closed.... Amid the vile scene children were playing, their young lives being slowly but surely sapped by the noxious vapours they were forced to inhale.... The lane ... is a disgrace to civilization.

No wonder Montreal was menaced. "One need be at no loss to account for the infant mortality of this city," the *Herald* wrote on its editorial page, "when he finds out what kind of air so many of the children are compelled to breathe from the moment they are born. The wonder is not that so many die but that any survive. The germs of disease ... are wafted to the cleaner parts of the city, and bring death and disease into households in which every precaution is taken.... The reeking lanes and alleys described by our reporters are nurseries of disease." The *Herald* was ready to give up on council; it wondered whether citizens should take the situation in hand by forming their own sanitary organization.

The city's eldest, most prestigious newspaper, the *Gazette,* was just as outraged:

> Canada, so far as Montreal is concerned has two wars on her hands, one against the rebels in the Northwest and the other against the filth of her streets; and, of the two, the latter is, by far, the most to be dreaded. It is a matter of profound astonishment to us that the inhabitants of this city do not realize the absolute peril of its position and proceed at once to deliver it therefrom. Is there any sane man among us ... who can walk through the streets of the city and not realize, as surely as the sun rises and sets and its heat is poured down, so surely shall the pestilence descend upon us unless the city is washed and cleansed? ... Many will be the graves and long the mourning among us before Autumn unless we act quickly and act all together.

Beaugrand called Grenier, Gray, and doctors from the city's four medical schools into an emergency meeting. He called a special meeting of council on Monday the 18th, at which he announced that Gray's resignation would be a "public calamity." Dr. Larocque had failed to respond to an ultimatum to return to work; Beaugrand fired him. The mayor recommended that a special board of hygiene be appointed to supply scientific expertise to the Health Committee. Action must be taken against the scavengers. Council should not accept Gray's resignation.

Most of the aldermen supported the mayor, although Beausoleil still could not understand the fuss about scavenging. Montreal always had these problems in the spring, he claimed. With council pledging its support, Gray agreed to return to the health wars.

¤   ¤   ¤

"The public will not be surprised to find that the city smells as badly as ever this morning," the *Star* wrote the next day. But it was soon evident that Dumaine & Larin were putting on a herculean burst of scavenging activity and by the fulness of May even Gray came to believe they were making progress.

Advances in the campaign against smallpox were not so easy. Not only were no public vaccinators at work but citizens were not cooperating with the sanitary authorities. More instances were reported of families and friends who did not want to send the sick to the smallpox hospital. One patient fled from her residence rather than accept isolation. Police detectives were set to work tracking her down. Other families ignored the board's rules and moved around freely. When policemen tried to enforce isolation one family fled the moment their backs were turned. Montreal's police were the laughing-stock of the city, anyway, for their central station had just been robbed. The acting medical health officer, Dr. Bessey, was unpopular as well. Tainted with the reputation of his bad vaccine, Bessey was like a general who had fired on his own troops. And the unilingual Bessey literally did not speak the language of the French Canadians, who seemed most vulnerable to the smallpox. "Assez curieux" to make him acting medical health officer, *La Presse* noted.

In the language that Dr. Bessey did speak, Dr. Alexander Milton Ross continued to attack vaccination. In a second letter to the *Herald,* he called it "the direct means of poisoning the lifeblood of our race with foul and dangerous diseases ... diseases peculiar to cattle ... the physical taints of the beast ... I believe vaccination to be a monstrous fallacy and vulgar error, unworthy of the intelligence of the nineteenth century. To fathers, mothers and nurses, I appeal— do not permit your precious little ones to be contaminated with the filthy virus of a beast." Ross had an alternative, the cleanliness that everyone was talking about as a defence against cholera. If only Montrealers ate wholesome food, drank clean water, washed once or twice a day, changed their underclothing freely, and cleaned up their houses, yards, and lanes, Ross wrote, "you may defy smallpox and other epidemics and save your children from the defiling impurity of vaccine virus." To Ross, a sanitarian of the old school, smallpox was another "filth disease," just like cholera. With sanitation and right living you could be invulnerable to both.

The filth of the back lanes overcame the scavengers. On June 1, the day the city was supposed to be officially clean, a citizen wrote in the *Gazette* that "Vacillation rules in all health deliberations, rubbish and filth meet the eye on every hand, butchers ply their offensive trade through the length and breadth of the city, the offal from which, with its death-dealing odors, must rot and decay in our yards, stables and by-places.... These pest places hold high carnival without let or hindrance, whilst scavenging contractors play fast and loose." The Health Committee began to explore ways of suspending the scavenging contract. Concern was mounting that the city, so attractive in the odourless, clean cold of winter, would get a reputation for being a filthy summer place. American newspapers were starting to reprint some of Montrealers' comments about their lack of sanitation.

For no obvious reason, there seemed to be more success in the battle against smallpox. The epidemic had caused sixteen deaths in the city, plus a handful in St-Jean Baptiste. But hardly any new cases were reported in the last ten days of May. The number of patients in the civic hospital shrank to about a dozen. On June 1, the health workers congratulated themselves that, except for convalescents in the hospital, there was not a single case of smallpox in the city of Montreal. With the North-West rebellion put down, Louis Riel in jail, the cholera not having arrived in Canada, the scavengers on their way out, and the smallpox almost extinguished, the two wars seemed to be over.

> All that could conceal their distempers did it, to prevent their neigh-
> bours shunning and refusing to converse with them, and also to
> prevent authority shutting up their houses; which, though it was not
> yet practised, yet was threatened, and people were extremely
> terrified at the thoughts of it.

— Daniel Defoe, *A Journal of the Plague Year*

CHAPTER 4

RITES OF SUMMER

S*unday, June 7*

The body of Christ moves through the streets of Montreal. Under blazing golden banners, the oriflammes of Catholicism, two hundred girls from St. Peter's parish lead an immense procession of the faithful. They are followed by bands, temperance societies, student societies, benevolent organizations, men's and women's groups, members of the clergy— from St. Peter's, St. Brigid's, St. Joseph's, St-Jacques, Notre Dame de Montréal, St. Patrick's, St. Anne's, and St. Mary's parishes. The marchers carry flags, banners, insignia. Many wear gowns or other costumes. Throngs of solemn onlookers pack streets garlanded with greenery and bunting, flags and triumphal arches. Hymns, chants, prayers, fill the air. His Lordship, Bishop Edouard Fabre of Montreal, flanked by two assistants, carries the Holy Eucharist, bread and wine that for Catholics is the body and blood of Jesus Christ. The sanctified Eucharist is guarded by a corps of pontifical zouaves, French-Canadian volunteers who served as soldiers in the struggle to defend papal territories in Italy from the encroachments of the nation state.

This is the high point of La Fête-Dieu, also known as the feast of Corpus Christi, Catholicism's spring celebration of earthly blessings. It has begun with tolling bells and a grand mass at Notre Dame, the parish church of Montreal. The procession's route is from there to St. Patrick's Church, where a grand outdoor altar has been erected. Fabre is carried on his bishop's throne to the dais where he delivers the solemn blessing of the Holy Sacrament to an immense throng. The parade reforms in its original order, and wends its way back to Notre Dame for a final benediction.

The ceremonies take six hours. Many of the onlookers have assembled six or seven hours before they begin. A small band of Salvation Army adherents marching up a nearby street are driven away by good Catholics from St. Anne's. Some say this has been the grandest Fête-Dieu procession yet, a powerful public witness to the faith of a Catholic city in an age of materialism and impiety. It might also be something of a Catholic answer to the rites of Winter Carnival season.

❂   ❂   ❂

Less than twenty-four hours later, the man who did more than any other to strengthen Catholicism in Montreal, Bishop Ignace Bourget, died quietly in his eighty-fifth year.

A French Canadian, the eleventh of thirteen children in a farmer's family, Bourget had been ordained in the 1820s and become bishop of Montreal in 1840. His zeal for his diocese, for the faith, and for French Canadians as a Catholic people, was as boundless as his energy. Before Bourget the Roman Catholic Church in Canada had not been strong. It had been short of priests, nuns, teachers, and money, and ever since the British Conquest had been feeling its way through the difficulties of co-existing with a secular power habituated to distrusting the Roman Church. During his forty years of untiring service Bourget presided over a remarkable transformation in Quebec. He brought out large numbers of priests and other religious workers from France, built new churches, founded new societies and communities, raised money, recruited the zouaves to be literally the soldiers of God, and fiercely advanced the claims of the Church in relation to the civil power.

It was during Bourget's episcopacy that Catholicism in Quebec finally reached the heights of power and influence churchmen had longed for since the days of F.-X. Laval, the first bishop of New France. In 1875, for example, the Quebec government abolished its Ministry of Education. For most Quebeckers education, like the care of the sick and the nourishment of the poor, would be handled by the servants of God. Societies of religious workers, priests, nuns, and lay brothers now ran the schools, hospitals, asylums, and other welfare organizations of the Catholic province. The image of Quebec as a society permeated and dominated by the Church began to fill out.

Ignace Bourget was a great ultramontane churchman, uncompromising in his support of the rigidly conservative positions Rome was taking in what was otherwise an age of liberal thought. On the other hand, Bourget did not follow the simple, austere rituals of the old Norman church in Canada. For the bishop and his followers, religion was public in the fullest sense, and if it was going to compete with other popular diversions in the nineteenth century, it would have to be truly popular. As in Italy, as in the Vatican, a Catholic society displayed its faith through ornate buildings, statuary, public ceremonies, zouaves, and colourful costumes and flags. Cults of the saints, adoration of relics, multiplication of shrines, emphasis on popular prayers, devotion, healing, miraculous cures— all brought religion closer to the people and their folk instincts.

Bourget wrought what has been called a "devotional revolution" in Quebec. There were new ceremonies, pilgrimages, celebrations, and holidays, public carnivals of prayer and worship—the procession of the Holy Sacrament on the Fête-Dieu being one of the most impressive. To be a good Catholic was to live and demonstrate and even revel in your faith. Montreal Catholic architecture in Bourget's age was opulently baroque, as in Italy, and the greatest stone demonstration of French Canada's faith was to be its own replication (somewhat scaled-down) of St. Peter's Basilica in Rome. The bishop decided to build his cathedral on Dominion Square, right in the centre of English Montreal. In your face, Protestants.

Bourget's funeral rites, held in the same week as the Fête-Dieu, were a grand public demonstration of Catholic Quebec's love and respect for its greatest bishop. First the bishop's body—bathed in light and incense, guarded by the ubiquitous zouaves—lay in state in his little parish church at Sault au Recollet. Then the remains were placed in a casket in a sitting position, open to the air, and carried in a huge procession, some four hundred carriages long, into Montreal to the Hôtel-Dieu. (Bourget's devotion to the sick and to Catholic hospitals was another of his many acts of witness.) The body lay in state for an afternoon in the hospital, then was taken to Notre Dame Church for viewing by thousands more.

Church officials used the occasion to exhume the remains of Bourget's predecessor, Jean-Jacques Lartigue, who had died forty-five years earlier. The two churchmen would rest together in the still unfinished cathedral. After being exhumed, Lartigue's body was also made available for viewing, in the Church of Notre Dame de Pitié. Observers remarked that Lartigue's remains bore "only the slightest resemblance to the human frame, the features being quite indistinguishable." Mourners pressed their heads or their prayer books or their rosaries to the clothing or faces of these holy men, drawing sustenance from the bodies of those closer to God.

Notre Dame was filled with humanity, perhaps as many as fifteen thousand people, including four hundred clergy and a seven-hundred voice choir, for the requiem mass on Friday, June 12. Black and orange banners hung from every beam and pillar. After the chanting and singing and the funeral oration, another solemn procession formed:

Cordon of police
Grand marshals
The Normal school
Students of St. Mary's and Montreal colleges
Band of Montreal college
The School of Doctors and Surgeons of Montreal
The Papal standard
The hearse, drawn by four horses
Papal Zouaves

His Lordship Bishop Fabre and the Rev. Mr. Marshall,
Vicar-General of Montreal
Visting bishops
The clergy to the number of eight hundred
The students and professors of St. Lawrence college
Judges and members of the Bar of Montreal
The Ministers and members of the Federal and
Provincial legislatures
His Worship the Mayor and aldermen
Representatives of the various municpalities
Representatives of St. Patrick's society
St-Jean Baptiste society
St. Joseph's union
Representatives of other societies
Citizens and carriages

The funeral procession numbered almost four thousand. It went first to the Church of Notre Dame de Pitié where Bishop Lartigue's body, carried in a separate hearse, joined the procession. No one had ever seen such public mourning in Montreal. The crowds could barely be kept from interfering with the procession. All flags flew at half mast. Public and private buildings—English and French, Protestant and Catholic—were draped in black and orange. Notre Dame Street in particular was transformed with beautiful displays of flowers and banners inscribed with mottos of grief and hope. At one point the procession passed under an arch of ladders, from which a triple crown was suspended. At times the journey resembled a triumphal procession more than a funeral march—another demonstration of the power of God and the achievements of Bourget in Montreal.

At the cathedral there were more masses, more eulogies, and more viewings. Finally, on June 13, the two bishops were buried in a special vault in one of the pillars of the edifice. Visiting faithful would kneel and pray and light votive candles at their tomb. These were men whose spirits could wield great influence and power. Would people be healed, perhaps, by the intercession of the bishops? According to *Le Monde*, a twelve-year-old girl who had touched the prelate's cheek as he lay in state had her sight miraculously restored.

Imagine those crowds that week. Tens of thousands of Montrealers attracted to the street processions because they are devout, because it is their duty, because they are curious to see the show, because there's nothing else to do. Such big events in the streets. Maybe once in a lifetime. The kind of occasion where you got up from your sick bed to take in the ceremonies. You shrugged off the tiredness or the flushed feeling of something coming on. Maman gave in and let Jean-Paul or Thérèse, who seemed so much better, go out to see the bishops go by. When the holy processions came in sight you shoved closer, rubbing shoulders with total strangers, feeling on your neck the hot breath of the people behind you.

*　*　*

No sooner had the health officers congratulated themselves on defeating the smallpox in the streets around Hôtel-Dieu, than they realized it had ignited in other places. Three or four new cases were being reported daily, mostly in crowded, shabby tenements just over the invisible boundary between Montreal and the poor village of St-Jean Baptiste. (Well, the boundary was visible in the sense that Montreal's water and sewage systems stopped at the city limits. St-Jean Baptiste, a poor village on thin soil over bedrock, had no running water or drains. Privvy pits were shallow; after a heavy rain they would be flooded and the village would be awash in faecal matter and garbage.) The Montrealers had no authority in St-Jean Baptiste. They could only hope that patients and parents would avail themselves of the opportunity to use the city's hospital.

Vain hope. No one wanted to go to the smallpox hospital. To ordinary people the hospital seemed to be the place where the disease raged, throwing off stench and fumes and poison. Going there would be like plunging into the pit of the furnace. From time immemorial people had gone to the house of pestilence or pesthouse to die.

The Montrealers did what they could. Drs. Bessey and Nolin visited the St-Jean Baptiste sick in their wretched dwellings—four families in one, twelve families in another, no plumbing, no ventilation—and said the patients and all the inmates must be isolated. But they knew the isolation would never be enforced. There was no board of health in this swollen, poor village of some seven thousand souls, many of them illiterate former country folk. A few overworked police constables and clerks said they would act, and then did next to nothing.

The people of the infected quarter, which quickly spread back across the boundary into Montreal, seemed hostile to attempts to help them or contain the disease. Placards identifying infected houses were being torn down. One Montreal sanitary policeman who was trying to placard a house found himself surrounded by a crowd and told he was risking his life. People were not reporting cases of smallpox either. When asked about sickness, residents and their neighbours, sometimes their doctors too, would suddenly become mute, evasive, or simply untruthful. Many children in the area were said to be sick with measles. No one would try to carry measles patients to hospital, imprison their families, or burn sulphur in their rooms.

On June 3 Beaugrand, Gray, and Bessey decided to ask the clergy to use their influence to encourage use of the smallpox hospital. Bessey visited Bishop Fabre with the request. It was not unusual to ask for the help of those with constant access to and the trust of the masses (only a few weeks earlier churchmen had read a circular from the pulpit urging their parishioners to take sanitary precautions against both cholera and smallpox). Fabre promised to do all in his power to help.

Dr. Bessey's efforts as medical health officer were hindered by stories and rumours about harm done to children he had vaccinated. Bessey was not popular in the East End. He did not speak French, and he was known to be abrupt and authoritarian. Bessey was a true believer in vaccination, intolerant of the fearful and sceptical, determined to do his duty, apparently unrepentant about the complications his vaccine had caused. It was said that he had sometimes forcibly vaccinated people who did not want the operation.

Public vaccination was still suspended, pending improvement in the weather and trust in the vaccinators. People could be vaccinated by their own doctor, but the Health Department was not vaccinating anyone, either in St-Jean Baptiste or in Montreal. And now there were rumours of smallpox in the village of St-Henri, another poor working-class quarter two miles away on the other edge of the city. St-Henri's council said it would launch a major clean-up, particularly to suppress bad odours. Councillors said the alleged smallpox case had turned out to be only measles. Dr. Nolin said he doubted that story. On June 5 Gray admitted that Montreal still had a smallpox epidemic.

During the week that Bishop Bourget lay in state, the Reverend John Casey, an Irish immigrant who had left the Catholic Church and become a Presbyterian minister, died of smallpox. Casey died at home, having refused to go to the smallpox hospital. Gray said Casey's refusal set an unfortunate example. Bessey muttered about the need for legislation to strengthen the department's authority to compel removal of patients. St-Jean Baptiste's council did seem to be moving towards getting some health regulations in place, though no village by-law could take effect until posted for a certain time on the doors of the parish church. Some residents thought the best way to drive away smallpox would be to close the private slaughter-houses that contributed so sharply to the community's stench.

Bishop Fabre assigned the task of visiting smallpox patients on the island of Montreal to Father Zephyrin Auclaire, curé of St-Jean Baptiste Church. Auclaire was given three assistants. Other clergy were discouraged from making visits for fear of transmitting the disease. Auclaire's group wore special soutanes during visits and carried the Host in a special bag. We know little about their work—the Church did not court publicity for doing its duty to the afflicted. Later it emerged that Auclaire and his helpers were not pleased with conditions in the smallpox hospital. Unusual for the province of Quebec, it was a civic, secular institution, run by the Health Department with whatever staff they were able to hire. On at least one, perhaps several occasions, priests were not summoned in time to give the last rites to dying Catholics.

There is no evidence that the Roman Catholic Church in Montreal ever discouraged vaccination or isolation. But Auclaire and his assistants did not encourage Catholics to use the civic hospital. Probably no one did. In a July editorial, the *Canada Medical Record* referred to the Hill house as an *"abominable* hospital.... We cannot conscientiously advise anyone to go ... we would not go, that is certain.... Patients in all the various degrees of malignity are crowded into rooms, each having a much smaller cubic space than is necessary for persons in good health, and each is obliged to breathe the poisonous emanations of others."

Home remedies were widely used to treat all diseases. In June the newspapers began to carry occasional suggestions about therapies for smallpox. According to an entrefilet (which may have been a paid advertisement) in *La Minerve*, Indians had found that the pitcher plant (*saracenia purpura*) helped draw the poison of variola out of the body. The *Gazette*, Montreal's establishment newspaper, printed a Parisian treatment: mix one grain sulphate of zinc, one grain foxglove (digitalis), half a teaspoon sugar, two tablespoons water; then add four ounces water. Take one spoonful every hour and both smallpox and scarlet fever will disappear in twelve hours. A correspondent to the *Herald* recommended one ounce cream of tartar in sixteen ounces of water. One tablespoon three times a day and you could sleep with a smallpox patient with perfect immunity. If everyone took cream of tartar for fifteen days, Montreal would be free of smallpox.

On June 10 Bessey issued a Health Department circular recommending vaccination as the best preventive against smallpox. All danger from erysipelas had passed away with the cold and damp spring weather, he claimed, and anyway there had only been thirty cases of it, with no deaths, in three thousand vaccinations. The Board of Health recommended that all unvaccinated children be vaccinated. But it did not resume public vaccination, probably because it doubted there would be a demand for the operation. Certainly A.M. Ross was doing all he could to reduce demand, as he countered Bessey's advice with his own:

> I trust there will not be found one medical man in the city who will heed the request of the Board of Health.... The dreadful experience of the past month with *foul vaccine* will not soon be forgotten. There are at present in this city scores of persons

struck with loathsome diseases from vaccination!!! ... Were I to relate a few cases that have fallen under my observation ... it would fill the mind with horror.

Instead of vaccination, which is *not* a preventive of small-pox, I advise the people to cling to sanitation.... Cleanliness and not vaccination is our salvation from smallpox and other filth epidemics.

                                         ✿ ✿ ✿

The summer tourist season was almost at hand. Out-of-town news-papers began to pick up stories about the smallpox and suggest that Montreal was unhealthy. Hotel owners worried about the summer trade. Why not say less about smallpox? It was not much of a prob-lem, was it, except in one distant quarter of the city and among a certain group in the population? Why alarm the general public and give Montreal a bad name?

Proprietors of several hotels, including Montreal's two biggest, the Windsor and the St. Lawrence Hall, mentioned the problem to Alderman Grenier, who agreed to take it up with the Health Committee. On June 15 Grenier suggested that the department stop giving reporters daily bulletins on contagious disease in the city because they were causing undue alarm and bad publicity. Alderman J.-W. Mount, a French-Canadian physi-cian and a member of the committee, agreed with him, com-menting that he could not understand what the press wanted with such news.

Henry Gray was not impressed with the implication that facts about the smallpox could painlessly be concealed. He argued that unless the staff told the truth about the epidemic, the rumours would become more sensational and the department would lose its credibility. This had happened in Chicago recently, where an attempt at suppression of news about smallpox had destroyed public confidence in the health authorities. Gray told his committee he did not believe a few dollars' worth of trade was more important than keeping the public accurately informed.

Grenier wanted it understood that he was not raising the matter in connection with his own interests as a wholesale merchant. His trade was not in any way at risk from the smallpox, he said. French Canadians would continue to come to Montreal if the disease was far worse than the cases now in the city. They weren't afraid.

Exactly the problem, Gray replied. He wished French Canadians were more frightened of smallpox. The disease was spreading only in their part of the city, while the English were almost completely untouched. The department had discovered a case where three mothers dropped in to keep company with the mother of a sick child. "Was there anything more frightful?" the *Witness* reported Gray asking: "It was this dense ignorance they had to contend against, for if the people whose houses were infected were only a little more enlightened, the disease would soon be stamped out."

There was some press support for Gray's view of openness, but Gray himself decided to back-pedal. He ordered Bessey and the staff not to talk so freely to reporters. On the other hand everyone was upset to learn about the housepainter who had just come down with smallpox after working in a residence where an unreported case existed. This was the human price of concealment. This was the month when the statue of "Liberty Enlightening the World" arrived in New York harbour from France.

❊ ❊ ❊

The village of St-Jean Baptiste celebrated St-Jean-Baptiste Day two days early, on June 22. The holiday honouring their patron saint had special meaning for the townsfolk. But for all French Canadians this had become a special day, the occasion for festivities marking their survival as a race or nationality in North America. Because the various patriotic societies were holding province-wide celebrations on the 24th in the town of St. John's, near the American border, St-Jean Baptiste invited everyone to their services and procession on the 22nd. As usual, the village streets would be handsomely decorated.

Prayers for good weather went unanswered. The day began with driving rain and high winds. While celebrants were attending pontifical high mass in the Church of St-Jean Baptiste, conducted by Father Auclaire, the wind tore down the street decorations, demolishing many of the special arches. Some were re-erected, others cleaned away. In the afternoon the weather cleared and the procession went ahead—yet another parade of dignitaries, religious societies, floats ("allegorical cars"), bands, fire brigades, patriotic societies—with flags, banners, and high spirits appropriate to a happy occasion. There were crowds of witnesses, many Montrealers having come out to the suburb. The procession wound through the streets of St-Jean Baptiste and the neighbouring village of Côteau St-Louis, ending at the provincial exhibition ground for an evening of patriotic speeches and a concert. We are not wrong in imagining that some of the children, let out to see the funny floats in the parade, still had scabs on their faces.

While national pride was the order of the day in St-Jean Baptiste, the race question hung in the air like musk at Montreal's City Hall. Council was wrestling with the problem of appointing a new chief medical officer. There had been thirteen applicants for Larocque's old job, temporarily held by William Bessey. Bessey himself had applied. The advisory board that Beaugrand had appointed a few weeks earlier to strengthen the Health Committee was supposed to suggest which of the candidates was most qualified. It could not agree on a name, forwarded the whole list to the Health Committee, and was never heard from again. The Health Committee could not agree either. Each alderman seemed to have his own candidate. Gray in the chair tried to stay neutral during an interminable discussion, but when pressed for his opinion said it was clear that Bessey, who had made hygiene and vaccination his specialty, was by far the best qualified for the job—"irrespective of nationality, as he did not care if Dr. Bessey was a Frenchman, Englishman or Turk."

Others did care. When the deadlocked Health Committee passed the buck to Council by submitting a list of ten names, the aldermen fell into a fierce, convoluted debate about the relationship of nationality to competence, and vice versa, in the matter of public health. Should the new medical officer be English? Alderman Archibald thought so, all else being equal, because all the city attorneys, notaries, and other prominent officers were French. And things were not equal, anyway, he thought, because Bessey was the best qualified candidate. Council knew Gray's opinion of Bessey and had before it a petition from scores of prominent Montrealers, mostly English, expressing confidence in the doctor and supporting his candidacy.

Some aldermen thought it important that a French Canadian be appointed to fill a position formerly held by a French Canadian. Others pointed out that Bessey had not only made mistakes with his vaccine, but did not speak French. Surely the French-speaking population of Montreal had a right to expect that the chief health officer would speak their language. Now if a truly outstanding candidate like Dr. Osler (who had left a year ago for the United States) could be found, Alderman Mount said, he could understand making an exception. Everyone regretted that nationality had been introduced into the debate, everyone denied voting on racial grounds, no one accepted Gray's plea that a board being criticized for incompetence should choose the most competent candidate. The idea of Bessey as assistant to a French-speaking chief medical officer, or vice versa, got nowhere. The debate bogged down in charges of bad faith, procedural wrangles, and Alderman Jeannotte's refusal to accept the mayor's rulings. After hours of arguing and voting on the various names, City Council finally selected the candidate advanced by Alderman Grenier, Dr. Louis Laberge, to be the new chief medical officer.

The procedure, the wrangling, the raising of the nationality question, had done credit to no one. But the appointment seemed not bad. Bessey was so unpopular in the East End as a result of the vaccine fiasco and his arrogance that he would have had an impossible time. He left Montreal that summer, and moved to Toronto. Laberge was a thirty-four-year-old physician who had made a special study of hygienic questions and was serving as secretary of the Societé d'Hygiène de la Province de Québec.[*]

---

[*] Like many of Montreal's young French-Canadian physicians, Laberge was technically a graduate of Toronto's Victoria University. The reason for this was that the Montreal School of Medicine and Surgery, where Laberge had studied, happened to be serving as Victoria's faculty of medicine in a strange marriage of convenience relating to Bishop Bourget's determination to stave off expansion by the Catholic liberals who ran Laval University in Quebec City.

He was bilingual and energetic, a respected practitioner, and took up his duties immediately. He announced that he was an advocate of thorough isolation for the smallpox, would strictly enforce the by-law requiring placards, and was having a more visible placard designed. He inspected the civic smallpox hospital, reported good conditions there, ordered a yellow flag, signifying pestilence, to be flown from it, and announced that he would have a telephone installed connecting the hospital, the health office, and his residence. He would work hard to remove the misapprehensions about the Health Department that were hampering its work among the French Canadians. Why just the other day the disinfectors had been harrassed by ignorant citizens who believed that disinfection meant burning clothes and furniture and pulling down houses.

❄ ❄ ❄

This looks like a case of the incident of the dog in the night. As Holmes told Watson, what was curious about it was that the dog did nothing in the night, did not bark to sound the alarm. Here in Montreal Dr. Laberge was not barking at all about the need for vaccination.

It was probably because the memory of the May incidents, and perhaps the identification of vaccination with the Bessey regime at the Health Department, was still so strong in the East End. The anti-vaccinationists were not going to let that memory fade. The problem was not just the penmanship of A.M. Ross—prolific as it was, and he did not subside—but also the activities of Montreal's French-Canadian "vaccinophobes," led by the venerable Dr. Coderre.

As a young medical student in Montreal in the 1830s, Joseph Emery Coderre had been involved in radical politics as a member of the Fils de la Liberté. He was briefly imprisoned in the aftermath of the 1837-38 Patriote uprisings in Lower Canada. In the early 1840s he completed his medical training through apprenticeship and settled into a long career. He was a professor of *materia medica* and botany in the Montreal School of Medicine and Surgery and served for forty years as the school's secretary. He was an active, important member of the medical staff of Hôtel-Dieu and a founding member of several Quebec medical societies and professional organizations—in short a leader in Montreal's French-Canadian medical community.

Coderre was also a relentless anti-vaccinationist. After seeing some patients die after vaccination, apparently of smallpox, Coderre had become convinced in the 1860s that vaccination was nothing more than inoculation with the germs of smallpox. He denied that cowpox and smallpox were different. To vaccinate, he believed, was deliberately to spread smallpox, as well as all the other diseases that might go along with it.

During the 1870s Coderre and several like-minded French-Canadian physicians spoke out constantly against the activities of the Montreal Board of Health, Dr. Larocque, and the other vaccination-ists. In letters to medical journals and newspapers and in broad-sheets distributed on the streets, Coderre claimed that vaccination was responsible for creating more smallpox, that it could cause any number of other diseases, including syphilis, that Montrealers were being killed by the operation—he would give names and addresses; he and his friends even displayed pictures of grotesquely diseased vaccinated arms—and that no one should subject themselves or their children to the dreadful operation. In those years medical anti-vaccinationism and the prejudices of lower class French Canadians fed on one another to create the ongoing resistance to the Health Department and its work. In 1875 the prospect of City Council implementing a compulsory vaccination program had sparked demonstrations that led to a night of rioting. Orthodox medical opinion tended to blame Coderre and his friends for poisoning the minds of the credulous.

In his early seventies now, Coderre was a more seasoned campaigner than A.M. Ross and he had better contacts in the French-Canadian community. Bessey's contaminated vaccine seemed complete vindication of his past warnings. Now he weighed in with new admonitions against "cette pratique meurtrière [murderous]" and the "charlatans" who were trying to carry out "l'empoison-nement de nos enfants." In long letters to Le Monde at the end of June, Coderre did all he could to fan the flames of resistance to vaccination, claiming that the cause had never been so strong. He was at least partially right about the strength of anti-vaccination sentiment in East End Montreal. After the episode of the bad vaccine even the enlightened editors of the *Journal d'Hygiène Populaire* stopped preaching about the need to vaccinate, and concentrated on calling for better placarding, isolation, and disinfection. French-Canadian doctors in the East End were said to be so distrustful of side-effects from suspect lymph that they were not vaccinating their own children.

* * *

This was the milieu into which Laberge stepped. He ran into trouble right away. On the first Saturday he was called to a tenement house in the rear of Roscoe's Hotel on St. Paul Street. The doctor and sanitary constable Moran found eighteen families living in a tiny tenement, six and seven to a room, filth and dirt everywhere. In one of the rooms, in the midst of all these people, was an eighteen-year-old male, sick with smallpox. His parents flatly refused to have him removed to hospital. Laberge did not back down. He ordered Moran and his assistant to carry the patient downstairs and summon the ambulance. There was scarcely any resistance to the determined doctor's orders. The house was then fumigated.

That night Laberge was called out after the sanitary police had gone off duty. He ordered a sick child removed to hospital. The parents refused. There was nothing to do but call for help from the regular police. Two constables came to the house, saw what was expected of them, and refused to enter the premises. A job for the sanitary police, they said. Police chief Hercule Paradis supported his men, saying it was certainly wrong that they should become contagious with smallpox. Others said the policemen were afraid.

Three new cases on Sunday, one a sick child at Phileas Quintal's saloon, which was part of his residence at 318 Mignonne Street. Quintal refused to allow his child to be removed. The board could neither take away the patient nor close the saloon. They placarded it. Quintal laughed at them. The placards disappeared. The saloon stayed open for business. "Moi, je n'ai pas peur de la picotte," a customer told the health officers. In another East End case a father would attend to his sick child and then return to work selling beer and rum. Gray and Laberge began drafting new by-laws to give the Health Department the right to remove patients and close infected multiple-use dwellings.

Now it was high summer in Montreal. People with smallpox in their dwellings were seen going about their business in the market and on streetcars. Children with smallpox marks on their faces—hideous in appearance, but feeling better now—went out to play. If their scabs had not dropped off they were still contagious.

Dr. Laberge claimed his department was fighting the pestilence "inch by inch" and with good success. Since April 1 there had been eighty infected houses in the city and thirty-three deaths. Most people thought the epidemic was spreading. "If it was," Gray told council on July 6, "it was entirely owing to the pig-headed views of people in the city who had small-pox in their families." The next night there was a fire at 620 St. Lawrence Street, next door to a house with smallpox. The mother and the nurse went outside to join the neighbours watching the flames. Some of the neighbours came in to visit the sick young man. The blaze went out, the disease had made new contacts.

❖   ❖   ❖

Up on the hill, in English Montreal, the health of the city was much, much better. Nothing to worry about, really. The well-to-do lived in handsome, uncrowded accommodations on high ground. Many of them followed the general rule that cities were good places to get away from in the summer, for even mountain-dwellers found that a foetid, overheated climate oppressed body and soul. Montreal's elite had any number of summer retreats: south to resorts in the Eastern Townships or Vermont; east to the Atlantic in Maine; northeast down the river to the popular Laurentian watering spots, Murray Bay, Tadoussac, Cacouna, Little Métis; perhaps over to New Brunswick or the Gaspé for the salmon fishing. Get the wives and children out of town for the season. Attend to business, but escape on weekends and for a few weeks in August. The servants could look after the residence; if they had gone to be with madam and the children, hire a man to stand guard. Pity the poor people condemned to sweat their days and nights in the city below the hill.

For the less affluent Montreal's environs offered several agreeable respites. Take a train excursion for the day, a steamer for an evening in the moonlight, the ferry to St. Helen's Island for a picnic. Walk up the mountain to feel the cooling breezes in the park (later this summer the first inclined railway will open, its base not far from the smallpox hospital). Go on a pilgrimage. If you have time go all the way to Ste-Anne de Beaupré, below Quebec City, the Canadian Lourdes where thousands of faithful assemble every summer and miraculous cures are said to be commonplace. The young English athletes play lacrosse and baseball endlessly, or join the roller-skating craze at the Victoria Rink. Butchers, bakers, grocers, firemen, policemen, Protestant Sunday schools, Catholic benevolent societies, licensed victuallers, the Hackman's Union, all organize grand summer picnics, some by train, some by boat, all featuring 100-yard sprints, fat men's races, prizes, and cooling refreshments. The Salvation Army plans an all-night prayer meeting.

Everyone talks about hours of business. Why can't merchants find a way to close a little earlier in the summer, say at six or seven on warm summer nights, maybe at noon on Saturdays? Clerks take the lead in this year's "early-closing" movement, organizing campaigns to have employers agree on common closing hours in the evening and/or a Saturday half-holiday. The problem is what to do about the mavericks: one hold-out can keep everyone scrambling for business late into the night. Will publicity work—give the old scrooge a bad name? How about a boycott? If only everyone will jump on the early-closing bandwagon—sign the pledges and stick to them—everyone will be the better and healthier for it.

After work there is always the saloon. For the poor there is the life of the street. In good summer weather Montreal's streets are always crowded, often late at night when the drinking spots empty. Lewd singing, swearing, street fights, saloon brawls, disturb the peace of soft weekend nights. Women are insulted, peaceful citizens knocked aside by gangs of rowdies. The police do not always find it easy to break things up and arrest the miscreants. Sometimes the roughs turn on the policemen themselves. On Saturday, June 27, Constable Hanson is badly beaten. Constable Malone is beaten in a mêlée on July 19 and dies from his injuries. Constable Beattie is killed trying to break up a street fight on August 21. The English newspapers are incensed about lawlessness in Montreal and the incompetence of Chief Paradis' men (another whiff of racial musk, particularly in the *Herald*: Hercule Paradis is Montreal's first French-Canadian police chief; his greatest problem is dislike of the police in the Irish neighbourhoods, where much of the violence erupts).

The city seems to be a haven for crooked Americans, second-hand dealers fencing stolen goods, and assorted footpads, pickpockets, stowaways, runaways, and prostitutes. Only the efforts of a handful of city detectives, particularly the industrious, self-promoting Cinq Mars, seem to keep Montreal from disintegrating into a city where no man's property or person is safe.

Even the dead are at risk. No one steals bodies any more in Montreal, but this summer some of the graves in the old Protestant cemetery near Dufferin Square are accidently opened by workers laying gas pipes. In early July they unearth thirteen coffins. At quitting time the decayed boxes and their contents are left in the open. A bunch of idlers come along, open the caskets, and make sport with the bones, tossing skulls from hand to hand. Finally the police stop the midsummer entertainment.

✤ ✤ ✤

Except for the smallpox, Montreal was not unusually unhealthy in the summer of 1885. Most of the city was not unusually unclean. The spring's scavenging crisis was finally solved in June when the Health Committee refused to give Dumaine & Larin a better price on their contract, declared it forfeit, and turned the job over to William Mann. The efficient Mann, whose night soil incinerator was now in full working order, finished cleaning the city.

The smells of summer could never be completely swept away. They included offal steaming in the sun wherever the keepers of private slaughterhouses dumped it; manure on fire at the old city dump at the Papineau Road end of Logan's Farm (now Lafontaine Park); loads of peas from a wrecked barge fermenting on wharves on both sides of the river; garbage-laden waste water running down from St-Jean Baptiste into Montreal streets; barrels of decaying fish and rotting fruit and vegetables in the markets; sewer gas and water closets; animal shit and dead animals; cooking odours and unwashed people.

Middle-class journalists had a sensitive nose for summer stories. The *Gazette*, July 15:

> HEALTH AUTHORITIES ATTENTION—A pool of water is lying in the unused railway track oppose the Beaver Line company's sheds, which is green with stagnation, and which is most dangerous to health, especially in these days of contageous diseases, and the health authorities should see to it that this nuisance is not allowed to remain there any longer. The stench from it, especially on a hot day, can be more easily imagined than described.

Fear of cholera lingered into the summer. The disease raged in Spain and Portugal that season, killing thousands in what North American newspapers described as "A Dance of Death." Early in the summer it was said that fear of cholera was causing a marked exodus from eastern seaboard cities. On July 28 in Montreal Dr. Archambault of St. Catherine Street reported a case of the dreaded *cholera morbus* to the Health Department. A man named Drolet had died a horrible death after six hours' sickness. It apparently had come on him after eating a "black" or "blood" pudding purchased in St. Lawrence market.

Nobody seemed to get particularly upset about the report, which was a false alarm. Drolet evidently died of violent food-poisoning. The cholera did not reach North America that season or any year afterwards. There was no new visitation of the great nineteenth-century plague. One doctor advanced the theory that Montreal had nothing to worry about from cholera because it was seldom found in cities where "eruptive fevers"—like smallpox—were present.

Hints appeared in the press that the smallpox epidemic was hurting the summer tourist trade. On July 8 Thomas Rodger of the Grand Trunk, the doctor who had first seen smallpox in the city, wrote the Health Department asking for comments in view of alarming stories being published in American newspapers. The railroad's business was beginning to suffer, Rodger claimed. Messrs. Cook & Co., the tour operators, also inquired, for they were getting cancellations. The London, Ontario, *Advertiser* published one of the typical exaggerations, claiming "on good authority" that Montreal had at least two thousand cases of smallpox and ought to be shunned until it cleaned itself up. This was too much for the conservative, commerically oriented *Gazette*. On July 16, under the heading "An Outrageous Falsehood," it editorially set the record straight:

> There are not two thousand cases of smallpox in Montreal, nor the tenth of two thousand, nor the fiftieth part of two thousand. The smallpox hospital at this moment has twenty-five inmates, many of whom came from outlying municipalities, and those from within the city limits are drawn from the remoter and poorer localities. There is no alarm felt in any quarter and there is no cause for such. Smallpox is a disease common to all large cities ... the disease is never epidemic.... There is not the remotest danger to be apprehended of contagion by those who visit Montreal, or those within it who are decently clean in their persons and their homes.

       ✿   ✿   ✿

Statistics about the inmates of the smallpox hospital were meaningless. Most of the sick were not going there. The Health Department's reports of a few new cases each day were also meaningless. People and their physicians were simply not reporting new cases. The health authorities found out about some sufferers only from the death certificates required for burial. There were about four deaths a week through June, then fourteen smallpox deaths in the week ending July 5, and ten the next week. Deaths, too, were probably under-reported.

The Health Department tried to fight the smallpox case by case, street by street, through the heat of summer. People paid as little attention as they could to the rules and regulations the department tried to enforce in the cases it knew about. Gray, Laberge, Radford, and staff must have known they were losing (both the *Canada Medical Record* and the *Journal d'Hygiène Populaire* told them they were), though they could not have had any idea of the consequences of defeat. On the weekend of July 11-12 it was confirmed that the smallpox had metastasized right across the city into St-Henri. Cases were reported in the outlying village of Vaudreuil, apparently brought back from Montreal by students who had attended the Fête-Dieu. The captain of the Laprairie boat turned back a lady with two sick children trying to get out of the city. What was she doing out of doors at all? Laberge said it would take a hundred sanitary police to track movements in and out of sick houses. In the same breath he assured the press that there were only about fifty cases in the city; Montreal was as safe for visitors as New York or any other city on the continent. The department dared not black out all reporting about the epidemic, or the public would become even more alarmed.

By mid-July the civic smallpox hospital was full to its twenty-five-patient capacity. Montreal notified the suburbs that it could no longer take their cases. Gray talked about the need for a new hospital, and the city secretly purchased a site out at Côte des Neiges Road near the cemeteries. But there was no time. More accommodation had to be found right away. The garrett of the Hill house was opened to take eight more patients. Early in August the department began planning a fifty-bed addition. "We do not know the moment the disease may break out in a large hotel in the city or in an educational establishment," Gray told Council. Notre Dame cemetery was asked to stay open extra hours for emergency burials.

The board's most important allies were frightened citizens. Only certain Montrealers took the disease calmly. Many others were terrified when they learned that smallpox was on the street, next door, downstairs. Sometimes no one knew until the black wagon appeared. This was the four-wheeled, enclosed vehicle, resembling a hearse, that the department used as an ambulance to take the sick to the hospital. When families tried to hide the disease, the neighbours might hear children's talk, pass on rumours, catch glimpses of marked faces. It was often suspicious neighbours who made the first report to the Health Department. Sometimes they were wrong. By July the department distinguished between reported and confirmed cases.

Was there smallpox in the family of the local grocer? Down at the saloon? Could you go anywhere without being on guard? Miss O'Connor of the Wanzer Sewing Machine Company entered a house on Montcalm Street on a normal business visit and found herself in the same room with a sick child. She almost fainted with revulsion, and, according to the *Witness*, ended up in the smallpox hospital.

That house had been placarded with the black-and-yellow warning: "SMALLPOX-PICOTTE." But the placard had been torn down. People who were frightened of smallpox wanted placards put up and wanted the department to disinfect wherever the pestilence was found. Others were not frightened of the disease and did not care. Some were frightened of what the board would do to them and their children. Nobody liked to see the black wagon in their streets. When you were put in it, the door was locked from the outside in case you became delirious and tried to escape.

To protect the innocent and the frightened, the department determined to use all the powers the law permitted. Gray and Laberge decided to test their authority by prosecuting a physician, Dr. Jacques, for failing to report a case, and a carter for taking a smallpox patient to the civic hospital in his hack. They knew that citizens, including doctors, would grumble about despotism by the health authorities. Laberge said he would willingly become as despotic as the czar of Russia in order to get ahead of the disease. The Recorder fined the offending carter (whose hack had become a potential source of infection), but delayed judgment in the Jacques affair while he reflected on the law.

People tore up placards right before the eyes of the sanitary police. They refused admission to their dwellings. When Chief

Benoit of St-Henri entered a house in which a boy had died from smallpox, one of the inmates threatened to shoot him if he attempted to disinfect it. A Montreal police sergeant had a case of smallpox in his own house on Wolfe Street. It was not reported; the house was not placarded.

Augustin Deseve kept a little grocery at 1617 St. Lawrence Main. Late in July one of his children died there from smallpox. The Health Department ordered that the child be buried at once and the store disinfected. A placard was put up. Nothing happened. The body lay in an open coffin all night. The placard disappeared. A few days later, another Deseve child took sick. Another placard was torn down. The city attorney told Laberge that if he closed the store he might be liable for Deseve's loss of business. A third placard was torn down. Laberge went into the store to reason with Deseve. They argued. Deseve hit the health officer and drove him out of the store. Laberge had Deseve arrested for assault and brought before the Recorder. The aggrieved storekeeper used "strong language" to the Recorder and spent a day in jail for contempt. He finally paid a ten-dollar fine for assaulting Laberge. The health officer thought Deseve's store did more to spread smallpox than any building in the city.

*　*　*

Maybe the climate was to blame. Everything seemed a bit demented in the blazing days and stifling nights of that summer of 1885. Tenement rooms were like ovens. People took to their balconies and to the streets for relief. Infants gasped for air and wailed in the dark. Tempers snapped. Brains feverish with heat and drink, some men beat their wives. Street gangs clashed and brawled. Even drygoods clerks went on a rampage: roving bands of them cursed storekeepers who upset early closing agreements; someone threw acid on goods in one store. The police asked for the right to carry guns. The manure dump in the East End burned and smoked and people could not stand the stench. No one knew how to put out the fire.

Montreal had a taste for the grotesque and fantastic. Crowds packed Doris' Circus and Menagerie to see John W. Coffey, "The Ohio Skeleton," Krao the missing link, and an Egyptian bovalapus. Chang the famous Chinese giant—eight feet two inches tall, said to be the eighth wonder of the world—came to town and exhibited himself at Messrs. Sparrow & Jacob's pavilion. He was a well-dressed, scholarly, most gentlemanly giant, particularly popular with the fair sex. Other circuses and shows were coming later in the summer, including the greatest of all, P.T. Barnum's extravaganza, complete with Jumbo the elephant, Jo-Jo the Dog-Faced Boy, Arada the Wild Guatemalian, and much more.

"What is the resemblance between Riel and a picture?" asked a humorist one night at the theatre. And answered: "They both must be hung." To its credit the crowd, mostly English, hissed. In Regina, North-West Territories, Louis Riel was on trial for treason. Madness was his only possible defence. We now know that Riel had taken ultramontane Roman Catholicism, including the teachings of the man he most revered, Bishop Bourget, to insane lengths. In 1885 Riel thought he was "David," prophet of the new world, charged by God to create a new haven for the Métis and for European Catholics in the North-West because of the corrupt liberalism of Rome. His chosen pontiff had been the dying Bourget. After Bourget expired it was Archbishop Taché of St-Boniface. Bourget had once told Riel in writing that he had a divine mission. During the rebellion Riel had spent much of his time in prayer or serving as a priest to his people.

The lawyers who went out from Quebec to defend Riel argued that he was mentally unbalanced. Most French-Canadian Montrealers thought he was a befuddled champion of a poor people who had probably needed help in the face of mistreatment by callous governments. There was no doubt that Louis Riel's visions had led to rebellion and bloodshed. At his trial Riel undercut his defence lawyers by giving a lucid speech contrasting his sanity with the lunacy of the government of Canada.

The return of the militiamen who had helped stamp out Riel's rebellion was in keeping with the season. Oh, it was meant to be a splendid civic occasion when the 65th Regiment came home on July 20. There was nothing wrong with the decorations, the immense crowds, the lusty cheers for the conquering heroes, the evening fireworks. A credit to their race, the speech-makers said in honour of the conquering heroes. But their uniforms were not a credit to anything. The men of the Carabiniers Mont-Royal paraded through the streets in dirty, discoloured rags, homemade slouch hats and cloth caps. Their uniforms had disintegrated during the campaign and no one had supplied new ones. At best you could say that their appearance showed the hardships they had been through, these brave soldiers "more shabbily and more grotesquely dressed than are the tramps and loafers of the east."

They were still ragged and shabby at the end of that week when Montreal held a civic holiday review and dinner for all its volunteers, soldiers said to have given the city a name in military annals as prominent as its commercial glory. The regiments paraded to the exhibition grounds in blazing heat and humidity. "Through the torrid July weather the troops marched with even step to the alternate music of the different bands. Sweltering beneath their uniforms, they advanced steadily, dropping a man [with sunstroke] here and there, until the parade ground was reached." There was no water at the parade ground. Crowds of spectators ruined the march past and smashed through the entrance turnstiles. At dinner time the soldiers broke ranks and rushed thirstily for their grub. Many got none. Speeches and toasts were cancelled. Veteran North-Westers declared this was the hottest, hardest day's campaigning of all. When a sweating trooper, bugle in one hand, bottle in the other, sounded the "fall-in" for the homeward march, the men had had enough. The planned route and all pretence of military order was abandoned. Exhausted soldiers straggled back to their armouries and dispersed.

That night's fireworks spectacular—summer's answer to the Winter Carnival—also went awry. The timing was bungled and everything was set off in a rush. It seemed as though the city was being assaulted with fire from the slopes of the mountain.

After the festivities the men of the 65th waited weeks for their back pay. Some were unemployed and homeless. One volunteer who had gone west to fight Riel, a young man named Parent, put up at Roscoe's Hotel. There he contracted smallpox and died.

On August 3 Montrealers learned that out in the Canadian west Louis Riel had been convicted and condemned to death by hanging. French Canadians held a serious mass protest against Riel's death sentence on the Champ de Mars—the parade ground behind City Hall—on the night of Sunday, August 9. One fiery speaker suggested that if anyone should hang it should be Sir John A. Macdonald, the prime minister of Canada.

Two days later Buffalo Bill's Wild West Show opened at the Driving Park in Point St. Charles. It featured Sitting Bull, Buck Taylor ("The King of the Cowboys"), Annie Oakley, the Deadwood Stage, the Wild West Cowboy band, Mexican vaqueros, Wichita Indians, Mustang Jack, Master Johnny Barker ("the Cowboy Kid"), and last but not least the renowned scout and Indian fighter, Bill Cody himself. The company played to packed stands in this first Canadian appearance. Bill announced that he hoped to engage Riel's former lieutenant, Gabriel Dumont, and some of the Métis to restage the battle of Batoche (Dumont eventually toured as a marksman with the Wild West Show). Sitting Bull, victor at the Little Bighorn, offered little more than scornful shrugs for the poor showing Poundmaker and Big Bear had put up against the whites. Bill visited Notre Dame Church. He and Sitting Bull pow-wowed with Canadian Indians at the Caughnawaga (now Kahnawake) reservation. The troop delivered a new baby elk into the world. And the Wild West Show gave a special dinner for the mayor, aldermen, and press. It was held in Sitting Bull's tepee. Buffalo steaks were served by cowboy waiters. As they ate, the diners passed around one of the Wild West Show's artifacts— the scalp of Yellow Hand, a Sioux chief slain in revenge for General Custer's death.

✿ ✿ ✿

Through all these days the black wagon trundled up and down the long, straight streets of the East End—Cadieux, Sanguinet, Hypolite, St-Dominique, St. Lawrence Main, now Wolfe, Montcalm, Visitation, Mignonne. Every night a few more bodies were hauled up to Côte des Neiges cemetery in hearses specially marked "SMALLPOX-

PICOTTE." Every day more people appeared in public wearing the hideous mask of the disease.

Montreal was slowly awakening to the menace: Every single one of these gatherings to witness processions, military parades, Riel demonstrations, and Wild West shows had helped to spread the sparks. The day of Buffalo Bill's press dinner there were nine deaths in the city from smallpox. Thirty-eight patients were in the smallpox hospital, 106 houses wore placards. Henry Gray urged public-spirited citizens to form a relief committee to help the needy. The health authorities were finally proposing to recommence public vaccination. Gray was visibly angry and tight-lipped at City Council on the 10th when he explained that the opposition of East End physicians had prevented their resuming the practice earlier. Now there was a shortage of vaccine in the city. More was on order from Boston.

Some readers of *L'Etendard* might be excused for believing that Ayer's Sarsparilla would work as a substitute for vaccination. It was advertised as a remedy for "les Scrofules et toutes les maladies scrofuleuses, tèlles que Ulcères, Plaies, Erysipèles, Eczéma, Pustules, Impétigo, Tumeurs, Charbon ... et Eruptions de la Peau." The *Star* urged the clergy to help save lives by extolling the virtues of cleanliness for the next few weeks. Editorially it advised Montrealers to "see the necessity of living temperate, cleanly, healthy lives, at least while the epidemic continues." At last the Recorder, moving suspiciously slowly in the matter, had upheld the prosecution of Dr. Jacques for failing to report a case of smallpox.

But the sanitary police told reporters that isolation had failed utterly. It could not be enforced. Some ignorant mothers would take their children to visit neighbours with smallpox and laugh at the idea of danger. The *Witness* interviewed a sanitary inspector:

Q. What class of people up to the present have been attacked?

A. The poorer classes of French. That they are attacked is very much their own fault. They will not adopt the most simple precautions. I have often posted the usual notice on the door of a house affected, and the woman has said, "I will soon tear that down." "Tear it down now, then." "Oh, no, I am not such a fool as to tear it down now, but, all the same, you will have to put up a new notice to-morrow morning." And a new notice I had to put up in many cases, as the people persist in tearing them down.

I passed a house recently in which there was small-pox, and found quite a number of women and children round the door talking to the resident of the house. When I remonstrated with them, they replied that it was the "good God" who sent the disease, that there was no use in fighting against it, and that if the good God willed it they would take it, and if not, they wouldn't.

There is no use in reasoning with them. English-speaking people will do what you tell them, as they appreciate the necessity for precaution. There are some parts of the East End crowded in a way which those who live in better parts of the city have no notion of. When any of these people are attacked it is very hard to isolate them.

*　*　*

William W. Robertson has had enough. He lives at 2444 Notre Dame, near Richmond, and has learned of one case of smallpox after another in his neighbourhood. His home is literally surrounded by the disease. On August 10 his servant came down with smallpox. He had her taken to the hospital and called the health office to ask for fumigation. When no one came—the department can't keep up with the demand—Robertson got directions from his doctor and did the disinfecting himself. The employer of one of his children, learning that the lad came from an infected house, then insisted that Robertson produce a Health Department certificate indicating satisfactory disinfection. Laberge's office refused to supply the certificate, because it had not witnessed the fumigation and does not credit private disinfection.

Robertson is incensed. A barrister, he is also a minister in the Seventh Day Adventist Church. They are a Protestant sect whose obsessions include personal hygiene because they pride themselves on treating the body as a living temple. Most Adventists abstain from alcohol, coffee, tobacco, and all other stimulants. Many are vegetarians. They come out of the same North American reform ferment that so entrances A.M. Ross.

The Health Committee is to hold a special meeting on Friday afternoon, August 14, to plan the resumption of public vaccination and the tightening and improvement of its procedures. Robertson appears at the City Hall office. A reporter overhears snippets of this well-dressed anglophone's agitated conversation with Dr. Laberge: " ... The people are dying like sheep in the city, and this in an enlightened and civilized age.... The very savages remove from their dirt, we hug our filth.... The system is rotten to the core.... I care nothing for your committee."

Laberge remains calm as Robertson gets angrier and angrier. Just before the meeting is to begin, Henry Gray comes over and asks about the trouble. When Robertson tells him, Gray explains that the disinfectors are working as hard as they can. People must be patient.

ROBERTSON: Patience! If fifty men cannot do the work a hundred should be appointed. If a hundred is not sufficient five hundred should be appointed. The lives of the people are at stake.

GRAY: But all these people cannot be appointed in a moment, nor could they be taught their duties in a moment. The calamity has come suddenly upon us. We are doing the best we can.

ROBERTSON: The system is all wrong. The department is asleep. Competent men should be appointed.

GRAY: ... You are excited and hysterical. You have no right to make such remarks. They are utterly unfounded....

ROBERTSON: The people are dying....

Robertson's voice is one of the stronger in a rising chorus of fear and anger. The plague is loose in the city and the authorities seem powerless. At the Health Committee meeting Henry Gray admits that Montreal faces "a great calamity," a more formidable threat than the North-West rebellion. The truth is about to be told about the menace of the smallpox.

PART II

*On the day when the death-roll touched thirty, Dr. Rieux read an
official telegram which the Prefect had just handed him, remarking,
"So they've got alarmed—at last." The telegram ran: "Proclaim a
state of plague Stop close the town."*

— Albert Camus, *The Plague*

CHAPTER 5

A STATE OF PLAGUE

THERE HAD BEEN 120 ACKNOWLEDGED deaths from smallpox since April 1. On Saturday, August 15, the Montreal *Star* sounded the alarm. "In our opinion the condition of Montreal has become such that it would be criminal to keep silence":

OUR SCOURGE

PROGRESS OF THE SMALLPOX IN
THE CITY

Not Less Than Four Hundred Cases in
the City—Forty Cases in the Small-
Pox Hospital—Twenty-five or Thirty
Cases in St. Jean Baptiste—Eight
in St. Henri—A Great Many
Cases Not Reported at all—
Apathy and Carelessness
in the East End of the
City, and Neglect of
Sanitary Precau-
tions—Notes
and Inci-
dents.

The *Star* had a daily circulation of more than twenty-five thousand copies, easily the largest in the city. Its proprietor, thirty-seven-year-old Hugh Graham, was a Canadian equivalent of Joseph Pulitzer or William Randolph Hearst. He was a man of immense energy and determination, utterly devoted to his newspaper. The *Star* was the leading Canadian exponent of the new "people's" journalism. Fiercely independent of politicians and political parties, it pioneered in the coverage of local issues affecting ordinary Montrealers. The health of the city was one of the paper's main concerns. The five thousand words of coverage it gave to the smallpox in four columns on August 15 was far longer than any story in any paper since the beginning of the epidemic. "During the early progress of the smallpox epidemic now existing in the city, the *Star* has carefully refrained from making sensational or alarmist reports on the subject, and has not felt justified in even discussing it freely," its report began. "The epidemic has now reached a stage at which it becomes necessary that the public should fully realize its extent and gravity."

The coverage included a capsule history of the epidemic, statistics, a summary of the Health Committee's work, an account of the "wisdom and charity" of the Catholic Church in ministering to the sick (Curé Auclaire and his three assistants were worn out by their work; one had been sent to Murray Bay to recover), and alarming anecdotal descriptions of the condition of the city and suburbs:

> A reporter was informed the other day of a serious outbreak in a little street in the vicinity of St. Jean Baptiste.... A walk through St. Jean Baptiste street is far from pleasant, the stench being simply abominable. Filthy, putrid matter has been lying in the gutters at either side of the street, exhaling the most disgusting smells, while the stench from some of the outhouses is almost unbearable....
>
> The wife of a member of the staff of the *Star* visited the St. Jean Baptiste Market the other day ... in the midst of the crowd was a young girl, whose face was completely covered with the marks of the disease, presenting a most sickening sight, her

friends apparently gathering round to gaze upon her affliction, and all eagerly commenting upon it....

It is within a hundred yards of the Windsor Hotel, at 1436 St. Catherine St. that the five children of a sergeant of police are suffering from smallpox.... The house is not placarded, and the parents declare that the children shall not be removed to the hospital. The neighbors are in a state of considerable alarm....

In St. Henri ... the people pay no more heed to a case of smallpox than they do to a case of rheumatism.... In St. Jean Baptiste it is exceedingly difficult to get at the facts; the popular impression is that there are at least a hundred cases.... One thing, however, there is no disputing, and that is that the sanitary state of the village is deplorable.

The story focused on the lack of vaccination in the East End and the ambivalence of many French-Canadian doctors to the operation. Quoting a prominent French-Canadian medical man, it chastized "the French Canadians of Montreal, not all of them, but the majority of them" for their indifference to the dangers of contagion, and their resistance to vaccination and isolation. A lead editorial attacked the "astounding apathy of a large section of the population.... Every possible influence should be brought to bear upon the people to arouse them to a sense of their danger and their responsibilities." There was no doubt that the *Star*'s considerable influence would now be brought to bear.

o   o   o

English-speaking Montrealers rushed to be vaccinated or re-vaccinated. Henry Gray and William Robertson rehashed their confrontation at the health office through letters to the press. Robertson called for a public meeting to consider the menace of the disease and the "utter incompetence" of the Health Department. "This is not an easy job to perform," Gray commented. "MANUFACTURER" wrote to the *Star* suggesting that it "now lead the citizens in a crusade against this scourge." Montreal faced commercial ruin, he argued, unless drastic action was taken. People would not buy goods made in the city, for fear of being infected with smallpox. Why not coerce French Canadians into getting vaccinated? Employers should simply fire anyone who could not produce a certificate showing that they and their families had been vaccinated. "HEALTH," on the other hand, thought the *Star's* coverage would "make very little difference to the great mass of the more ignorant portion of our French population." They could only be influenced through the clergy, he claimed. But it might help if money was available to assist breadwinners forced to stay away from work while their homes were isolated.

The *Star* continued its frank coverage of the epidemic on Monday the 17th, but with a certain editorial caution. Many of its correspondents wanted strict prosecution of people who tore down placards, for example, but the *Star* thought they showed "a misplaced confidence in the power of the law to make people obey the law ... it is not half so easy to secure this punishment of offenders as it is to write about it." The newspaper reasoned that the creation of "a healthy public opinion" would be better than attempts at rigorous law enforcement.

The *Witness* became the second paper to join the crusade that day, trebling its coverage under the alarming heading "VACCINATE! VACCINATE!" It printed detailed instructions from the Health Department on sanitation and disinfection, advice on vaccination, and a long letter from William Robertson. To expose the enemy, it also printed the text of a broadsheet, embellished with a skull-and-crossbones, that was said to be widely circulating in the city:

DON'T!!

Don't permit your precious little ones to be vaccinated! Vaccination is not only unnatural, filthy and unclean, but positively dangerous to health and life.

Scores of children in Montreal have been poisoned with a loathsome disease by vaccination. Don't allow your children to be poisoned with the vile putrescence of a beast, or the syphilitic poison of unclean men.

... For other poisons there are antidotes, but for vaccine poison—none!! The audacity, whether of ignorance or craft, with which vaccination is now being recommended in Montreal is almost incredible.

Vaccination is outside the range of science; it may properly be classed with "charms," "incantations" and "witchcraft." It is in no sense a preventive for smallpox—for hundreds have died with smallpox who had the mark of the beast on their bodies.

Cleanliness is the only scientific, because natural, preventive of smallpox. Clean bodies, clean clothing, clean living, clean homes, clean food and clean water are nature's prophylactics, and nature is always right!

It was not an anonymous production. The author, who had the courage to put his signature to the document, was the energetic A.M. Ross, carrying on his crusade for health reform and right living. "DON'T" was one of at least two new anti-vaccination tracts he wrote that month. By his estimate he distributed twenty thousand copies of each.

Robert White, a concerned businessman, decided to investigate the situation for himself. He visited the Health Department that Monday, and came away convinced that the city was hopelessly unready to fight the epidemic. The addition to the smallpox hospital was not yet finished. The hospital had no well or running water and no telephone connection with the Health Department. The department was trying to fight a major epidemic with one doctor, nine sanitary policemen, and three clerks. When the new wing opened, the hospital would still be able to handle less than one hundred patients. The department now admitted there were at least four hundred cases in the city. White estimated that the real figure was closer to six or seven hundred. Drastic steps would have to be taken, White concluded. He doubted the Health Committee would act without pressure from citizens.

So he decided to make pressure. White called a meeting of Montreal's leading boot and shoe manufacturers for Tuesday afternoon, August 18. Montreal was the centre of the boot and shoe industry in Canada; the employers who attended White's meeting were among Montreal's largest and most influential. White explained the situation, and the manufacturers supported his sense of urgency. One reported that one of his employees had taken sick with smallpox just half an hour ago. They had to protect the reputation of the city, the reputation of their products, and the health of their workers. It was resolved to give all employees ten days' notice to produce certificates of vaccination for themselves and their families or face dismissal. A second resolution urged persons in districts affected by the smallpox to abstain from attending churches and public gatherings. The boot and shoe men appointed a deputation to confer with City Council about the best means of stamping out the smallpox.

* * *

The most prominent citizen of Montreal was seventy-seven-year-old Sir Francis Hincks. Hincks was a former prime minister of the pre-1867 Province of Canada, a former finance minister of the Dominion of Canada, former governor of Barbados and British Guiana, an architect of Canada's banking and railway systems, in many ways an architect of Canada itself. Few anglophone politicians had been as concerned as Hincks about the need for racial tolerance in Canada. As a leader of the Reform party, he had worked tirelessly to persuade French Canadians—crushed and demoralized in the aftermath of the 1837 rebellion—that their language and identity would be respected in Canada, that they could wield political power in alliance with other liberal-minded Canadians. Hincks' long career in public life had been always turbulent, almost always distinguished. Now Sir Francis lived quietly in Montreal on St. Antoine Street West, indulging his considerable literary and scholarly interests, widely honoured as one of the young Dominion's few venerable statesmen.

On Sunday, August 16, Hincks became ill. By Tuesday morning it was clear that he had smallpox, a severe case. It was the fulminating "black" smallpox. Hincks died Tuesday night.

His funeral would have been one of the largest in the city's history. Thousands would have come to pay their last respects to the statesman, whose body would have been beautifully dressed and at rest. Instead the hideous, stinking corpse was buried at five in the morning, with only his immediate family present. It was later determined that Hincks had caught the smallpox from a servant who had visited a sister in an infected house.

News of Hincks' sickness and death completed the awakening of English-speaking Montreal. The *Herald* and the *Gazette* joined the *Star* and the *Witness* in expanding their coverage of the epidemic and demanding action (a fifth English daily, the *Times*, was utterly without influence and dying. It finally collapsed that fall after its managing editor died of smallpox). The press in other cities, which had been watching Montreal closely, was now fully alert. In the week of Hincks' death all of North America read that smallpox was blazing out of control in Canada's largest city. Montreal instantly became a place to be shunned.

Were people who had come from Montreal infected with small-pox? Toronto had just such a case, in a family named Merrick who had fled from Montreal two weeks earlier to escape the scourge. They were being thoroughly isolated in their residence in their new city. How eagerly would other Torontonians—thoroughly alarmed about a single case of imported smallpox—or people anywhere else, welcome Montrealers into their lodgings? How eagerly would anyone buy clothing, shoes, dry goods made in Montreal? Was everything and everyone from Montreal contaminated?

❖   ❖   ❖

"How's your arm? Did your vaccination take?" the English ask one another on the street. At Notre Dame Church on August 19 a special grand mass is celebrated to invoke the intercession of St. Roch. Roch was a fourteenth-century French nobleman who survived the plague in Italy, devoted himself to its victims, and wrought many miraculous cures. Canonized, he has become Catholicism's patron saint of plague victims. There is a special altar to Roch at Notre Dame, and on this day it is decorated with flowers and coloured lights. "O Lord, we, thy servants, pray that you may keep your people, by continued piety and through the prayers and merits of the blessed St. Roch, make them secure against all contagion of both soul and body through Christ our Lord. Amen."

This is the prayer for the festival of St. Roch, recited by Father Picard. He urges the congregation to take all possible precautions against the epidemic. It might well be considered a just punishment from God for their numerous sins, Picard tells the faithful, and suggests they amend their lives to be more deserving of mercy. All day long the believers come to kneel before the altar and petition the intervention of St. Roch. As in the days of the Black Death, hundreds of years earlier, plagues seem to be sent from a wrathful God.

Henry Gray thinks the *Star* and the other newspapers are having the good effect of making Montrealers conscious of the need to be vaccinated. Public vaccination has resumed, and private physicians are always willing to vaccinate. The city has fresh supplies of vaccine brought up from Boston. Henry Gray himself has just vaccinated his own children with some of the new lymph. Yes, he tells reporters, it's true that an 1861 statute of the Province of Canada, which has never been enforced, requires the vaccination of all children in certain cities, including Montreal. But surely there will be no need to enforce it now, thanks to the publicity. The Health Department also offers free carbolic acid for disinfection purposes. The way the Hincks case was handled also helps, for it showed the East End that the same rules apply for rich and poor. Hincks' house had been immediately placarded; burial was immediate; the house was fumigated. This week there is also a placard on the servants' lodge up on the mountain at Ravenscrag, the city's most imposing mansion, where one of the millionaire Allan family's servants is infected. On the other hand, the Health Department apologises profusely to Dr. Molson for the way in which over-zealous officials slapped a placard on his house one noon-hour on hearing a mere rumour that his wife had died of smallpox.

Many employers follow the lead of the boot and shoe makers and announce that all their workers and workers' families must be vaccinated. Employees with sickness in their homes must absent themselves on pain of instant, permanent dismissal. But how will they live without wages? Everyone knows that the fear of having to lose three or four weeks' pay is helping drive poor people to resist placarding and isolation and causing them to lie to their bosses. Shoe manufacturer William Holden discovers one of his woman workers falling asleep at her machine. He learns that she has been up all night burying one of her children, just dead from smallpox. The sickness had been in the family for a week.

Holden and a few other employers promise to pay the wages of those who have to stay away. That could become an expensive proposition if the smallpox increases. Surely it is a job for the city. Mayor Beaugrand announces that as treasurer of the Patriotic Fund, raised to help families of the North-West volunteers, he proposes to use the remaining balance in the fund to help compensate sufferers from the smallpox. No one objects. Some companies offer free vaccination for their workers. Dr. Rodger vaccinates everyone at the Grand Trunk, for example. Hotel workers and the staff of the English newspapers are all vaccinated.

On Thursday afternoon the delegation of boot and shoe manufacturers meets with the Finance Committee of City Council. Beaugrand attends and announces that he is requesting the closing of Montreal's theatres and cancellation of the visit of Barnum's circus. The streets will be sprinkled daily with thymo-cresol as a kind of public disinfectant. Money is available for relief. Beaugrand and Alderman Grenier, chairman of the Finance Committee, assure the manufacturers that the city is doing everything in its power to contain the epidemic. Grenier explains that the civic hospital will have all the beds it needs. Many people with smallpox don't want to use it, he argues. The richer, more intelligent section of the population, such as the late Reverend Casey, set a particularly bad example. Plans exist for the erection of a new smallpox hospital, to be ready next spring. The manufacturers' idea of converting one of the exhibition buildings to an emergency hospital seems unduly alarmist, and will certainly not help attendance at the exhibition.

Dr. Laberge has told the aldermen that the disease has stopped increasing. Both Grenier and Beaugrand tell the manufacturers that it is important not to be too frightened. Beaugrand tells the story of the leper who infected fifty people in Damascus. Five hundred then died of the disease—four hundred and fifty of them from fright. We must face the epidemic "in a manly way" the mayor suggests. He and Grenier fully support manufacturers who require their employees to be vaccinated.

Whatever the mayor says, many citizens are frightened and are keeping their eyes peeled for faces masqued with smallpox—doing spot checks, as it were. The victims can appear anywhere—in the parks, on the streets, even in church. A poor imbecile wanders around the streets of St-Jean Baptiste with the marks of smallpox on him until the police take him in. See that man getting on the streetcar ... *look at his face!* ... hands snatch at the bell rope, the car empties. The City Passenger Railway Company, whose business is falling off drastically, announces that conductors will turn away people suspected of having the disease.

What about people who have been in contact with and could be carrying the plague? Should the sanitary policemen, for example, be allowed to ride the streetcars, as they did on their way back from fumigating Sir Francis Hincks' house? The CPR announces the sanitary police will not be allowed on board. What about people carrying packages of clothing or linen? Are they coming from infected houses? The company bans packages on the streetcars, just in case. Which leads to this scene at the corner of Craig and Bleury:

A tall man wearing muttonchop whiskers, a threadbare Prince Albert coat, and a melancholy air, a paper bag under his arm, begins to board a car:

"No passengers with parcels allowed on board," the conductor says.

"Why not?"

"Superintendent's orders on account of the smallpox."

"But I have only a bag of flour."

"Can't discriminate; you will have to get off."

"I won't do it."

Eventually a policeman is called: "Come now, get off this car."

"I won't. I call the other passengers to witness if this is not tyranny."

A crowd has gathered. "Is it smallpox he has got in the bag?" says one bystander. "No, it's not; it's dynamite," says another.

Finally persuaded to leave, the man sticks out his tongue at the departing car, and utters a loud "Bah!"

Can you trust the servants? Think about the Hincks case! Should you hire a cab? Who knows who's been there before or if the hackman's family is sick. What about the tradesmen? There are stories of milkmen and bakers and grocers who come out of smallpox houses to do their daily rounds. The Health Department's offices in City Hall are headquarters in the campaign against the epidemic. The obvious place to go to get vaccinated. Also the obvious place to go to report a case in the neighbourhood (suddenly dozens of new cases are reported, many of them unconfirmable), to report a case in your own house (every little chill becomes a harbinger of smallpox), to go for help when you feel sick and don't know what to do. Reporters see several marked faces in the crowds outside the offices. There may be more smallpox germs at City Hall than in any other public building in Montreal.

Except for the smallpox hospital itself, of course. Certainly a good place to stay away from. If only it didn't sit there overlooking Fletcher's Field right by the main path up to Mount Royal Park from the eastern sections of the city. Thousands pass right by the hospital every week. Many would hardly notice the single placard on the broken-down fence beside the parkway. Some promenaders are probably tempted to hop over that fence and sample the apples ripening in the orchard on the hospital's grounds. Could the apples be infected with smallpox? Does the hospital infect everything and everybody near it?

Look at the pattern of cases, so many of them in the vicinity of the hospital, so many of them in St-Jean Baptiste village which is directly down wind from the hospital. Many of the villagers and some of their physicians believe that the hospital itself is causing the outbreak of new cases. It is, after all, the centre of the fire. Does the burning there generate miasmic gases? Are these spreading over the city from the pest-house, causing the sickness and death?

Surely the offensive odours that seem to lurk everywhere are warnings that must be heeded. Montrealers' old and instinctive identification of bad smells with disease and danger is now acutely tuned. Newspapers print more complaints than ever about putrid places—the vacant lots where the illicit butchers dump their offal in the dead of night, the stinking water closets in the Grand Trunk's Bonaventure Station (which the *Herald* labels "Death's Right Bower"), the "pest hole" of Ste-Anne's market.

Some American visitors and one of the public vaccinators are reported to be doing a good business selling little packs of compressed camphor to counter bad odours. "Citizens walk in fear and trembling through streets the usual unsavory odors of which are now mingled with whiffs of carbolic acid, thymo-cresol, chloride of lime and camphor," the *Gazette* notes. The smell of disinfectant is itself a danger signal.

With smallpox the nose is not always enough. Barber shops are full of the good smells of shaving cream and tonics and lotions. The man who goes into the shop on St. Catharine Street and waits his turn is probably off guard. Then he steps up to his chair and gets a good look at the face of the customer before him. *But he is fully recovered,* the barber pleads. *There is nothing to worry about.* His new customer flees in horror. Are barber shops infected? An anxious St. Catharine Street barber writes to the press saying this did not happen in his shop, which is perfectly safe.

o   o   o

From the beginning of the scare, some citizens and editorial writers called for drastic action. Enforce the placarding law. Barricade people inside houses to make isolation work. Institute house-to-house inspection and compulsory vaccination. *Stamp it out!* Stamp it out hard and fast.

Well, perhaps draconian measures would not be needed. As August drifted to its end, the alarm gave way to a kind of lull. Surely the newspaper campaigns, the vaccinations, people's new sensitivity to the smallpox—perhaps the fervent prayers and special masses being offered in the churches—would have their effect and the epidemic would fade away. The health authorities claimed the disease was or soon would be under control. Many rumoured cases were proving to be unfounded. Even though there were an astonishing seventy-four smallpox deaths in the week of August 17-24, bringing the official total to more than 250, the menace to sensible people was not great. The recently vaccinated or those who had survived a case of smallpox had absolutely nothing to fear, and could carry on undisturbed. Anyway, this brief outbreak did not compare with the epidemics of the 1870s, which never seemed to end.

Montreal's five French daily newspapers seemed hardly to notice the epidemic. True, they gave fairly short shrift to local news at the best of times, for all of them were still traditional journals of opinion rather than new-fangled *news*papers on the model of the *Star* and its English competitors. Editors whose passion was party politics and political ideology were obsessed with national politics, provincial politics, international affairs, the future of the French race, the fate of Louis Riel, and similar topics. Here and there in their dense columns of small print they would insert occasional notes about items of municipal interest, often rewritten from other papers. Otherwise editorial pens would take up a local issue only when it was being well-agitated.

All the fuss about the smallpox still seemed fairly inconsequential. "La petite vérole, cette année, n'est past très maligne," scoffed *La Minerve* in an editorial attacking the exaggerations of out-of-town newspapers. Most Montrealers, it claimed, were calmly going on with their business. *Le Monde* still ranked the cholera as an equal menace with smallpox, and urged sanitation as the way of dealing with both diseases. Dr. Coderre contributed to *Le Monde*'s columns a translation of A.M. Ross's circular as well as his own warning of the folly of forgetting last spring's disasters with vaccination. To Coderre it was evident that vaccination had spread smallpox, and much else, then, and that more vaccination would lead to more smallpox now. Even Mayor Beaugrand's own newspaper, *La Patrie*, declared on August 26 that "Il n'y a pas d'épidémie, proprement dite." In a real epidemic of a disease as contagious as smallpox, the writer thought, there would be many more cases.

The world was not impressed with such sang-froid. Outsiders' alarm about Montreal as the centre of a modern plague continued to mount. Merchants reported that customers were cancelling business trips to the city; some were said to be cancelling orders. The

Independent Order of Foresters, the First Regiment of the Hartford Light Guards, the Supreme Court of Canada, and other groups, cancelled plans for meetings in Montreal. American tourists bypassed the city on their way home from Canada. Why take your chances going through an infected place? At seaside and country resorts, vaccination was all the rage (at Tadoussac the summer people held a "vaccination bee"), and many summering Montrealers decided to stay on a bit longer.

Travellers from Montreal were not greeted with the usual *bonhomie*. "On registering from Montreal we scarcely received civility, and were in doubt whether we could get accommodation," a merchant reported after a trip to Portland, Boston, and New York. "We heard of others who failed to get into any of the first-class hotels at all. In social circles, also, Montreal men and women do not get invitations as of yore, and as for the clubs, it is useless trying to get admission into them.... Last week friends of mine were about registering at a leading hotel in Quebec as from Montreal, when an acquaintance said unless you want to be sent to the top of the house don't do it, so he entered as from New York. At a lakeside hotel in Ontario, a family from Montreal intending to spend a week or so were so ostracized by the other visitors as to make it impossible to remain."

Excursion parties from Montreal were definitely not wanted and had to be cancelled. No one proposed to cancel the visit of an important delegation of French politicians to the city, but their steamer stopped short of Montreal for fear of being quarantined in other ports. The railroad companies were alarmed too. Could they afford to be seen to be carriers of smallpox on their Montreal runs? Not only would passengers react with horror, but public health authorities in neighbouring provinces and states would not stand idly by and let the plague spread along the arteries of commerce. The city of Port Huron, Michigan, on the Grand Trunk line from Canada, was second only to New York in the numbers of immigrants to the United States that it received; thousands of French Canadians entered each autumn to work in northern lumber camps.

On August 25 the United States Marine Hospital Service established a train-inspection system at both Port Huron and Detroit.

People travelling from the Montreal area would not be allowed to cross unless they could furnish proof of vaccination and permit their luggage to be fumigated. (One of the first big jobs was clearing the eighteen-car special train carrying Buffalo Bill, Sitting Bull, Annie Oakley, all the cowboys and Indians and their paraphernalia. An Ontario surgeon gave the troupe a clean bill of health, counter-signed by a U.S. consul, so they were allowed to cross without spe-cial disinfection of their saddles, scalps, and other gear. Back in the U.S.A., the Wild West band could relax, safe from the terrors of Canadian smallpox. The other travelling extravaganza, Barnum's Circus, had escaped exposure when its Montreal visit was cancelled. But it then suffered a major catastrophe in St. Thomas, Ontario, when a Grand Trunk locomotive killed its giant elephant, the origi-nal "Jumbo.")

But only outsiders and certain Montrealers were alarmed. Smallpox divided the citizenry into two camps. One group was terrified of the disease, ran and hid from it, got vaccinated, and sup-ported its forcible suppression. The other group accepted the pres-ence in its midst of one of God's scourges that sadly carried off some of the children *de temps en temps*. There was little sense of urgency about smallpox where the epidemic was most severe—in poor neighbourhoods in the East End and in the suburbs of St-Jean Baptiste, St-Henri, and Ste-Cunégonde. In the West End the huge crowds pressing to be vaccinated sometimes had to be controlled by police. The very sight of the black wagon struck terror into their hearts. In the East End crowds of children traipsed after and played around the black wagon. Sometimes boys climbed aboard to hitch a ride.

At the Recorder's court the clerks were very nervous about the daily string of miscreants. How many of them had been in contact with the smallpox? This and all other courtrooms were regularly dis-infected. On the other hand, Recorder B.A. Testard de Montigny seemed almost nonchalant about upholding the health laws. Colonel G.E.A. Hughes, second-in-command of the 65th Regiment, had been caught personally tearing down a placard on his house on St. Denis Street. The Recorder, who had taken his time in the Jacques case, seemed again in no hurry to pass judgment. Did this man, an arch-conservative ultramontane French Canadian, believe in enforcing these public health laws at all?

Work on the addition to the smallpox hospital proceeded slowly. When one of the workmen came down with the disease, it became almost impossible to hire any others. Despite the belief that the smallpox was abating, it seemed wise to delay the opening of the public schools for a couple of weeks and to require vaccination certificates when they did open. Confident that the epidemic would be beaten, the English newspapers defended their coverage as responsible and necessary, and were steadfast in condemning Montreal's dirt and disease as a disgrace to its civilization.

The French press, unconvinced that the smallpox was serious, poured scorn on sensation-seeking English papers. Exaggerations about the epidemic, stemming from a blind desire to increase circulation, were doing immense harm to Montreal's business and its reputation, the francophone writers claimed. "Des millions de dommages à la ville pour des centins de profits à quelques boutiques!" sniffed *La Minerve*, in an obituary editorial for this "légère épidémie." *La Presse* barely deigned to notice "ce *puff* intempestif," blown out of all proportion by the *Star*'s infernal lust for melodrama. What a ridiculous mistake the *Star* had made in reporting all 224 burials at the cemeteries last week as having been caused by the smallpox. If the sensation-seeking reporters had checked the facts soberly, they would have realized that there were only 109 deaths from smallpox in the city during the final week of August.

❖   ❖   ❖

To Hugh Graham and his staff at the *Star* it hardly mattered whether the death count was 224, 109, or its own corrected figure of 154 (including the suburban municipalities). This was an intolerable toll of death and suffering. The newspaper continued its detailed coverage, now called for compulsory house-to-house vaccination, and demanded an emergency meeting of City Council to strengthen the Health Committee. Yes, outsiders were foolishly panicking and exaggerating conditions in Montreal. But it would be simply criminal for newspapers to stop writing about the epidemic and limit themselves to publishing statistics:

> During the nine years in which the smallpox was here before, the press contented itself with giving the occasional statistics of the disease, and the city contented itself with receiving these statistics in silence. Year after year passed by, and year after year hundreds died, and hundreds more lived pitted and unsightly. What effect had the "statistics," forsooth, on the public mind here? They had none. The disease had its will.
>
> Yet now, when, after a temporary peace, we have another carnival of death and filth threatening us again, it is urged that the press should confine itself to now and again giving "the figures" and keeping silent about every other aspect of this crisis. And not only is this line of argument put forward as logical and as Christian—for we have had it from the pulpit in one instance—but as justified by the facts. And what are these facts? They are that during the little over two weeks since the truth was first fully exposed here, there have been close on two hundred lives sacrificed.

The other English-language papers shared the *Star's* outrage. The death toll was rising astonishingly fast. The Health Department's inability to persuade people to take precautions was obvious. Here was a city some of whose people believed that they should bring their children into contact with smallpox—even making the request at the civic hospital itself—in the hope of giving them a mild case. Respect for placarding was non-existent. Nothing was being done by the magistrate himself in the case of Colonel Hughes. The Health Department had run out of placards.

Convalescing patients at the smallpox hospital wandered through the orchard chattering and laughing with friends on the other side of the ramshackle fence, making a joke of security. Vaccination affected only those who allowed themselves to be vaccinated. One public vaccinator estimated that 75 per cent of his work was re-vaccinating people who did not need it. He did it to reassure them. The city had no power to force any public health measures on suburban villages that were more stricken, more helpless, less health-conscious than Montreal itself.

The outside world decided to intervene. In early September officers of the railway companies and outside boards of health came to the city and met with Gray and other Montrealers in the American consul's office. Some of them toured the infected areas. "It is our opinion that the Canadian authorities cannot handle the epidemic within their own borders," the secretary of the New Hampshire State Board of Health wrote to Washington, "much less serve us in any marked way in keeping the disease out of the New England States." A lacrosse team from Toronto refused to come to the city. If Montreal's lacrosse men wanted to come to Toronto they would have to be disinfected first. North America prepared to put the whole city of Montreal in quarantine.

Even the *Gazette*, the most cautious of the English newspapers, flip-flopped yet again and decided the end of the epidemic was not in sight. It charged that the French-speaking population was "singularly callous to the deadly character of the disease" and called for compulsory vaccination, proper isolation, and drastic improvements in the hospital. The bitterness and frustration of English Montreal welled up in letters to the editor. In the *Star* "CITIZEN" offered biting sarcasm about the view of Montreal that the group of visiting politicians from France would take home:

> The interments in the Côte des Neiges Cemetery will tell loudly of the way in which the French in Canada have kept pace with advancing science in France....
>
> The delegation will be able to report that in Montreal every one is expected to have the smallpox. That is, every one who speaks French. It is patriotic, for was not Jenner an Englishman? It is perhaps a way of testifying affection for *la mère patrie*, and even if *la mère patrie* has no such prejudices we can show the delegation that we can not only be more Catholic than the Pope but more French than the Frenchmen themselves.
>
> ... The delegation will be able probably to report, as an interesting fact, that whenever they have met Canadians who are pockmarked they always understood French.

In the *Herald* on September 2, "PRO BONO PUBLICO" contributed a long meditation on the smallpox and boycotting. The letter, unusually positioned on the newspaper's front page, would become notorious. Here it is, in part:

> Montreal is at this time experiencing in its fullest significance the meaning of the term "Boycotting".... In Halifax last week I was surprised to hear at the cigar-stand in one of the hotels a gentleman remark, "Is that cigar from Montreal?" "Yes." "I don't want it. All the cigar makers are *French*; they have the smallpox; won't vaccinate; these cigars carry it." Result, cigar seller at once cancels all orders from that city. The same scene took place in a boot and shoe store there, with similar results— "*French* operatives." In the dry goods trade even, it is seen in all parts of the country. In the ready-made clothing departments business is absolutely nullified, *again*, it is "*French* sewing women." Along the lines of railway are large posters, black and yellow, notifying passengers to "avoid Montreal, turn off at Prescott and go by Ogdensburg to the east...." Outsiders seem to think that smallpox microbes are crawling along the streets and sidewalks, like potato bugs, and nearly as large. Hence the city is practically being shut off from business by, and with, the world....
>
> It is notorious that doctors do not hesitate to say "it is far worse than reported," taking care to add, "*Vaccination is imperative to stop it.*" All right, gentlemen, that may be true ... Then, on the other hand, we have the priests saying, *we don't believe in vaccination*, and so between the two demoralization exists, and we are forced to the conclusion that it is a question of money; sordid selfishness on both sides, the one class, medicos, making a bonanza out of those *already* vaccinated at a dollar a head.... The other the priestly class (R.C.), make a harvest through the number of burials; for each one means five dollars and upwards, hence you see the *golden calf* may also have something to do with its exaggeration.
>
> Then, our Council is a combination of jobbers, who care more for feasting and money making, at the expense of the

community, than for suppressing disease. Their efforts to put down this are simply childish. No attempt is made to enforce sanitary observances, either in the public matters or private places; filth! filth! everywhere, notoriously so in the Eastern section of the city. It is the French part of the community who are responsible for the present condition of things; call a spade a spade and place the blame where it properly belongs. It is everywhere the cry: "Your French operatives, they are dirty, they do not vaccinate, and you have this pestilential disease always with you, and always will so long as your Council and English-speaking people act as they do."

There is one very strong preventive that has not yet been tried; put *that* in force and it will soon work a revolution, viz.: let English capitalists, manufacturers and employers of labor, drop off all the French help, have only English-speaking people who are vaccinated, and who are not afraid to use *soap* and *water*, and it will soon be seen how it will stir up action.

North America began to treat Canada's largest city like one of the cholera-stricken places in Spain. A party of American tourists across the river in St. Lambert awaiting a train connection wrapped their throats in damp clothes saturated with camphor to protect themselves from "smallpox air" being wafted across the river. No tourists were coming to the Windsor Hotel, which was said to have laid off forty workers. You could go to the Windsor or to the *Star*'s office to sign a petition for a public meeting to discuss the epidemic. The out-of-town officials' first requirement was that the city station medical men at the train stations check for proof of vaccination. United States postal authorities were about to require fumigation of the mails from Montreal. Much more was about to follow. Would the world out there refuse to accept telegrams from the stricken city? people joked.

You could take the smallpox lightly, in a macabre sort of way. Patients at the smallpox hospital would taunt skittish passers-by with gestures and cries of "You've got it!" "There was a seeming propensity or a wicked inclination in those that were infected to infect others," Defoe wrote of London during the great plague. In

Montreal a young lady, the daughter of a clerk for the Grand Trunk, went walking in the East End that week with some friends. At the corner of Notre Dame and Champlain streets they were approached by three French-Canadian women. One woman's face was covered with the pustules of smallpox. The young lady and her friends got out of the way.

"What! frightened?" cried the woman with the smallpox. "I'll let you see!"

She ran at the girl, grabbed her, and rubbed her pustules against the captive's cheek.

The victim fainted. The companions looked on, struck with horror. The woman with the hideous face walked away, laughing.

Reporters demanded that the sanitary police apprehend the "fiend in human form" who had assaulted the girl. Henry Gray commented that he was not sure what could be done to the assailant, except send her to the smallpox hospital.

Gray was privately more worried than he appeared. On August 31 he wrote Quebec's lieutenant-governor, L.F.R. Masson, asking him to create a provincial board of health because of the outbreak. It had already spread to Sorel, Lachine, Vaudreuil, St-Hilaire, St-Pocoma, and many other places, Gray wrote, and a "serious disaster" was in the making.

On September 1 the council of the Montreal Board of Trade called for a special meeting to discuss the reputation Montreal was getting as a "pest-hole," an "unclean city." All of the English papers were demanding action. The French went along, grudgingly. *La Presse* grumbled about exaggerations, the generally stable mortality in the city, and the difficulties of the working class, but supported a public meeting to clear the air. *La Patrie* argued that exaggerated fears were now abroad in the world, "soit mauvaise foi, soit calcul, soit maladresse," and something had to be done to restore the city's good name. "Si nous ne prenons pas des mesures énergiques, capables de rassurer nos voisins et de rétablir la confiance dans nos produits manufacturiers, l'hiver sera rude et la misère effrayante." It supported a public meeting to take "des mesures propres à fermer la bouche de ceux qui nous ruinent dans notre commerce." The most eloquent statement of the situation was in the *Gazette*:

We are not sure ... that a heavy responsibility does not rest upon the press for having so long refrained from raising the voice of alarm and goading the authorities into an activity to which the warnings of the mortality rate failed to stir them....

The lamentable feature of the situation is the apathy of the civic authorities and of the French-Canadian population, among whom the disease lives and moves and has its being. The Church, which ought to be foremost in thundering against the criminal indifference of the French to the adoption of approved precautions and sanitary regulations, remains silent ... the City council has not deemed it worth while to convene a special meeting to devise means of grappling with the disease; the Finance committee has made no recommendation of an expenditure of money ... for the provision of an efficient corps of sanitary police, the erection of a proper smallpox hospital, and the enforcement of sanitary reglations. One-half the citizens, in fact, appear absolutely callous to the dreadful ravages of the disease and the incalculable mischief it is working to the city in a hundred and one ways....

Montreal is at this moment placarded in every newspaper in America as a city afflicted with a dread and terrible disease—a place to be avoided by all who value their health, to be shunned by businessmen as they would the leprosy, and yet we have in our midst, nay, in the seat of authority, men who supinely fold their arms, call the scourge the visitation of God, and coolly abide the time when it shall have spent its course. Is this to be? Is there no public sentiment that can take shape in active aggression against this apathy and overwhelm it with repressive deeds?

◊　◊　◊

Time to act. On the morning of Friday, September 4, the governors of the Quebec College of Physicians and Surgeons held a special meeting at Dr. Hingston's house and prepared recommendations to put before a gathering of Montreal's physicians later that day. In

Quebec City the provincial government responded to pleas from Gray and Beaugrand by issuing an order-in-council creating a central Board of Health for the province. Its members included Hingston, Gray, Beaugrand, and several Montreal and Quebec physicians. At noon, in the Corn Exchange building, one of the largest and most representative meetings of Montreal merchants that anyone could remember convened in response to the Board of Trade's summons. Virtually the whole mercantile elite of Montreal came out to discuss the peril. There was immediate agreement, "That in view of the fact that smallpox is, by the consent of medical authorities, regarded as a preventable disease, this meeting urges upon the authorities to use the most vigorous measures for its eradication."

William Hales Hingston—doctor, former mayor, public health reformer, smallpox expert—was the logical man to come to the fore in the crisis. Ever cautious, he was not quite willing to commit himself on the seriousness of the crisis. Asked to address the merchants, Hingston steered deftly between the alarmists and the now-discredited forces of complacency. "With a little delay, a little calmness and wisdom from men who in ordinary times are remarkable for these qualities, the disease which I should say is not as great as is imagined by people at a distance, will be stamped out from our midst. I am afraid that a large section of the people have lost their heads, and are at present acting in a manner which a couple of weeks from hence they will not consider wise or prudent." The measures that the medical men would recommend that evening, Hingston said, would "go a great way towards putting an end to this epidemic and relieve the anxiety in the public mind."

The merchants were confused about the epidemic and the anxiety. They applauded speakers who attacked the apathy and incompetence of the civic officials. They also applauded speakers who attacked the press for damaging the city's reputation. Above all, they were worried about Montreal's future and about the Health Department's inability to get sanitation by-laws enforced. The Recorder's indecisiveness in the Hughes case seemed to mean that the law itself was being suspended, apparently because M. de Montigny did not believe in arming the state to stamp out smallpox. The merchants called on Council to spare no expense fighting the

PLAGUE: A STORY OF SMALLPOX IN MONTREAL

epidemic, and they called for stringent enforcement of the law. William Clendenning, a stove manufacturer and one of the meeting's organizers, spoke for many:

> CLENDENNING: ... The disease is now raging in one end of the city.
> DR. HINGSTON: I would prefer you should qualify the word raging.
> CLENDENNING: I say when the disease is so bad it is a disgraceful thing the magistrates of the city should set aside the means the law has put at their disposal to cope with the disease. When such a thing comes to pass it is time for us to be alarmed (Applause).
> A MEMBER: Three groans for the Recorder (Applause).
> THE CHAIRMAN: Order, gentlemen.
> CLENDENNING: When the law is set aside by the mandate of the city, it is time for us to take the matter into our own hands, unless we are willing to see the people die off by scores and our trade ruined (Applause). Have the people who make the trade of the city no power to see that the law for the protection of the people is honestly administered? (Applause).... We must let it be known to the city officers, from the worthy city Recorder down, that there is a public opinion in the city and that we have the power to compel him to do his duty without reference to race or religion.... A magistrate who would not do that is not worthy to be a magistrate, and he should not hold his position long (Applause and cries of "Quite right").
> MR. D.A.P. WATT said that what stamped Montreal was the filth and dirt of the city.
> A CITIZEN: No, no.
> MR. WATT maintained that he was right....

The merchants called for compulsory vaccination and isolation, and appointed fifteen of their number to meet with provincial and municipal authorities and the clergy to urge all possible support for the sanitary authorities.

Later that afternoon virtually every prominent physician in Montreal, French and English, attended the meeting organized by the College of Physicians and Surgeons. Hingston was in the chair.

He spoke in character, saying that no one present believed the smallpox was as prevalent as the public were led to believe. Still, it was in the city and steps should be taken.

The doctors reaffirmed their faith in vaccination, called for every possible means of isolation, for ample hospital accommodation, and for a campaign by physicians against the anti-vaccination "prejudice" among the public. They also passed a resolution expressing their regret "at the exaggerated fears of a section of the population, and the exaggerated reports that have been circulated regarding the disease." A.M. Ross and Dr. Coderre dissented from the resolution supporting vaccination. Coderre's position had already been undercut by an endorsement of vaccination by most of the staff at his own Montreal School of Medicine and Surgery. Ross was singled out for special condemnation, as the meeting labelled his anti-vaccination circular "an unprofessional act, and one which places him outside the recognition of the profession." Like the merchants, the doctors decided to seek the cooperation of the city's clergy.

On that day the Health Committee was unable to hold a scheduled meeting. It lacked a quorum. The newspapers let Montreal know about it. The next morning the Recorder finally released his decision in the case of Colonel Hughes, who had been caught in the act of tearing down a placard on his house and had called a sanitary policeman a pig. The Recorder admitted that the by-law seemed to be valid; he lashed out at the English newspapers for daring to criticize the judicial process; and he dismissed the case against Hughes, and all other pending cases, on a procedural technicality. A week later M. de Montigny sentenced Joseph Paquet and Horace Laframboise, both aged twelve, to two and three years respectively in a reformatory for stealing fruit from the garden of the Sisters of Providence.

On Saturday morning, September 5, Honoré Beaugrand chaired the largest meeting yet of prominent Montrealers, in Nordheimer's Hall. The platform was packed with dignitaries from the churches, universities, manufacturing, financial, and mercantile houses. Beaugrand told the assemblage that he had called the meeting because all over the continent it was believed that the people of Montreal were dying like sheep in the streets. The mayor censured the speakers at the Corn Exchange meeting who had called Montreal a dirty city and had attacked Gray's Health Committee. They had no idea, Beaugrand said, of how strongly outsiders were reacting to exaggerated reports of the peril. Certainly the epidemic was bad enough, but after all there had only been about three hundred deaths in Montreal beyond normal during the past four months. Furthermore, many French-speaking citizens were outraged at PRO BONO PUBLICO's attack on their nationality in the *Herald.* Insulting the French people, Beaugrand argued, was no way to stamp out smallpox. For emphasis, he repeated his comments in French.

Most of the speakers, English and French, dissociated themselves from the PRO BONO PUBLICO letter. Virtually everyone pleaded for racial cooperation, praised the church's efforts to encourage vaccination, and denied that the French of Montreal were dirty. With so many strong feelings having been aired the day before, there was little more to say. Beaugrand supported a merchant proposal to have a volunteer citizens' committee created to help the civic authorities stamp out the epidemic. The meeting approved a list of twenty-eight names for the Citizens' Committee, including the mayor, Hugh Graham, prominent garment manufacturer Hollis Shorey, a sprinkling of French Canadians, and many significant employers. It was not quite clear whether the citizens thought they were also endorsing compulsory vaccination.

Within hours the leading spirits in the citizens' movement presented themselves at the bishop's palace for their audience with Monsignor Fabre. His Lordship the Bishop of Montreal had called his parish priests to join him for the encounter. Twenty-two prominent Montreal merchants, three of whom had French names, laid their concerns before the ecclesiastics. The businessmen represented institutions employing some ten thousand French Canadians. Their spokesman was George Hague of the Merchants' Bank, one of the city's most respected financiers. The meeting was conducted in English. Hague "very courteously but forcibly" (according to the *Star*) drew the bishop's attention to the seriousness of the epidemic, the damage it was causing to Montreal's reputation, and the possibility that a boycott of the city's products would lead to immense unemployment and destitution in the coming winter. The merchants hoped that all the clergy would recommend vaccination and isolation from their pulpits.

Bishop Fabre "cordially" told the merchants that his priests had already urged their people to obey the advice of physicians concerning vaccination. Several clerics, led by Father Auclaire, spoke of the need for better hospital accommodation, making clear that neither the Catholic laity nor the Church had confidence in the civic hospital. Montreal's most important parish priest, Father Sentenne of Notre Dame Church, wondered whether the local and foreign press had not exaggerated the truth about an epidemic which was chiefly affecting the very young, "who were at all times peculiarly susceptible to any specially unwholesome condition." Fabre drew attention to the odious charges about the Church made in the PRO BONO PUBLICO letter. Everyone supported William Clendenning's denunciation of the letter as untrue, brutal, and unchristian.

Fabre had met earlier with the delegation of physicians. He promised the merchants that his clergy would repeat their advice to the people to follow the instructions of the doctors. The priests would not formally advocate vaccination because they were pastors, not physicians. The pastors would tell their people to obey the physicians, who were responsible for medical science. Immediately after the meeting Fabre issued this letter to his priests:

> I consider it my duty to make known to you several resolutions adopted at a meeting of the medical men of Montreal, which resolutions refer to the smallpox epidemic which is now raging in the city and vicinity. You will inform your congregations of these resolutions and urge upon them to conform thereto.... You will show them that they must respect and esteem medical science, and that they must not allow themselves to be influenced against its teachings by mere prejudices....
>
> Get them also to understand that it is their interest and a duty for them to contribute, as far as each one is personally concerned, to diminish or prevent the ravage of this epidemic, by taking all the precautions suggested by the Faculty. Obedience to the orders of the medical men who are bound,

before God, to employ the most efficient means of preserving
health, will have good results....

Among other means of prevention, you must urge isolation
of the patients themselves and those who attend them. On this
point you will tell your flock that, as soon as the disease has
made its appearance in a household, all the members of the
family must even abstain from coming to church, for there is
there a sufficient reason for not hearing Mass.

Above all, tell your congregations to abstain from all
excesses, to be temperate in their habits, both as regards eating
and drinking, and to pray fervently that this scourge may soon
cease.

The bishop himself set an example by addressing the congregation
at the cathedral at early mass the next morning. He and most of
the priests went further than the cautious language of their circular. They advised their people to get vaccinated and to practise
perfect isolation.

◦   ◦   ◦

It seemed that Montreal had awakened to its state of plague. The
leading newspapers had sounded the alarm. The leading citizens
had responded. Physicians had spoken out. Employers of labour
were requiring vaccination. The Church was advocating vaccination.
Volunteer citizens would work with City Council to pour resources
into the fight. The province had created a Central Board of Health
with sweeping powers. Vaccinations were going on at a wonderful
rate. There would be immediate improvements to the smallpox hospital. "In the course of a few days we may fairly hope to see the
progress of the smallpox blocked," the *Star* enthused on the
Monday after all the meetings and the sermons in the churches.
Earlier it had hailed the many signs of progress with a nineteenth
century's equivalent of our "light at the end of the tunnel"
metaphor: "One begins to see daylight through the bush."

> They therefore walked abroad, carrying in their hands flowers or
> fragrant herbs or divers sorts of spices, which they frequently
> raised to their noses, deeming it an excellent thing thus to comfort
> the brain with such perfumes, because the air seemed to be every-
> where laden and reeking with the stench emitted by the dead and
> dying, and the odours of drugs.
>
> — Petrarch on the Black Death

CHAPTER 6

THE WAGES OF SIN

Monday, September 7

Corner of Victoria and Sherbrooke streets, a fashionable intersection near McGill College:

A crowd of little boys and female domestics watches a party of official-looking men making strange preparations. They don bright yellow oilskin jackets and pull on high rubber boots. Some put on rubber fishermen's hats, the rest make do with felt chapeaux. Each has a stout stick and a lantern. When everyone is properly attired, and the lanterns are lit, the leader hands out big cigars. Everyone lights his cheroot. In a cloud of smoke the men disappear through a manhole into Montreal's underworld.

The city surveyor, P.W. St. George, has arranged a special sewer tour. The party consists of St. George, three helpers, and reporters for the *Star* and *Gazette*. St. George will lead them on an inspection of the "Coteau Barron," one of Montreal's oldest main sewers. It drains some 910 acres running from the central slopes of the mountain through the East End to the river

129

at Monarque Street near Molson's brewery. The aim of the "petite promenade" is to confirm or deny the common belief that the city's drainage system is helping to cause the plague because of blockages, bad construction, or other noxious problems.

Will it be a hazardous journey? The main danger seems to be of being poisoned by the foul vapours in the infernal tunnels. The cigars are a counter-device, their smoke being healthy vapour. St. George tells the men to keep smoking if they value their lives. All the manhole covers have been removed along the route to drain off some of the sewer gas. Above ground a city employee tracks the voyageurs, carrying a ladder from manhole to manhole in the event that they have to be suddenly evacuated.

The men walk fifteen feet below the street, on the floor of a tubular brick sewer about six feet high and four feet wide. The brickwork seems new at first, for they are in a northern extension, added in 1870, of the main East End drain. After crossing the intersection of Berthelet Street and Union Avenue they are in the old sewer, built in 1862, and it starts to conform to the popular idea of sewers (formed for many people in this era by Victor Hugo's description of the Paris cloacae in *Les Misérables*). The bricks are brown, their mortar discoloured. Sediment has oozed through chinks in the mortar. Carbonate of lime stalactites hang from the roof. No one describes the darkness as Stygean, possibly because there is light from the open manholes every two hundred yards along the tunnel.

In a few places the men have to bend double to make their passage, but there are no blockages in the drain and it seems to be doing its job remarkably well. About six inches of fast-moving water flows through the sewer. Practically no sediment or foul deposits are noticed—indeed the sewer seems to be just carrying dirty water until the men make a small dam with their boots and observe some of the solid particles coming down. This drain is in good working order, and it is not evident that anything would be gained by the special "flushing" of the main sewers that some health-conscious Montrealers are demanding.

The travellers inspect the entrances of the principal side sewers, finding perfect drainage and good flows in all cases. St. George shows the party a number of old wooden drains, a few of which are from smaller streets, most the connections from private homes. From these the flow is usually sluggish and putrid. Such pollution as occurs, then, seems to take place before local refuse reaches the city's sewer. Wooden drains are no longer permitted in new construction, and all street drains are being modernized, but Council does not require property-owners to replace their old wooden connections. Tramping and splashing and smoking, the men pass the Jeanne Mance, St. Urbain, St. Lawrence, Amherst, St-Denis, and St-Hubert cross-drains. St. George observes that the system drains the whole smallpox region of Montreal, a fact which is not immediately reassuring. The party carries on virtually to the end of the tunnel. After a three-mile, three-hour subterranean passage through the entrails of the city, the men climb their ladder into the light and fresh air.

*   *   *

So the people of East End Montreal did not live on top of a swamp of pullulating, fermenting poisons. Nonetheless, almost all of the East Enders believed the smallpox was related to bad sanitary conditions, for which somebody was to blame. A number of English Montrealers, who shared the notion of there being an intrinsic connection between smallpox and dirtiness, were quick to fix the blame on the East Enders themselves. PRO BONO PUBLICO had spelled it out in blaming filthy French operatives from the East End, and then going on to attack venal priests, venal physicians, and an incompetent City Council. His roundhouse assault, aimed mostly at French Montreal, was a highly visible tip of the iceberg of ethnic and religious antagonism plaguing Montreal before and during the smallpox epidemic.

Suspicion between the English and French racial groups in Canada went back to the British Conquest. It was renewed every few years as the tensions of sharing a single state led to disputes about constitutions, representation, language, schools, taxes, subsidies, appointments, railway charters, and power. Most often the races had become tangled in religious disputation, as French Canada became the centre of Canadian Roman Catholicism in a sea of English-speaking Protestants. Resisting assimilation came to be a cause that many French-Canadian clergy, especially those influenced by Bishop Bourget, virtually equated with defence of the Church. It was by no means a perfect fit (think of all the English-speaking Irish Catholics), but in a simple, fundamental way it seemed that the central fault line of Canada, Quebec, and Montreal was between French Catholics and English Protestants.

Through the 1870s and early 80s there was a tendency for division to harden. Religious conflict sharpened as aggressive evangelical Protestants confronted an aggressive ultramontane Catholicism in Quebec that seemed to turn its back on the separation of church and state, toleration, and most of the liberal values and achievements of the modern world. New theories of racial and cultural evolution coloured old quarrels with a patina drawn from pseudo-science. Canada's westward expansion also opened fields of opportunities for cultural conflict about religious, educational, and linguistic practices. Would new territories and provinces be cursed—or blessed—with Catholic-Protestant/French-English duality?

Inside the province of Quebec, French and English struggled to maintain a state of uneasy co-existence. Provincial and municipal governments juggled representation and policies to accommodate the numerical majority of the French on one hand, the wealth and commercial dominance of the English on the other. The two most powerful social groups in Quebec were the Roman Catholic Church and the English commercial elite, the latter centred in their "Square Mile" of fine homes on the slopes of Mount Royal. In the years after Confederation the English enjoyed considerable political power in the provincial government. The treasurer of Quebec, for example, was always English, and in 1885 it happened that the premier of the Conservative provincial government, J.J. Ross, was English on his father's side. Ross was also a physician.

Quebeckers of both nationalities were involved in endless debates about the provision of social services, particularly education and health. The Church insisted that its mission to teach the young and care for the sick took precedence over any secular activities of the state. Most English-Protestant Quebeckers could agree with Catholics on the importance of religious institutions. Normally the province made do with separate-but-equal Protestant and Catholic hospitals, schools, orphanages, and asylums. Sometimes the balance could not be maintained. In 1884-85 English-speaking Quebeckers were particularly agitated by charges of overcrowding, neglect, and callous use of physical restraints in the treatment of inmates of the province's two principal lunatic asylums, both operated by Roman Catholic religious orders.

Dr. Daniel Hack Tuke, a noted Quaker and asylum reformer from England, had published a scathing report on the Quebec institutions, including Montreal's Longue Pointe asylum, implying that French-Catholic Quebec was unbelievably backward—positively mediaeval—in its treatment of the mentally ill. Tuke could not believe that "a colony of England, so remarkable for its progress and intelligence as Canada, can present such a spectacle ... in the year of grace 1884, in the Montreal Asylum." One result of the storm of controversy was Quebec legislation attempting to tighten controls on the asylums. The operators declared the new laws a violation of their contract and refused to be bound by them. Ultramontane Catholics, such as the writers for Senator Trudel's newspaper, *L'Etendard,* anathematized the legislation as state interference with the autonomy and liberty of religious groups.

Louis Riel's North-West rebellion in 1885 was more important in the history of Canadian race relations than in the annals of the West or the Dominion's military traditions. The Riel affair touched off passions that continued to flare long after the fighting had ended. Riel was French-speaking, of French blood, and insanely Catholic (he had in fact spent some time as a patient in both of Quebec's lunatic asylums in the 1870s). Fifteen years earlier, during his first insurgency, he had deliberately taken an English-Protestant life by ordering an execution. Now he had tried to set the whole of the Canadian prairies ablaze with Métis and Indian violence. Not surprisingly, the North-West rebellion aroused English-Canadian extremists to more alarm about the machinations of French Catholics—the people responsible for Riel's milieu, the people who after his capture argued that this rebel and traitor should be given clemency.

Some newspaper comment on Canadian racial issues was particularly inflammatory that year. A Toronto paper, the *Evening News*, was using the style of the new mass journalism to conduct a populist, nativist crusade against French influence in Canada. Its portrayal of Canadian issues was crude, simplistic, stereotyped, incendiary, and apparently in tune with the views of many of its readers. This is how the *News* saw relations between Ontario and Quebec in May 1885:

FRENCH AGGRESSION

Ontario is proud of being loyal to England.

Quebec is proud of being loyal to sixteenth century France.

Ontario pays about three-fifths of Canada's taxes, fights all the battles of provincial rights, sends nine-tenths of the soldiers to fight the rebels, and gets sat upon by Quebec for her pains.

Quebec ... has been extravagant, corrupt and venal, whenever she could with other people's money, and has done nothing for herself or for progress with her own earnings.

Quebec now gets the pie.

Ontario gets the mush....

Hundreds of thousands of dollars are spent in maintaining the French language in an English country.

Ontario is getting sick of it....

If we in Canada are to be confronted with a solid French vote, we must have a solid English vote.

If Quebec is always to pose as a beggar in the Dominion soup kitchen, she must be disfranchised as a vagrant.

If she is to be a traitor in our wars, a thief in our treasury, a conspirator in our Canadian household, she had better go out.

She is no use in Confederation.

Her representatives are a weakness in Parliament, her cities would be nothing but for the English speaking people, and today Montreal would be as dead as the city of Quebec but for Anglo-Saxons, who are persecuted and kept down by the ignorant French....

Quebec could go out of the Confederation to-morrow and we would not shed a tear except for joy.

To the *News* and many other English Canadians, Riel was a symbol of French-Canadian aggression. In its coverage of the North-West rebellion, the *News* seemed to single out Montreal's 65th Regiment for special scorn, publishing a particularly stinging accusation that the men were a bunch of drunken incompetents led by worthless, drunken officers. Nineteenth-century newspaper controversy was often sharp-tongued and long-winded. Several French newspapers, particularly the rabidly ultramontane *L'Etendard*, responded to journals like the *News* in kind, raging against francophobia, English aggression, Protestant fanaticism, and other aspects of a satanic conspiracy to destroy French Catholics in North America. The slurs on the 65th had been too extreme, however, even by the loose standards of the time. They resulted in a criminal libel suit against the *News*'s proprietor, Edmund Sheppard, scheduled to come to trial in Montreal in September.

French Canada was already feeling aggrieved and defensive, then, when the *Star* broke the Montreal smallpox story, the other English papers followed suit, and English newspapers throughout North America took notice. Smallpox was killing French Canadians in Montreal, everyone read. Not English-, Irish-, or Scotch-Canadians. Listen to *Grip*, Canada's (Toronto-based) national humour magazine:

"Fumigated Verses from Montreal"

Tommy Ruggles,
Mother's joy!
Vaccination!
Healthy boy.

Alphonse Daudet,
Mother's pet!
Smallpox patient;
Dead—you bet!

The Daudets and other French families seemed ignorant of the benefits of vaccination, unconcerned about the loathsome disease they spread among themselves and to others, and they lived in some pretty nauseating slum conditions. It was an image of French Montreal that reinforced the idea of backwardness spread by the Tuke report on Quebec's treatment of the mentally ill. It was an image reinforcing Protestant stereotypes of Roman Catholics as unprogressive (forget the Irish Catholics for now). It was an image of French Canadians as poor peasants who lived close to the earth, bred lustily, and were content to live in ignorance of the progressive outside world. An image caricatured in PRO BONO PUBLICO's talk of filth, priestly domination, and boycotting.

Everyone, English and French, denounced that letter and the *Herald* for publishing it. In denouncing the letter, the French newspapers translated and circulated it throughout the community. As *La Patrie* put it, the letter was a species of "fanatisme qui n'a jamais été surpassé pas les insulteurs de notre race." To *La Presse* it was "le libelle le plus atroce qui ait encore été publié contre les Canadiens de race française et les catholiques." It was outrageous to be called a dirty people by members of the same race that inhabited the slums of London, Manchester, and Sheffield, and whose own reformers wrote so eloquently of their uncleanness. It was odious to suggest that the French Canadians should be boycotted and shunned in their own country. "Let us be ready for a life like Southern blacks," UN CANADIEN-FRANÇAIS wrote in French in *Le Monde*, "because soon they will dream of barring us from their hotels, expelling us from their schools and public places, anywhere where the English wish to tread."

L'Etendard, zealously Catholic, zealously French-Canadian, raged at slurs against the priesthood by descendents of Cromwell's bootlickers, sons of Luther, Henry VIII, and Queen Elizabeth. The republican *Patrie* was appalled at the assumptions of Anglo-Saxon superiority underlying the PRO BONO PUBLICO letter. "Since the Conquest," it wrote, "they have unceasingly portrayed us in Europe as a stupid and degraded race, a degenerated fragment of the French race whose future is to enter a state next to savagery." *L'Etendard* made bitter mockery of Anglo-Saxon attitudes:

Just imagine, English eyes, English ears, and, worse than all, English noses, to have unceasingly to see, to hear, to scent French Canadians.

It is really shocking.

Ah! we are very guilty. Not only do we circulate in the streets at the risk of profaning the ground that our masters alone should tread, since they valiantly conquered it at the point of their valiant swords ... we even breathe the air that their superiority should insure them the right of breathing before us.

The air that the cession made exclusively British.

And in spite of all this, English though they are, they sometimes have to breathe second-hand air. Just fancy pure-blooded Saxons having to breathe an air that has already been vitiated by French lungs!

Shocking! shocking!

Alas! yes, we who never wash; whose epidermis shrinks from soap and water as much as a good son of Luther shrinks from holy water; we, shaking with fever, perspiring cholera, covered with the hideous pustules of the smallpox, we throng around the counters of the English gentlemen, we buy their goods, for which we even pay cash....

Paranoia begat paranoia. A columnist in *La Patrie* claimed that the English were intent on genocide: they were creating the smallpox panic so they could boycott and starve the French. To *L'Etendard* the English were practising germ warfare:

We will no longer have even the right to earn our livelihood in our own domain if we are not ready to accept from their doctors, with a vaccine more than suspect that they bring among us, the germ of the frightening malady which is a part of their national heritage and which, as late as twenty years ago, was so appropriately called "*le mal anglais.*"

The newspaper suggested that French Canadians should boycott English shops and stores, and thus save the "gallophobes" from being bothered by their dirt, smells, and filthy money.

French Canadians remembered that "le mal anglais" had come to Montreal from Chicago on the Grand Trunk, carried by "un Yankee," a member of "la race supérieure des Anglo-Américains." The fate of Sir Francis Hincks was proof that smallpox did not kill only poor and dirty French Canadians. *La Patrie* thought the Hincks and Ravenscraig cases showed it was a threat everywhere in the city. *La Presse*, on the other hand, thought the English were relatively free from it only because they did not have to live in conditions like those inflicted on the people of St-Jean Baptiste. "Deposit the same amount of excrement near Beaver Hall, give it time to ferment and to generate and throw off myriads of microbes, and we would see whether the English resisted better than the Canadiens."

Why was St-Jean Baptiste so foul and smallpox-ridden anyway? Surely because the English caused it. The English aldermen on Council had opposed St-Jean Baptiste's requests to connect with the Montreal drainage system; they were opposing proposals to annex the poor French-Canadian village to Montreal. How could it get rid of its poisonous vapours if it could not get sewer connections? *L'Etendard* spelled out why English-ruled Montreal was to blame for the smallpox in French Montreal:

> You not only wished to stop St-Jean Baptiste from cleaning itself up, but you have for years deposited your manure two paces from its borders! You have put your hospital in its parish and almost on its territory, you have forced its priests to serve there to keep it clean. Your slaughterhouses border on it, and your butchers who still break your rules and slaughter in them, hurl into its streets the bloody refuse of their animals.
>
> The city of Montreal has done everything in its power to make St-Jean Baptiste a hotbed of epidemic disease....

No one defended PRO BONO PUBLICO's charge that the French Canadians were a dirty people. The *Witness*, normally a voice of aggressive English Protestantism, criticized this libel on a race whose poor people were notably clean in their habits. They could not afford rugs on their floors, but they kept them swept. Editorially the *Herald* apologized for inadvertently printing the offensive letter, dissociated itself from its contents, tried to explain that letters did not reflect the newspaper's opinion, and apologized profusely several more times. French anger gradually subsided, as the journals accepted the opinion of the doctors, supported by the Church, and recommended vaccination and all kinds of cleanliness. It was more important to unite to drive the smallpox out of the city than to continue these newspaper spats.

But the resentment lingered. The world was, in fact, threatening to boycott Montreal. Outside journals did think the worst of the French Canadians. The *New York Times,* for example, wrote of them as a people who were accustomed to having the plague. If only the English newspapers had not sensationalized this minor epidemic. Most of the city's French-Canadian aldermen still believed that more damage had been done by the English press than by the smallpox itself. Jacques Grenier could not understand why the same papers that had said next to nothing during the much worse epidemics of the 1870s should now be so frightened. He could only think that the *Star* and the *Herald* were pursuing a vendetta against French Canadians or were the agents of outside interests, or both. Perhaps they were doing it for "Toronto gold."

To Grenier this was just another visitation of smallpox, like the ones he had seen so often in the past. Father Sentenne of Notre Dame Church, who took an interest in health matters, had begun to realize that it might be a more serious time of suffering, and he was stung by the criticisms of his people. From the pulpit and to reporters Sentenne said that the Church did not need the press to tell it how to do its duty. For weeks he had been advising his flock to take precautions. He thought the smallpox was severe in St-Jean Baptiste not because the people were dirty but because most of them were desperately poor newcomers from remote rural parishes, some without a change of clothes, who were simply unable to take precautions and who had weakened constitutions. Sentenne shared the belief that the civic hospital was probably causing some of the disease in the area. He thought the summer's fire on Logan's Farm might also have spread the vapours.

The priest had been studying the death toll. He hit upon the important realization that the great majority of victims—some 278 of 323—were young children. If one looked only at the forty-five adults who had died of smallpox, there were as many English and Irish victims as French. Sentenne's statistics were used in the French press for more special pleading—the epidemic wasn't so bad after all, and where the most important people were concerned, those in the prime of life, the plague seemed to affect all races equally. In any case, as Sentenne argued, the people would soon take the good advice they were being given and the smallpox would cease to trouble Montreal. No need to be so alarmed.

○　○　○

The alarmists would not calm down. When the *Star* began publishing the facts on August 15 there had been a total of 120 deaths. In the next twenty-four days there had been 296 more deaths, which was surely justification enough for its course. The defence that mostly children were dying was hardly impressive. "It seems to be assumed by the clergy and physicians that those who are losing the children can well spare them to the Kingdom of Heaven," the *Witness* wrote, "and that their willingness to expose their babes to so horrible a death is more or less warranted by the bliss which must follow. We have not so learned Christianity."

The *Star* ignored the PRO BONO PUBLICO controversy as largely an affair of cranks. To be attacked by Grenier as a mouthpiece for "Toronto gold" was another matter. Hugh Graham's newspaper struck back:

> Nobody is more to blame than Alderman Grenier, the man who has more influence over the City Council than any other alderman and who, had he cared more for the interests of the city and less for cheap popularity, might have saved Montreal much of the loss it has suffered. If there has been anything shameful in connection with this great public calamity it has been the inaction, the negligence, which has pervaded the City Hall. Nearly all that has been done yet to check the progress of the smallpox has been due to the influences of the

newspapers which Alderman Grenier so grossly abuses.... What has Alderman Grenier done? What has the Council done? If the matter were left entirely to Alderman Grenier the epidemic would last as long as did the epidemic of 1873-1878, of which he is so proud. Does he suppose that in the year 1885 Montreal can enjoy in secret the luxury of an epidemic killing hundreds? ...

We have not so much respect for the traditions of 1873-1878.... We do not believe it is necesssary to sacrifice another 4911 of our citizens during the next eight years.... Another such calamity would be the ruin of Montreal, and public feeling in Monteal is such to-day that, if the Aldermen contemplate a repetition of their brilliant performance ... the citizens themselves have a very different programme.

That program had been spelled out at the public meetings. It was time to get on with it. On September 7 and 8 the new Provincial Board of Health organized itself (Hingston was elected president) and ordered all municipalities in the province to appoint local health boards. The Montreal Health Committee held a fully attended meeting, which got right down to business. The first addition to the smallpox hospital was finally finished; a second addition would be commenced immediately. Henry Gray admitted, for the first time, that it had been hard to find competent nurses and attendants for the hospital. The city now intended to turn its management over to the Grey Nuns, assisted for Protestants by the Anglican order of Sisters of St. Margaret. Steps would be taken to build a new hospital on a new site. Itinerant vaccinators would begin going from door to door in the East End offering free vaccination.

Henry Gray drew the line at compulsion, telling his committee that it could never be enforced. Alderman Mooney, his predecessor as chairman, agreed. "The country has just got over a North West rebellion and could not stand another one in Montreal East," Gray said.

The new Citizens' Committee also met to discuss how to help. The municipal authorities had not asked for help, and many of them did not welcome this kind of outsiders' intervention. Beaugrand decided to abandon his chairmanship of the Citizens' Committee and was seldom seen again at its meetings. The citizens discussed where to build a new hospital (they could not agree: some favoured a rural setting near the cemeteries, others an island in the river or a converted ship), how to help with relief (for now Beaugrand, through the religious orders, was dispensing the $1,285 left over in the Citizens' Fund for the North-West volunteers, augmented by donations of $25 from Alderman Stroud and $500 from Donald Smith, a millionaire fur trader and partner in the CPR syndicate), and the questions they wanted Council and the Health Committee to answer about the epidemic.

The most forceful action was taken by the government of Ontario, influenced partly by Michigan's regulations, which passed a tough order-in-council that week aimed at quarantining Montreal. No rags or newly made clothing from Montreal or any other infected locality would be landed in Ontario without inspection and certification from an Ontario-appointed authority. No travellers would be allowed to enter Ontario from Montreal by boat or train without passing medical inspection. They would have to prove they had been vaccinated within the last seven years. Those who did not would be removed at the provincial boundary and turned back or would be vaccinated on the spot.

Inspection of the trains began immediately. On Tuesday night a woman bound for Chicago carrying a baby covered with the scabs and crusts of smallpox was discovered by the Ontario inspectors. Everyone fled from the car, which was disconnected and sent back to Montreal carrying the mother and child. A fair number of Montrealers, English and French alike, grumbled at Ontario's "insolent outrage" in bringing its inspectors into Montreal to do work that Quebeckers were perfectly competent to do for themselves.

The Ontarions were unbending. They had no faith in the Montreal or Quebec health authorities. Montreal itself soon withdrew its train inspectors, letting the railways and outsiders do the job. American authorities, who set up similar procedures on southbound trains, imposed a further humiliation by pressuring Canada's postmaster general, John Carling (a London, Ontario, brewer) to have all the outbound Montreal mail fumigated. Experts doubted that smallpox could be transmitted by letter over long distances, but they had to give in or face an American mail boycott.

The Health Committee began its experiment in voluntary house-to-house vaccination on Friday, September 11. A French-Canadian physician "of good address and polite manners" went from door to door on Visitation Street, in the heart of the infected quarter, using every argument he could to induce people to accept vaccination. Between 9 a.m. and 6 p.m. he persuaded only four people, all adults, to take the operation. On Saturday the Provincial Board of Health issued sweeping directions empowering local boards of health to enforce placarding, isolation, disinfection, and removals to hospital. Vaccination was not required.

The week featured the usual optimism from the Health Committee and much wishful thinking in the newspapers, particularly the French dailies, but there was no hard evidence of progress. Instead there were more horror stories of sufferers at large on the streets, the sick showing up at the Health Department, placards being torn down or ignored, and people holding traditional funerals for the smallpox dead (whose pullulating corpses were supposed to be disposed of immediately and without accompaniment). Forty-eight people died in the agony of smallpox on Sunday, September 13, bringing the week's official total to 128.

* * *

"The epidemic came upon us like a blasting wind—it came suddenly," Henry Gray claimed at City Council on Monday the 14th. It was Council's first meeting since June, and the English newspapers were screaming for drastic action. Gray defended his board's policies step by step. The smallpox had been beaten in the spring, he argued, and would have disappeared had it not been for the unusual crowds at the Fête-Dieu celebrations and Bourget's funeral. Dr. Hingston had recently told him that the mortality was less serious than during the last epidemic. Gray still felt that the situation did not warrant the "senseless excitement which prevails now in some quarters." Everyone's catch-phrase about the epidemic was "stamp it out." Easy to say, Gray told Council. "With animals it is done by shooting those afflicted, but you cannot shoot human beings, although I believe some would be inhuman enough to do so."

Politely but bluntly, Henry Gray maintained that neither vaccination nor isolation was possible without the support of the people affected. "It must be remembered that boards of health, here as elsewhere, can do but little without a healthy public opinion to back them. Laws cannot be enforced without the consent of the people." Gray suggested that the Citizens' Committee could usefully prepare literature, mainly in French, on the virtues of vaccination, isolation, and support for the public health authorities.

The Citizens' Committee wanted to go much further. It had adopted a sweeping proposal, drawn up in the form of a petition from some sixty prominent citizens (most of the moving spirits behind the original citizens' meetings), asking City Council to constitute their body as "The Emergent Health Committee" and turn over to it the power and money necessary to stamp out the epidemic. The "vigilante" group, as the *Herald* called them, unself-consciously, deposited a $4,000 bond against its promises to provide a three-to-five-hundred bed hospital within six days, enforce isolation, carry on house-to-house vaccination—compulsory if necessary—and provide relief where needed.

The Citizens' Committee assured Council that it was not interested in rehashing the past. It wanted to help get the smallpox out of the city. Such bold, loud proposals from prominent citizens could not be lightly dismissed. Beaugrand had consulted widely about the situation and the Citizens' Committee's remedies. Civic officials and leading Montrealers agreed that the emergency justified extraordinary action. Council could not legally delegate the powers the citizens wanted, but there was a provision in Quebec's statutes enabling Montreal to enlarge its Board of Health in an emergency. After a long debate on numbers, Council agreed to enlarge the Health Committee by appointing six new citizen members to work with the seven aldermen. On the recommendation of the Citizens' Committee, City Council appointed to the Health Committee (now usually called the Health Board) Messrs. Adolphe

Levêque, Louis Perrault, Richard White (editor of the *Gazette*), William Masterman, G.E. Desbarats, and Hugh Graham.

The mayor and a party of seven aldermen left the city that night, September 14, for a junket to the Toronto Industrial Exhibition (forerunner of the Canadian National Exhibition). They went in a special Pullman as guests of the Grand Trunk. Their party was just starting, the smallpox forgotten, when a young man entered their car. "You come from Montreal?" he asked. He was an Ontario health inspector, requiring proof of vaccination. There was much merriment and aldermanic rivalry as arms were bared and the marks approved. Alderman Mathieu did not bare his arm, and suggested that "some extra large marks of former vaccinations" should do (he was probably marked from smallpox in his youth). The Ontario doctor insisted, pulled out his instruments, and rubbed the vaccine virus in the arm of the Montreal alderman. The group gave three rousing cheers for the most newly vaccinated man in Canada, and invited the doctor to join their party.

In the heart of the city the Health Department mounted its largest removal operation yet. Watched by a large crowd of onlookers, a posse of sanitary police raided the old Eagle Hotel at 31 College Street, now a run-down tenement nicknamed "Noah's Ark." Five people had died from smallpox there the week before. Now sixteen children with the disease were removed from the building. One corpse was found and taken away. It is not known how many inhabitants of the ark survived.

◦   ◦   ◦

"Whatever those new members of the board will ask I will vote for.... For my part they shall have plenty of rope...." Alderman Beausoleil launched the September 16 first meeting of the expanded Health Committee/Board of Health on a sour note. The citizen appointees represented the people who had spread libels about Montreal and the old Health Committee all over North America, he claimed. Well, Beausoleil was ready to let them prove they could do a better job, though he thought they should all personally have to visit the smallpox houses, handing out relief.

145

One of the citizen members remarked that he had come in good faith and a spirit of harmony to try to help defeat the smallpox. The board settled down to business, and showed a new sense of urgency. Reliance on private donations for a relief fund was abandoned, as $5,000 in civic funds was set aside to help afflicted families. Sub-committees, dominated by the newcomers, were appointed to study hospital needs and the best means of isolating victims. It was evident from this first meeting that Hugh Graham of the *Star* was the strongest champion of vigorous measures. He called for a house-to-house inspection of the city and the posting of a watchman at every infected house. Gray said this would require hundreds of men. Graham said the board should hire them.

The board began to meet daily. At the second meeting, the hospital sub-committee, Perrault and William Masterman, recommended that a third extension be added to the existing building. The isolation sub-committee, Graham, White, and Levêque, could not agree on recommendations. Graham and White submitted a thirteen-point proposal calling for compulsory isolation "without regard to cost." All homes would be inspected to discover "secreted cases." ("There are as many cases hidden as reported," Henry Gray wrote privately to the American consul-general.) All infected persons would have to choose between going to the hospital and being completely isolated at home, with round-the-clock guards. Levêque's minority report called for another appeal to clergymen, doctors, house agents, and others to report cases. Nuns should be engaged to help discover and care for patients. Isolation would be recommended, but not required. Complete isolation was impractical because of all the cases in the city, Levêque argued, and would be resisted on principle anyway.

The board agreed to a week's experiment with voluntarism in everything but placarding. If the trial failed, compulsion would follow. Levêque arranged with Bishop Fabre for the Grey Nuns and Sisters of Providence to begin visitation on the board's behalf. Fifty nuns started immediately and within hours were reporting scores of new cases. They also distributed relief on behalf of the city—under strict instructions, of course, not to give any cash to families that included drinkers.

The Provincial Board of Health, effectively run by Gray, Hingston, and Beaugrand, issued a stream of orders aimed at forcing suburban municipalities to fight the epidemic. Realizing that it might have to intervene directly, the board hired the ace detective of the Montreal police force, Cinq Mars, a man said to have "a good nerve and any amount of determination," to be chief sanitary policeman for the province of Quebec. The Montreal Health Department decided to open branch offices in both the East and West ends, where people could come to report cases, arrange for disinfection, get vaccinated, and do other business. When the landlord at 429 St. Catherine Street realized that his premises would become a "picotte establishment" for the East End, he objected violently. Higher rent and a promise of compensation if the upstairs tenant moved out soothed his troubled mind.

Public vaccination was now available at numerous locations from nine a.m. until midnight. Most of English-speaking Montreal had been vaccinated. The schools were opening. Most Protestant schools required proof of vaccination. Pleading the poverty of so many of their families, Catholic schools required certificates only from children who had had smallpox in their families. Attendance at the Catholic schools was very low, as priests advised keeping children at home if there was the slightest exposure.

To reduce exposure at the smallpox hospital, the department had tightened security. A constable now stood guard at the gate. The fence was repaired and strengthened and topped by barbed wire. On September 19 the Grey Nuns took over administration of the institution. They named it St. Roch's Hospital.

o   o   o

All that week a special novena to the Blessed Virgin had been held at Ste-Anne's Church. There were daily prayers begging the mother of Christ to intercede to bring about the end of the plague. Many Catholics believed that prayer and repentance were the preconditions for any lifting of the plague. At St. James Church on the 13th Abbé Filiatrault offered what became a widely quoted explanation of the descent of God's wrath upon Montreal:

> If we are afflicted with small-pox this summer, it is because we had a carnival last winter; feasting the flesh, which has offended the Lord by the crimes which we committed during that time. The city of Montreal endeavored to raise herself to as lofty a position as the Tower of Babel; she intended to spread her fame—not only in the United States—but also in the greatest cities of Europe. It is to punish us for our pride that God has sent us small-pox. He has punished us by keeping away from our midst the strangers who were in the habit of visiting us. Consequently a greater scourge afflicts us, that of misery, the wages of sin.

According to St. Paul, writing to the Romans, the wages of sin are death.

After I have told you ... how another, by the insufferable torment he bore, danced and sung naked in the streets, not knowing one ecstasy from another; I say, after I have mentioned these things, what can be added more?

— Defoe, *A Journal of the Plague Year*

CHAPTER 7

HEART OF DARKNESS

YOU AWAKEN IN THE NIGHT AT THE hospital to hear the noises of smallpox. "Water, water, water, for God's sake, give me some water!"

"Shut up."

The thump of a patient, writhing in pain and fever and delirium, who falls out of bed. "Now sit on her and keep her down. Tie her down."

"Water!"

The thump of a corpse, pushed off its bed. Wrapped in a white sheet for a shroud, it is dragged out. Bump, bump, bump as bodies are dragged down from the second storey.

More cries for water. Mugs clang on iron bedframes. At night there is only one man on duty for the whole hospital. He does not come. You get up, if you can, and get some water from the pail for your fellow patient.

If the cries are coming from the "bad" or the "black" ward, where they keep the worst cases, you are too frightened to do anything. "Healthy" patients don't go in there. Maybe an attendant will come, maybe not. They are often too busy for that ward. If the inmates stagger to the door or come out, the other patients run away.

The cries from the heart of the darkness sometimes fade to hoarse whispers. Eventually they stop.

"Close the window; I'm cold." It rains, and the rain comes through the open window. You shiver under your blanket, the wool fibres running into your pustules. When they close the windows, the stench is unbearable, the vile odours of smallpox mingling with smells of urine and faeces from the commode at the end of the ward. The stench comes up from the floor, uncleaned for days, from the mattresses, from the unchanged bedclothes, and the unwashed patients.

Rank grass and weeds overgrow the grounds outdoors. Heaps of barrels and piles of linen are strewn around the yard. The gate hangs open. Seventy-five feet away, liveried servants drive splendid carriages up the main road to the mountain park.

The delirious patients sometimes get up in the night and wander through the wards. Sometimes they fall on other beds, other patients. There are never enough attendants, and until the sisters take charge they are a strange lot. Why is the matron, Mrs. Gertrude Holman, dressed in nun's clothes? Why are her two servant girls dressed as men? Why are they "playing with one another" on the wards, as Lizzie Penfold saw it. Is it some strange masquerade of the smallpox hospital? Is Lizzie just delirious herself?

The cook is a drunkard, everyone knows that. Meals are sometimes hours late. The food tastes horrible—thin soup with a few chunks of boiled meat, tea that tastes like senna and salt, potatoes cooked without being cleaned. Is it the bread that is inedible, or is it the thought of taking it from the girl who brings it to you in bare hands covered with smallpox?

The food is put out on tables and patients help themselves. The convalescents are expected to serve the sick. Some do, with wonderful love and dedication—a little girl named Alberta, and young Miss Connor whose fiancé had taken smallpox and died in the hospital. Other patients take food greedily, until there is nothing left for anyone else. The sickest patients, or those without friends, often get the least. It is assumed that the very sick cannot eat or drink. No one feeds them or holds a cup to their lips.

The attendants are not nurses as we know them. It is assumed that nothing can be done for the very sick, and that the convalescents can look after themselves. "This is not the Windsor Hotel," Dr. Nolin tells patients who complain. He says they have no right to complain, and that they must look after themselves and the others who need help.

If you are brought to the hospital at night, the attendant will motion you to go and find a bed somewhere. It may be just emptied by death, the linen unchanged. The sheets might be taken away and a soiled blanket left. Some of the mattresses are made of straw and are verminous or maggotty. Every few days a servant will clean the floors or supply fresh linen. No one bothers to use disinfectants or any kind of deodorizer. Some of the male patients smoke to purify the air.

Dr. Nolin will notice you when he makes his daily rounds. He takes note of your name and passes on. Sometimes he prescribes a little cream of tartar, sometimes a cup of mineral water or a dose of castor oil. He always agrees to get the medicine you ask for, but often forgets. "Mrs. Gertie," the matron, is sometimes kind, sometimes brusque. If the patients complain too much at night she turns off the gas lights, leaving them in the dark. "Lottie" Larose, the most experienced nurse, lives in some kind of uncaring private world, and spends much of her time doing dishes.

There appears to be no remedy, no relief, for the victims of the black pox, many of whom are sick children. It is not thought wise even to wash smallpox sufferers, for fear of aggravating the pustules. The victims moan and cry out, die with no one by their side, not even a priest, and are carried off and jammed into coffins. Some say that two or three bodies are sometimes put in a single coffin. Some say they saw bodies stacked in the "dead house" awaiting a new shipment of coffins.

A father and son named Davis are both brought into the hospital suffering from the black pox. The father dies first. The boy hears his parent's body pitched out of bed and cries out, "If I live to get out of here I'll make this all known." He dies the next day. Those who did get out remember how the bowels of dropped corpses would open, and the fluids stain their shrouds and run onto the floors.

After mid-summer only priests and ministers are allowed to visit the smallpox hospital. Friends are encouraged to send gifts of fresh food and drink. Grapes are most common and are always appreciated. There are charges that the night men who carry off the corpses also steal delicacies, particularly wine. "Shut up, or I'll clout your ears," one of the thieves says to a complaining patient in the night. Other patients go out in the orchard and steal apples for their fresh fruit.

Each of the three additions to the original farmhouse is a two-storey box-like frame building, connected to the older wings by a common corridor. Each addition has four 15' x 20' wards. There are eight beds to a ward, four a side, two feet apart. There is no electricity or running water, and the commodes are just chairs with pails under them. The pails are supposed to be emptied twice a day, but sometimes they are not. Sometimes they overflow. Sometimes patients who soil themselves are left to lie in their piss and shit for days.

These were the memories of Lizzy Penfold, James Hancock, John Munroe, William Higgins, Joseph Coleman, George Woodfit, Joseph Brightman, Miss Hunter, Miss Hillier, James Wallace, Robert Watters, Mrs. Hemming, Miss Bush, Flora Campbell, Mrs. Mathers, and Mrs. D.R. Borland, all of whom were patients in the hospital between April and early October. Conditions were worst in mid-September, when the sick and the dying overwhelmed the handful of staff. Even when the Grey Nuns took over, St. Roch's hospital had a staff of six sisters and a few male night attendants to care for over one hundred patients. Afterwards Protestants and Catholics differed on how much of an improvement the change to religious operation brought about. Everyone agreed that the nuns worked like slaves.

The accounts of the horrors of St. Roch's hospital did not become public until later, and we will see that some of the patients' charges were flatly denied. Officially, almost insouciantly, the Health Department maintained that patients enjoyed the best possible care in the civic hospital, before as well as after it became St. Roch's. In fact, the Health Board knew their facility was shockingly inadequate, and it was this knowledge that lent urgency to their search for a new hospital.

* * *

Bad as it was in the Montreal hospital, the situation was worse in the suburbs. In St-Jean Baptiste it was "almost incredible," a *Gazette* reporter wrote on September 19. The village's feeble attempts at public health measures had broken down completely. Placarding and isolation had been abandoned. Children played freely in the streets with the marks of the smallpox on their faces. Heaps of dirt and refuse lay everywhere. William McNabb of 76 Pantaleon Street, who had often complained about the negligence of the authorities, could no longer be interviewed. "Don't come in; my child has taken the smallpox in spite of all I could do." Prisoners at the police station had complained that the the chief's two children were allowed to run around the station with smallpox. Both children had since died.

The nervous journalist went into a doctor's office, and found smallpox cases in the waiting room. He went into a cigar store, and saw more smallpox. Then he watched a man killing fowls on the sidewalk near the market. Their blood ran into the street to mix with the refuse and garbage. The reporter broke off his inspection and got out of St-Jean Baptiste.

At the other end of the city in St-Henri, the situation was "ten times worse than they have ever admitted," a resident wrote to the *Witness*. "The authorities know very little about the epidemic as literally nothing is done to secure returns ... nothing is done to isolate the patients or to indicate the houses.... There have been scores—if not hundreds of cases, not a house has been marked." When the first case broke out on a street nothing would be done. When there were ten or a dozen, someone would appear from the village, hose down the yards, and toss a packet of disinfectant on the doorstep.

St. Henri is in a sanitary state that would not be tolerated anywhere else in the world. On most of the streets there is no drainage, slops of all kinds being thrown out promiscuously. The only attempt at drainage is a narrow gutter covered with a board and most of these are choked up with filth. There is a sewer running from the Tanneries down the whole length of Metcalfe Avenue, open to the light of day and flowing two feet deep with black filth, poisoning the air for a long distance around.

... There are about one hundred English families in this neighbourhood, many of them living in infested localities, and they have not had a solitary case, while all around the French are dying like sheep.... A very large percentage of the people on the street are freshly pockmarked. I have been shaved by a barber and learned the next day that he had several cases of smallpox up stairs! I have been served in a dry goods store by a clerk apparently not long out of bed from small-pox! I have bought goods at a grocer's and had them brought home by a boy with the marks on his face! Only this afternoon I saw two girls carrying home a basket of washed linen, one girl covered with red scars.

Even the worst hospital would be better than nothing. In the village of Outremont a farmer's hired hand took sick. The farmer put him in a dilapidated shed with an old piece of carpet to lie on and arranged to have food left at the door. The municipality finally heard about the case and tried to get a doctor to look into it. Many doctors did not like to treat smallpox for fear of becoming contagious and scaring away their regular patients. The third doctor approached by the Outremont mayor finally went round. Dr. Lecavallier noticed untouched food set about thirty feet from the door of the shanty. The sight inside was "too dreadful to write about," he reported, "but to put it in a few words there was the body of a man dying of the small-pox lying on a piece of carpet, without water and there was no saying how long the man had lain without attendance, for he lapsed into insensibility. It so did for me that I had to go home." Lecavallier sent a letter to the mayor describing the case. By the time Outremont officials arrived to give help the lonely man had died. A few days later Outremont officially objected to a proposal that Montreal might build its new smallpox hospital within its boundaries. Henry Gray observed that Outremont was the town where they leave people to die in barns.

Nobody wanted a smallpox hospital anywhere near their neighbourhood. Every proposal for relocation foundered on municipal or
property-owners' objections. The people of the village of Côte-des-
Neiges pleaded with Montreal not to put a pest-house on property it
had purchased near the main road down which farmers brought produce into the city. The Montreal Golf Club's excuse was their club-
house's proximity to the mountain park. The provincial Bureau of
Agriculture would not allow use of the exhibition buildings (as Gray
learned by reading the *Herald*, whose reporter apparently stole the
letter of refusal from a desk in the Health Department). The merchants' association of Hochelaga protested against using an old barracks in their end of the city. Seven hundred citizens of Longue
Pointe met to consider every possible means of resisting any scheme
to take over the old St-Benoit asylum. Alderman Jeannotte protested
on behalf of East End Montreal against any expansion of an institution
that was already spreading the smallpox by sending poisons into the
air. If attention were paid to all of these protests, Gray told his board,
the only practical place for a new hospital would be up in a balloon.
There were serious suggestions that a hospital ship, moored in the
river, might be the answer. It would never do in winter. Finally it was
decided to add a fourth temporary wing to the existing St. Roch's.

"The Pale Horse Still Maintains His Gait," read the *Herald*'s
smallpox column on September 21, announcing the weekly death
toll. Two hundred and thirty-five deaths from smallpox in seven
days, almost double the week before. "It is a crime to trifle with the
epidemic any longer," the *Herald* said. "Lives are wasted by every
weak measure and by the non-enforcement or the partial enforcement of every good regulation." The Citizens' Committee had
stayed in existence to support its men on the Health Board and
keep an independent eye on the situation. At its meeting that afternoon, Louis Perrault introduced three priests, who joined the committee. Catholic authorities were obviously alarmed. Father
Leclaire of St. Joseph's parish told the committee that nothing was
working in his community. At least sixty of his families each had
three or four cases. People were concealing the smallpox, even
from Leclaire and the nuns. He had visited one family who insisted
on keeping the room in darkness. When the priest demanded light,

it revealed a person covered with smallpox. He had put up placards personally, and they had been torn down. Isolation was non-existent.

The priest thought better hospital accommodation was desperately needed and believed that vaccination, offered by trusted doctors, would now be better received. But he was also confessing failure—the inability of even the Church to persuade people to protect themselves from the smallpox. "He had exerted all his influence in favour of vaccination," Leclaire told the meeting. "The people, however, had got the idea that vaccination was simply a speculation of the doctors and some had even accused the priests of being in partnership with the doctors." The Citizens' Committee resolved to meet daily while the plague raged. *Le Monde* was about to publish another letter from Dr. Coderre blaming the spread of smallpox on vaccination, and vaccination on the venality of "messieurs les vaccinateurs."

❂   ❂   ❂

Tuesday, September 22

A cool, overcast day. Rain begins in the early afternoon. According to the Health Office there were twenty-seven deaths from smallpox in the city yesterday and nine in the suburbs. The Recorder's house on St. Denis Street is now placarded, as his daughter has smallpox. At the Board of Health's morning meeting it hears that the Canadian Pacific and the other railway companies will stop offering one-day trips out of the city. The Academy of Music, however, wants permission to reopen for a production of "The Rag Baby." Alderman Roy suggests that crowds should not be encouraged during the epidemic. In that case, Hugh Graham says, the churches should be closed. Others allude to gatherings of large crowds in the cemeteries on Sundays; these are Catholic processions reenacting the Stations of the Cross. The board agrees to let the Academy open. Its patrons are likely to have been vaccinated.

Another long discussion of the hospital situation. No progress on a new hospital. The need for Protestant nurses to look after the

Protestants at St. Roch's hospital is thoroughly aired; steps are being taken. Water closets will be installed at St. Roch's now that it is connected with the city water supply.

Is public vaccination working? Henry Gray admits it is not. Many do come to the thirteen vaccination stations, but those who most need the operation, the children, are not being reached. Perhaps house-to-house vaccination should be tried again. It had always failed, Gray admits, "owing to the contempt people have for corporation employees." Perhaps the Citizens' Committee would have better luck if it sent its own doctors, perhaps accompanied by priests. The board hears that the nuns have discovered 324 new cases of smallpox in their house-to-house visits.

Gray attends the Citizens' Committee's meeting in the afternoon. Some members think that employers are getting good results in compelling their workmen to be vaccinated. But one of the city's largest, most influential employers, tobacco magnate W.C. McDonald, speaks out for the first time. He urges the city to stop offering retail vaccination and go about it in a wholesale way. Go to work as if the city was on fire, he says. Divide it into districts, organize doctors to go from house to house, send priests with them. Stop trifling with the smallpox, for it will keep spreading until people rot above the ground as well as below it. McDonald prophesies ruin for Montreal unless the responsible authorities do their duty. He cannot accept the idea that the lives of little children are not as precious as those of adults. He calls on the mayor to become the Napoleon of the hour.

When Gray describes the work of the public vaccinators, handling one thousand to fifteen hundred persons a day, McDonald interrupts: "At that rate winter will be over before the work is accomplished."

"You can't help that," Gray replies. "There is strong prejudice against vaccination, so strong that even the clergy can not remove it. A large number of people will refuse to be vaccinated."

"A mere remnant only."

"Your only recourse is to get a law passed enforcing compulsory vaccination, but I warn you that if you try force you will be met with force. If our Board get an order to enforce vaccination, however, we will obey it. But it is my duty to warn you of the consequences."

Father Leclaire passionately defends the Church's position, throwing the blame on bad vaccine, and on greedy doctors who cannot agree among themselves.* The priests will try to persuade the people. They can do no more. It is clear that Leclaire and other churchmen do not believe they can make the difference in the struggle, whatever Protestants may fantasize about their power. The force of religion is blunted, dulled, in its collisions with class antagonisms, economic resentments, blind fears. The Citizens' Committee resolves to support compulsory vaccination, more or less along the lines McDonald suggests.

Henry Gray goes on to another meeting, the Provincial Board of Health. Drs. Hingston, E.P. Lachapelle, J.W. Mount, and Richard McDonnell are also present. They have a long discussion behind closed doors, which results in this order: "That vaccination being the only safeguard against smallpox, and the only measure likely to stay its progress in the present emergency, vaccination of all children and re-vaccination of grown persons is ordered to be enforced by all local boards of health."

The afternoon's rain is the beginning of a storm. In truth it is a dark and stormy night. By midnight the rains have become torrential. At 177 Dalhousie Street, near Haymarket Square in the heart of

---

* "The Bishop is no doctor and he can go no further than the doctors. We did what we could when the epidemic broke out but we had no help. I have given relief myself on condition that the families relieved should be vaccinated and isolated. Then no doctors were given to vaccinate the people. I have advised vaccination but can't wonder that my advice has not been adopted. The doctors charge one dollar for every one they vaccinate. If they give a certificate they charge a dollar more. You can't blame them because no man has a right to work for nothing, but what is the result? Suppose there are seven in a family, the cost of getting all these vaccinated and afterwards getting certificates may be $14. How many poor families do you suppose can afford this sum? What the priests could do they have done and done alone. The people of St. Joseph's suburbs are not unwilling to be vaccinated, provided it is done by discreet persons. The people are not altogether to blame, for their repugnance to vaccination. Their prejudice is due to the carelessness with which the work was formerly done. In my parish there are many who are willing to be vaccinated by doctors they know but not by strangers. Referring to the action of the bishop I wish to say that while there is no unanimity among doctors it is out of our sphere to preach vaccination as a thing which must be done as a matter of conscience."

the largely Irish quarter known as Griffintown, a man rushes into the street in his nightclothes. He is in a frenzy. His wife follows him, shrieking for help. Awakened neighbours know that Mr. Enoch Adams, a middle-aged man who works as a tinsmith for the Grand Trunk, has a case of the black smallpox. It was diagnosed last Saturday by Dr. Rodger. Now Adams is rushing about in delirium and agony. Some neighbours have resented the fact that his house has not been placarded. No one offers to help.

Adams collapses, writhing, on the sidewalk. His wife rushes to Number 7 police station to get help. Police Sergeant Crowe tells her it is a job for the health authorities and he will send for them. There is nothing more the police will do. The wife goes back to try to help her husband. No one comes. (Constable Hackett has gone to Dr. Laberge's house, knocked on the door, and been told by someone to come back in the morning. He has gone on to Sanitary Inspector Radford's home and told Radford that a man with smallpox has been turned out into the streets. Completely misunderstanding the situation, Radford told the constable that the people who turned him out will have to take him back in as there is no room in the hospital. Smallpox was not his business anyway, and they should consult a doctor.) Adams has been lying in the rain and cold for almost an hour when a passing stranger helps his wife drag the poor man back to the house. They get him to the doorstep, but cannot get him up the stairs. Lying in his hallway, his legs extending into Dalhousie Street, Enoch Adams dies.

The wife covers the body with a quilt and stays with it. All night long no one comes. Towards morning neighbours go to Number 7 station, Number 6 station, Central Station, begging for help. The police phone around, refer people to the health authorities, promise to send constables to send guard. At 7:15 a.m. two constables from Number 7 station finally arrive to keep the crowd away. A reporter comes and sees the weeping wife guarding her husband's body while the crowd watches from the other side of the street. Finally Sergeant Moran of the sanitary police comes and calls for a coffin and hearse. At 8:45 a.m. Enoch Adams's body is taken away for burial.

159

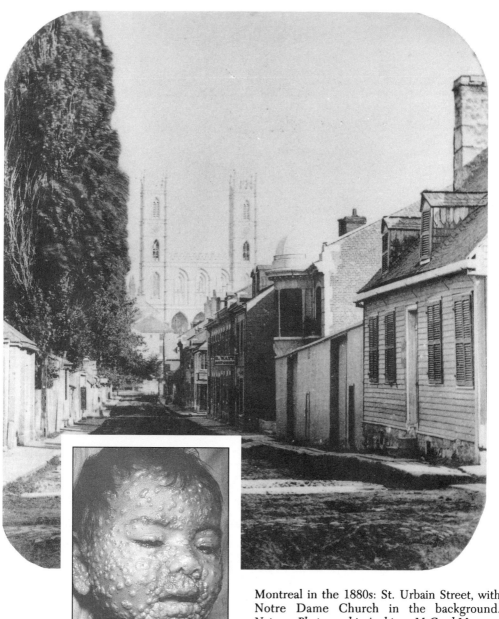

Montreal in the 1880s: St. Urbain Street, with Notre Dame Church in the background.
Notman Photographic Archives, McCord Museum of Canadian History
Insert: A twentieth-century smallpox victim.
World Health Organization

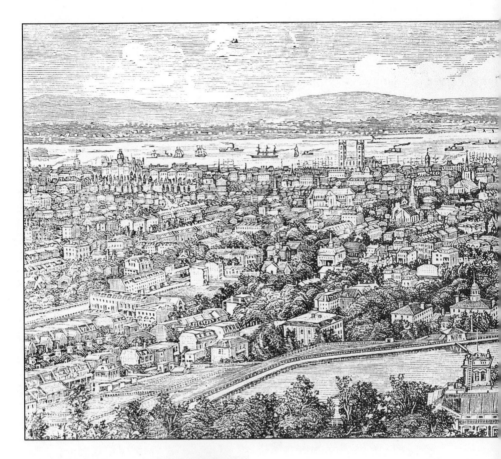

Left to Right: Henry Gray, Chairman of the
Health Committee of City Council (*Fraser-
Hickson Institute*), "Doctor" A.M. Ross, anti-vac-
cinationist (*University of Toronto Library*),
Honoré Beaugrand, Mayor of Montreal (*Notman
Photographic Archives, McCord Museum of
Canadian History*), Dr. J.-E. Coderre, anti-vac-
cinationist (*Fraser-Hickson Institute*), Dr. Louis
Laberge, Medical Health Officer of Montreal
(*Fraser-Hickson Institute*)

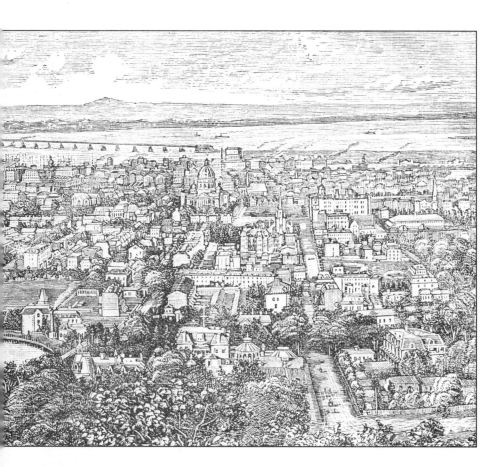

Top: Montreal from the mountain, showing Notre Dame Church, the river, the Victoria Bridge. The civic smallpox hospital was on the mountain slope to the left of the camera. *National Archives of Canada*

The Best Preventive Known FOR SMALLPOX,

DR. MORLEY'S
STANDARD ENGLISH REMEDY

During the epidemic Montreal's nine daily newspapers carried many notices for disinfectants, odoriferants, pure foods, and patent medicines. Vaccine shields, obliterators of smallpox marks, and tonics, such as Labatt's Ale, were also advertised. (*Fraser-Hickson Institute*)

MONTREAL DRIVING PARK.

SOMETHING NEW, REALISTIC, GRAND.

Six Afternoons Only, commencing Aug. 10th

Gates open at 1, performance at 3.30 p.m.,
Rain or Shine.

FIRST TIME IN CANADA!

The Greatest Novelty of the Century.

Buffalo Bill's Wild West

The following are a few of the numerous
FEATURES:

THE RENOWNED SIOUX CHIEF,

SITTING BULL.

And Staff, WHITE EAGLE and 52 Braves.

The One-Legged Sioux Spy, FRISKING ELK.

The Great Markswoman from the Western
Border, Miss ANNIE OAKLEY.

Largest HERD OF BUFFALO ever exhibited.

Grand Indian BUFFALO HUNT, known as
the "SURROUND."

CONDEMNED !

The City Council Protest in the Name of Humanity

AGAINST THE EXECUTION OF LOUIS RIEL,

The "Herald" Eulogized for its Stand !

AN OPEN AIR MEETING AT THE CITY HALL.

Liberals and Conservatives Unanimous in Denouncing the Government.

LARGE AND ENTHUSIASTIC DEMONSTRATION HELD LAST EVENING.

Sir John and the Quebec Ministers Burned in Effigy.

Left: Crowds attending Buffalo Bill's Wild West show probably helped spread smallpox. (*Fraser-Hickson Institute*)
Above: The condemned rebel, Louis Riel, received more attention than thousands of children dying of smallpox. (*Fraser-Hickson Institute*)
Right: A.M. Ross's scurrilous anti-vaccination propaganda, claiming that vaccination spread smallpox and enriched doctors. (*University of Toronto Library*)

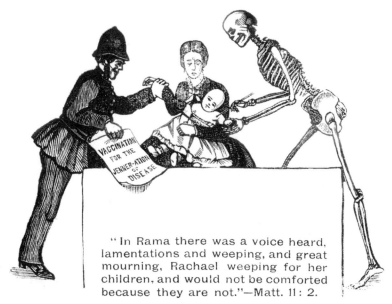

> " In Rama there was a voice heard, lamentations and weeping, and great mourning, Rachael weeping for her children, and would not be comforted because they are not."—Matt. 11: 2.

The City Papers Cry

VACCINATE! VACCINATE!! VACCINATE!!!

THERE'S MONEY IN IT!!!

TWENTY THOUSAND VICTIMS!!! will be Vaccinated within the next ten days in this City under the present **ALARM!!!**

That will put **$10,000** into the pockets of the Medical Profession.

CLEANLINESS, SANITATION AND HYGIENE ARE "NONSENSE," unworthy of attention by our Board of Health.

FILTHY STREETS, FILTHY LANES, AND FILTHY DRAINS help the Medical Profession.

THERE'S MONEY IN IT!!!

The City Papers Cry

VACCINATE! VACCINATE!! VACCINATE!!!

O tempora, O mores!

August

In late autumn the Board of Health forcibly
removed to the hospital smallpox patients who
could not be properly isolated. Families and
neighbours often fiercely resisted the activities of
the sanitary police. When Canadian artist Robert
Harris found his portrait business dull because of
the epidemic, he sketched this *Incident of the
ˆmallpox Epidemic, Montreal,* which appeared
Harper's Weekly. (New York Public Library)

> ...the yet unbroken spell of our helplessness, poised on the edge of some violent issue, lurking in the dark.
>
> — Joseph Conrad, *The Shadow-Line*

CHAPTER 8

EAST END REBELLION

THE STRONGEST POLICEMAN IN GREATER Montreal stood five foot ten, measured fifty-five inches at the chest, twenty inches around the bicep, and weighed 279 pounds. He was twenty-two-year-old Louis Cyr, a constable on the six-man Ste-Cunégonde force, who was rapidly developing a reputation as "Ste-Cunégonde's Sampson." It was said that he could lift 1,678 pounds and he had advertised his willingness to take on any man in the world in a weight-lifting contest for money. There was no man in Montreal he was afraid to arrest, Cyr boasted.

On Wednesday afternoon, September 23, Cyr and another officer were going from house to house ordering citizens to clean up their yards when they came upon Adolphus "Rouge" Paquette, drunk and throwing stones at passers-by near the corner of Workman Street and Atwater Avenue. The policemen arrested Paquette. As they marched him to the station, they were approached by Paquette's brother, Theophile, and two other men. A mêlée occurred in which a third policeman, Charles Proulx, was knocked senseless with an axe. Louis Cyr picked up his comrade with one hand, held fast to his captive in the other, and kept going for the station. He was brought down by a rock as big as a goose egg.

Before Cyr could recover, Proulx was beaten again by the axe-wielder. Reinforcements arrived, including help from the Montreal force. Three of the four offenders were apprehended—one by Cyr during an upstairs brawl in an Atwater Street tenement ("Ouellette kicked officer Vermet in the groin. Officer Cyr, however, came to the rescue, and lifting Ouellette up as though he were a cat, threw him down on a table and stopped his struggles"). Theophile Paquette, red-haired, face pitted with smallpox, escaped. Constable Proulx teetered on the brink of death. Cyr tried to resume his duties, but had to take to his bed to recover from "brain fever" caused by the rock that hit him.

That Wednesday was a busy day for Montreal police. At the courthouse that afternoon the criminal libel trial of Edmund Sheppard, proprietor of the Toronto *News*, finally came to an end. His paper was judged to have published blatant falseholds about the behaviour of the men of the 65th Regiment during the North-West troubles. Sheppard was fined $200. As he left the courthouse a mob surrounded him, hooting and howling, demanding revenge for the defamations. Lieutenant Normandeau, formerly of the 65th, rushed at Sheppard and tried to horsewhip him. Sheppard parried the first blow with his umbrella and knocked off Normandeau's hat. Major Dugas, the man who had charged Sheppard with libel, pushed Normandeau aside. Sheppard was reaching for a revolver in his pocket when police intervened, seized him, and headed for the station. They had to use their clubs to protect the Toronto journalist (who was given his gun back and got out of town). Unlike the villains in Ste-Cunégonde, the mob was said to be well-dressed, composed principally of men from the upper classes.

The Police Committee of City Council, chaired by Hormidas Jeannotte, met that day to consider complaints made by citizens in the aftermath of the Enoch Adams affair. Several constables were summoned to explain and justify behaviour that Alderman Grenier labelled "inhuman and stupid." Jeannotte defended the men, saying it was not their duty to touch smallpox cases. This was up to the sanitary police, who had been notified. Alderman McShane, who represented Griffintown, where many of the other clashes between police and citizens occurred, launched into a wild attack on the force: ... a pack of lazy vagabonds ... loafing instead of helping citizens fight the disease ... going into low shebeens and getting drunk ... bragging about arresting some unfortunate only a little less drunk ... clubbing unfortunate wretches on the street.... Jeannotte said it was the policemen who were being clubbed and murdered. Soon they would be armed to protect themselves. "That's right," McShane said. "Give them revolvers to shoot down the innocent citizens."

The police were ordered to be more diligent in reporting health problems to the health authorities. And they were told to exercise greater vigilance over the Salvation Army, whose meetings were often being disrupted these days, with assailants and defenders ending up in court. "Ce n'est pas de la religion," *La Patrie* commented sourly about the "maniaques" of the Salvation army. "C'est du cirque." A day later the Salvationists were attacked in Victoria Square by a mob wielding sticks and stones. Four of their men were injured, one of the female soldiers fainted, and a drum was stomped to ruins.

⚬ ⚬ ⚬

On Thursday morning, September 24, after a round of explanations and recriminations in the Adams case, Hugh Graham presented the Health Board with a detailed program for compulsory isolation and vaccination, the trial of voluntarism having failed. The board would be implementing orders of the Provincial Board, and would work with the Citizens' Committee. The unvaccinated would have four days to come forward while the operation was being organized. Compulsion would begin on Monday the 28th.

Nobody would be vaccinated by force. Graham and the other members of the board said this time and time again. People would be asked to prove that they had been vaccinated, asked to accept free vaccination if they could not, then have their names taken if they refused. Clergy would try to persuade them to cooperate. Only as a last resort would they be charged and, if convicted, fined in a special health court. The Health Board requested the loyal support of all classes in the community, urging "patriotic and quiet submission" to measures for the public well-being.

Catholic churchmen refused to accompany the vaccinators in their rounds. But they agreed to receive names of those needing persuasion and then visit them separately. Father Lonergan of St. Mary's Church told the Citizens' Committee that if priests went to the people with the doctors, the people would not listen to them.

Montreal's newspapers, French as well as English, supported the resort to compulsion. *L'Etendard*, for example, temporarily swallowed its indignation at everyone's insults to the French Canadians, admitted that the plague was serious, admitted that vaccination was recommended by the vast majority of medical men, and urged everyone to obey the authorities. At the other end of the political spectrum, "Cyprien" in *La Patrie* explained ruefully that while he had defended the liberties of the individual all his life, he could not support the idea of fathers denying vaccination to their children. That would be liberty to commit infanticide. On Saturday *La Presse* favoured vaccination, but opposed compulsion. By Monday it had fallen into line, but with much muttering about the East End being poisoned by bad drains and the refuse from the millionaires on the mountain. *Le Monde* decided the danger was too great to rehash the rights and wrongs of compulsion. Perhaps it would help if all the city's doctors were made public vaccinators, so that people could go to their family doctor for (free) vaccination, rather than have to submit to a stranger.

Hugh Graham's *Star* published long, eloquent editorials on the need for community support of the health authorities and on the goodwill underlying the board's program: "We want to hurt nobody; we want to do nothing unlawful or cruel to any one. We want to save the lives of the people and the city from ruin when we urge all classes, all races, all creeds to encourage the doctors in their visits.... When every body is vaccinated, we shall cease to be reproached and sneered at by the whole world, and not till then."

The smallpox both was and was not a menace to English Montreal. It was not killing many of the English, and you could live in Montreal through the whole epidemic without ever seeing a case or a placarded house (just as you could live in the city without ever speaking a word of French). But the plague's damage to the city was both material and moral. All citizens, the *Witness* thought, were mortified by outsiders' reaction. "We feel intensely the shame of being regarded by the world as contaminated, and of being open to the charges of tolerating a loathsome disease and of endangering a whole continent by breeding and disseminating a pestilence." On that day, Saturday, the city's attorney, M. R. Roy, Q.C., was ordered to leave the CPR's Ottawa train because he would not accept re-vaccination. He got off at Montebello.

*   *   *

On Saturday afternoon, September 26, the Board of Health started to remove patients from dwellings where isolation was obviously impossible. Trouble started right away. Five children in three families had confluent smallpox at 6 Berri Lane. The youngest was less than a year old. All three mothers were pregnant. The residents offered "determined opposition" to any removals. Dr. Laberge relented, placed guards at the tenement, and asked the Grey Nuns to help the people during isolation.

St. Louis Street runs east from the old parade ground, the Champ de Mars, which has since become the parking lot behind City Hall. In 1885 St. Louis Street contained Montreal's newest slum, a block of one-and-a-half storey tenements built on land owned by the St-Jean Baptiste Society. The buildings faced inward around a square; many had small shops on the ground floor. In the last few days smallpox had spread through the tenements with astonishing speed. On Saturday night Henry Gray accompanied Sergeant Moran and three other sanitary policeman to 165 St. Louis Street— a "foul slum," Gray called it, "which would never have existed in any city but this"—to remove patients who had not been isolated.

A large crowd gathered and barred the way to the health authorities. They sent to Central Police Station, which was in the basement of City Hall, for help to keep the crowd back. One constable arrived and refused to help. Gray and Moran told the residents they would return the next morning to remove the sick.

Sergeant Moran asked for police help in advance. At Central Station he was given two constables and told that Chief Paradis concurred in the view that they were not required to assist if it was a case involving smallpox. When Moran entered the house on St. Louis Street, a pregnant mother met him with an axe. She said she would kill him if he seized her child. The police constables refused to enter the house to help Moran. They told onlookers that they too would kill anyone who tried to take away their children. There was nothing to do but leave.

Aldermen Prefontaine, Dufresne, and Mount were at City Hall. They heard of the troubles and agreed that it would never do to allow the law to be defeated. The aldermen went downstairs to the Central Station, where they found no one in charge. Prefontaine, a member of the Police Committee, ordered the police to reinforce the sanitary men. A squad of ten policemen accompanied Moran back to St. Louis Street and blocked it off, keeping the crowd away, while Moran's men removed three children and two women in the black wagon. The axe-wielder offered no resistance.

In the East End that afternoon it took forty-five minutes for the Catholic procession of supplicants to St. Roch to pass. Thousands of faithful from St. Bridget's and other parishes, led by a beadle carrying a staff and a priest with a crucifix, wended their way through most of the infected streets in the city, chanting prayers. Hundreds of residents rushed to their doors to witness the scene. Thousands of children were part of the gathering. From pulpits that morning priests urged the people to support vaccination and the recommendations of the Board of Health. They also read a papal decree on the efficacy of prayer in crushing epidemics and plagues. About two thousand members of St-Jacques parish made a pilgrimage to Côte des Neiges Cemetery, kneeling, chanting, and praying at each station of the cross. L'Etendard claimed that this was the best way to restore healthy conditions in the city.

In the evening the Champ de Mars was the site of another public meeting on behalf of Louis Riel, whose execution was now scheduled for October 16. His defenders were raising money for last

166

desperate appeals. The fiery Liberal lawyer and agitator, L.-O. David, raised the matter of smallpox when he told the crowd of two thousand that while the English were blaming French Canadians for being uncivilized, without the French presence in Canada the English would still be living in their slums of London. If they wanted to blame the French Canadians for spreading smallpox, the French could just as easily blame them for having brought it to Canada "in their nasty poisoned rags from the slums of London."

In Longue Pointe seven hundred citizens held a meeting to protest the Board of Health's plan to use the old Christian Brothers' epileptic home as a smallpox hospital. They resolved to use all possible measures, including the enrolment of special constables, to resist Montreal's plans. Some talked of burning the building down rather than having it become a home for smallpox.

On Saturday and Sunday, September 26-27, seventy-three more people, mostly children, dead from smallpox within the city limits of Montreal, were buried in Côte des Neiges Cemetery.

¤   ¤   ¤

Madame Chaput was Montreal's equivalent of Dickens' Madame Defarge. She and her husband lived at 427 St. Catherine Street, next door to the East End offices rented by the Board of Health. Madame Chaput did knitting and ladies' fancy goods that she sold from her home. They had smallpox in the residence, but the Chaputs, probably fearing for their livelihood, were determined not to be placarded.

An earlier placard had been torn down. The sanitary officials lodged a charge with the Recorder. Monsieur Chaput bragged to them that he would pay $200 in fines rather than see his house placarded. On Saturday he had a momentary triumph when the acting recorder threw out all the anti-placarding cases on procedural grounds. First thing Monday morning the health police tried again.

Placarder Benoit was about to post the black and yellow notice on her door when Madame Chaput rushed out and tore it from his hands. A second one appeared ... she reached to tear it down ... her wrists were seized by a sanitary policeman who held her back. Her husband ran out of the shop shouting that they were assaulting his wife. A crowd gathered and the health officials retreated.

The crowd followed them to their office. People milled around outside, cursing the Bureau de Santé and its interference in their lives. "You loafers," one man cried, "You feast and revel in champagne while we die of starvation. Wait till to-night and we will clean you out and burn down your place." Police arrived and cleared away the mob. A *Herald* reporter who followed the placarders on their rounds that day saw resistance virtually everywhere they went, most of it from angry women like Madame Chaput. One of them ran into the street brandishing a carving knife and declaring that she was "a true Canadian" and would not let anyone put a placard on her house.

Honoré Beaugrand was sick with asthma and exhaustion, and under doctors' orders to rest. Henry Gray was the acting mayor. After hearing of the St. Louis Street troubles, Beaugrand had written formal letters to Gray and Chief Paradis. The laws must be upheld. The policemen were obliged to assist the sanitary police. Those who had not done their duty would be suspended. All policemen would submit to vaccination or re-vaccination, or be dismissed.

Alderman Jeannotte happened to appear before the Health Board at its daily meeting that Monday morning. He was leading a delegation from the East End objecting to a proposal to use the old female gaol in their quarter as a smallpox hospital. Jeannotte thought it would spread the smallpox further, and he told the board that the various rending, glue, and tallow factories in their part of the city also caused smallpox. Then he spoke in his role as chairman of the Police Committee and objected to the city police being used to assist the sanitary police.

This was too much for Henry Gray:

> I went to the place with my officers. I saw the children lying in smallpox and people all around them. In pursuance of a charitable and Christian-like law, we tried to send those children to an hospital, where they would be cared for, but we were resisted by force. I sent a policeman—not one of the cowardly

City policeman, but a Sanitary policeman—to the Central station for help.... We were not going to illtreat the children. We took them out of a filthy den and placed them with the nuns, ladies who devote their lives to charity and kindness.... In an emergency like this the bells of Notre Dame should ring the alarm and every police officer in the city should be sent to aid in the enforcement of the sanitary laws. They should be sent, not to club the people, but to show that the City council is doing its best. I am a Catholic, and I have defended the rights of the people of the East end, and I think they should look upon me as their friend.

Gray was called away to discuss the troubles at the East End health office, where the staff were being taunted and feared for their safety (one of the secretaries, a one-legged man, was told that his other leg might soon be broken). He suggested that they close the office. Jeannotte chaired a Police Committee meeting at which everyone else supported Beaugrand's position on the use of the police and passed appropriate resolutions. Then the aldermen assembled for the regular meeting of Council.

Jeannotte charged that the mayor was exceeding his power by meddling in the affairs of the police. His defence of police reluctance to deal with smallpox led him into comments on lawlessness in Griffintown, which aroused Alderman McShane to another roundhouse assault on the incompetence of the force and its chief. Jacques Grenier intervened, claiming that Chief Paradis was being abused because he was a French Canadian. The real problem, Grenier said, was the failure of the Recorder's court to support the police with strict penalties. McShane denied that he was a racist— he had supported Paradis for chief, he said, despite threats that he would be shot.

The Health Board needed money to pay for its vaccination campaign. Alderman Beausoleil announced that he was resigning from it because he did not agree with the policy of compulsion. Alderman Rainville, also from the East End, supported Beausoleil, telling Council that if vaccination were made compulsory it would provoke a civil war. The proof of that, Rainville claimed, could be seen in the disturbances at the East End health office that morning. He had been vaccinated himself, the alderman said, and he supported the practice. But he would allow no one to vaccinate his family against his will.

Rainville moved an anti-compulsion amendment to the motion releasing funds for vaccination. Beausoleil seconded it. McShane observed that the people of Montreal were dying like the cholera victims in Spain and it was not manly for aldermen to stand against the good of the city. It was as natural for an Irishman to vaccinate his child as to eat his dinner, McShane remarked. Alderman Stevenson said he could not believe what he was hearing: in the last seven days 238 people had died of smallpox, and the men representing the wards where the disease was worst were opposing strong measures! Even the city attorney was refusing to be vaccinated!

> JEANNOTTE: Good for him.
> STEVENSON: What can we say to the poor people now when they have such an example set them?

No wonder Montreal was looked on as a plague-spot and its citizens treated like lepers, Stevenson concluded. Everyone had tried persuasion. The time for persuasion had passed.

Aldermen Mathieu, Dufresne, Perrault, Rainville, Beausoleil, and Jeannotte voted for the amendment against compulsion. Aldermen Mount, Prefontaine, Archibald, Fairbairn, Rolland, Stroud, Roy, Holland, Robert, Wilson, and Grenier voted in favour of compulsion. The main motion was then carried, aldermen Rainville, Beausoleil, and Jeannotte dissenting. These were three of the four representatives from St. James' and Ste-Marie's wards, where smallpox was at its worst. The fourth, Alderman Roy, had originally opposed compulsion, but had changed his mind. He rented lodgings to some six hundred tenants; scores of them were dead. His brother, who had not believed in vaccination, had six children suffering from the disease.

❖   ❖   ❖

St. Catherine Street. That evening, Monday, September 28

Crowds have been reassembling in front of the East End health office, the site of this morning's disturbances. By seven o'clock the street is black with a throng of men and boys. Some would-be leaders orate. Hoots and yells increase as people mill restlessly. Someone casts the first stone. One of the health office windows shatters.

Police gather from all over the East End. They are equipped only with batons and Paradis does not want a confrontation with the citizens. He argues with those in the mob who can hear him, saying they will certainly wind up paying the costs of any damage they do. "The chief's oratory was interrupted at intervals," the *Star's* reporter observed, "by the music of the stone chorus on the panes of the Health Office windows."

Except for the stones, it was not an ugly or even a very unruly gathering. From time to time the police would clear the sidewalk in front of the windowless office. After about half an hour of desultory stone-throwing the cry went up "À l'Hôtel de Ville!" Most of the crowd moved off along St. Catherine. Some sang "En roulant ma boule." Others cried "Vive La France!", "Bravo Riel!", "Hurrah Canadiens-Français!" Not an unhappy throng: singing, cheering, people happy with drink, people filling their pockets with stones. About a thousand strong, their numbers growing as they paraded, almost entirely French-Canadian.

Rocks smashed the windows of several East End pharmacies that had been selling vaccine. Next was Dr. Lachapelle's house near Sanguinet Street. Dr. Lachapelle was a member of the hated Provincial Board of Health. The Lachapelle house was duly stoned. No one noticed until afterwards that these were two different Lachapelles. Number 951 St. Catherine was unmistakably the residence of Montreal's medical officer, Dr. Laberge. Voices shouted for Laberge to come out of his house and be killed. When he did not appear his windows were broken. On their way down St. Denis Street towards city hall the stone-throwers took out many street lights, more pharmacy windows, and some of the panes in Alderman Grenier's house.

The main health office was on the Gosford Street side of City Hall. A volley of missiles and flying glass sent clerks, placarders, disinfectors, vaccinators, and the rest of the staff scrambling for cover. One woman was felled by a stone. Policemen went out to calm the crowd, but got nowhere. The throng filled Notre Dame Street and Jacques Cartier Square; it stoned all the front windows of City Hall. "Down with compulsory vaccination!" According to *La Patrie*, a young Frenchman named Chappelier exhorted the crowd with wild denunciations of tyranny. Shots were apparently fired into the building. The party inside thought the mob might force the doors at any time. Aldermen Gray and Roy were the senior civic officials at hand. Gray phoned his home, told his daughter to take out their loaded revolver and fire it into the mob if they should attack the house.

Still sick, Honoré Beaugrand was taking a sulphur bath at home when he was called to the telephone. He ordered the tocsin—the alarm—to be sounded. The bells of Notre Dame rang out, calling police from all over the city. The mayor disregarded doctors' orders and said he would go to his office. He left his wife at home with the coachman, a double-barrelled shotgun, a revolver, and orders to shoot the first hostile person who opened their front gate. At City Hall Gray had called for help from the volunteer militia. Word spread from the armouries for men to muster, but it would take time.

As the defenders grew more anxious, two police detectives fired their revolvers out the window over the heads of the crowd. All the police in the building were issued rifles with bayonets. Suddenly Chief Paradis and the squad who had been defending the St. Catherine Street health office appeared on the scene. Paradis ordered his men to put guns aside. He organized sallies of baton-wielding constables who drove the crowd away.

"Au Herald!" someone shouted. A large group moved down Craig Street to Victoria Square, yelling, throwing stones, smashing the windows in the *Herald*'s offices. The paper was being well vaccinated, someone quipped. Printers and journalists went on with the job of getting out the next morning's edition.

Beaugrand had now arrived at City Hall. He ordered police to defend Victoria Square and began organizing reinforcements from the harbour police and the militia. The rioters were quickly driven away from the *Herald* building. "Au Star!" someone shouted, but the police had scattered the stone-throwers and they fled up Beaver Hall or along Craig, back to what a reporter called "their small-pox fastnesses" in the East End.

At the corner of Panet and Ontario streets the mob smashed into the drug store of Dr. Laporte, one of the public vaccinators. Someone started a small fire, but it was put out before much damage could be done. Down on St. Catherine the health office was trashed again. The stock of placards was dragged into the street, doused with sulphur from the disinfecting supplies, and set ablaze. Another smallpox bonfire.

Beaugrand, Paradis, and squads of policemen and firemen arrived on the scene. The firemen threatened to turn their hoses on the crowd. The crowd threatened to cut their hoses. As his men fought to clear the street, Paradis went inside the ruined health office where he found a man trying to upset the stove and start a fire. The man tried to flee. Paradis caught him.

"Don't let him take him to jail," he heard someone yell. Then he was attacked by several rioters, struck on the head, and kicked.

"Are you going to assassinate your Police Chief?" Paradis blurted out, his head covered with blood.

"Champagne, don't strike, it is the Chief of Police," someone said. Board in hand, Elie Champagne was berating his friends for using his name when he was arrested and taken away. Paradis, half-fainting, was carried into a nearby house.

Now more than one hundred strong, the police freely wielded their batons as they cleared St. Catherine, St. Denis, and Ontario streets. ("Sergeant Carpenter rushed forward, brandishing his stick above his head, and, almost before the rowdies knew it, he was in their midst, dealing terrible whacks in every direction and scattering them right and left. In another second some fifty policemen were also among them, using their batons with a most appreciable vigor.") By one in the morning the last of the rioters had been driven into the far suburbs and the city was quiet again.

About two o'clock people living near the corner of Dorchester and German, about four blocks from City Hall, were awakened by wailing and sobbing from outside. A woman, dressed in black, walked along the street carrying an infant who was dying of smallpox.

Mother and child had been turned out by the people at the house where they were staying. The onlookers heard the horrible story, shut their windows, and went back to bed. The woman wandered on, her baby in her arms.

o   o   o

"Hurrah for the French-Canadians; Montreal is no longer for the English nor Irish," an excited young man in the crowd outside the ruined health office exclaimed the next morning.° There was a buzz of approval, and the young blood, apparently not long out of a smallpox bed, took to a nearby saloon to drink to the victory.

The curious were out in force, of course, to survey the damage. As riots went (and Montreal had seen a fair share over the years, usually relating to religious passion), the September 28 affair was fairly modest: one ruined health office, several badly damaged drug stores, several score broken windows and gaslights, an incapacitated police chief. Property damage amounted to a few thousand dollars (the city eventually paid $1,971 compensation to private property-owners). No lives were taken in the rioting. Seventy-nine people died of smallpox in Montreal and its suburbs that day. There was some newspaper alarm about organized conspiracies and mob rule, but most post-mortems noted that the crowd had been relatively good-natured, with most of the destruction carried out by small numbers of hotheads, many of them young boys.

But was it only the beginning? "A number of men, who looked old and respectable enough to know better, while standing in front of Dr. Laporte's store, were heard to say that they hoped the mob would start out again to-night and do the city up more thoroughly." Beaugrand received five threatening letters that morning; Grenier and Gray were warned that their homes were in peril. The city

---

° The *New York Times*, which perhaps had a stringer covering the story, reported that in Victoria Square the night before a young man had mounted the pedestal of the statue of Queen Victoria and asked the crowd whether Montreal was to be ruled by the English or the French. "The French," they shouted back.

buzzed with rumours of *pieds noirs* and quarrymen from the outlying suburbs about to march downtown. Some of the sanitary police
were told to their faces that they would be killed. Dr. Laberge was
said to be going about wearing a disguise.

Mr. GRAHAM: We might just as well determine now and at
once whether the mob is going to rule the city.
Mr. ROY: We must rule or die.

Other members of the Health Board were venting their outrage that
morning when a man entered their meeting, identified himself as an
anti-vaccinationist from France, and suggested the board take steps
to appease the rioters. The intruder was probably Chappelier, the
Frenchman seen in the thick of things during the mêlée. He was
told to get out. The board was discussing a resolution urging the
mayor to call on the militia to keep order in Montreal, when
Beaugrand came into the room to say he had done just that.

Beaugrand explained to Council that afternoon that the threats
and rumours, supported by reports from plain clothes detectives
who had gone into the East End, forced him to act. As chief magistrate he was requesting the military to come to the aid of the civil
power, and had personally issued revolvers to the sanitary police.
The crisis had to be dealt with now. Yes, he would use those loaded
words and say the trouble had to be "stamped out." If the rioters
did not die of smallpox they were going to die of famine next winter
as the world shunned Montreal. As mayor, Beaugrand was determined to carry out his "sacred duty" to himself and to the people.

Most of the aldermen were in no mood to trifle with rioters.
Grenier moved a resolution endorsing the mayor's actions. The
letter of the law would be followed. The soldiers would be constantly under the supervision of the civil power, not permitted to
use force without the authorization of a magistrate and the reading
of the Riot Act. The Health Board had never wanted a show of
force, Gray told Council. They had just wanted to go "smoothly and
quietly to work as civilized people should." The trouble, he said,
came from the lies that unprincipled doctors had spread among the
people—"that the vaccinators lolled about in houses, smoking

pipes, penetrated into females' bedrooms, tied children down and forced them to be vaccinated, etc." Gray intended to go on with his duties that night, "but if the blackguards break into my home the women there are prepared to repel them."

Council was told that the Health Board had decided to end the hospital impasse. It had sent men that morning to take possession of the provincial exhibition buildings, a few hundred yards north of Fletcher's Field on Mount Royal Avenue in St-Louis du Mile End. The seizure had led to threats that the mob would burn the buildings. Beaugrand asked Council whether Montreal was going to be ruled by the mob or by Council. "The Council!" aldermen cried.

Some East End aldermen criticized what they saw as a series of provocations—first the decision to enforce compulsion, then the seizure of provincial property outside the city, now the calling out of the militia. Jeannotte blamed the Health Board for causing the unrest in the streets, denied that the situation was particularly menacing, but warned of very serious trouble if troops used their rifles on the people. Other aldermen blamed Jeannotte, Beausoleil, and Rainville for having taken anti-vaccination positions that had encouraged the mob. If only the police had been more efficient the day before, some thought, or if they could use firearms or horses to subdue the rabble, the whole thing could have been contained. "Ten policemen armed with rattan canes under a resolute man would have done more to inspire terror ... than all the militia force in the country," the *Witness* grumbled that afternoon.

No one endorsed tolerating violence or mob rule. Alderman Roy told Council that the city must spend millions, if necessary, to stamp out the smallpox and restore order. Personally he would shoot the first man who tried to attack his house again. (Odd, how many Montreal politicians kept guns in their homes.) The mayor's decisions were unanimously endorsed by Council.

The citizen soldiers of Montreal mustered at the armouries for the second time that year, received their ammunition, and began to drill. The men of the Victoria Rifles, supported by the Montreal Cavalry, were ordered to secure the exhibition buildings. All the other regiments—Montreal Engineers, First Prince of Wales Rifles, Fifth Royal Scots, Sixth Fusiliers, and the Montreal Garrison

Artillery, more than a thousand soldiers strong—stood ready. One regiment, the 65th, was conspicuously absent. These French-Canadian veterans of the North-West campaign would have been called out, their officers explained, but the men were still waiting for new uniforms. Perhaps it was just as well that the regiment was not used. Some of the men had smallpox. Some would have stayed home because of smallpox in their families. Others might have turned out anyway. Those who showed up would have certainly done their duty as soldiers, even against friends and neighbours, but perhaps the turnout would have been very light.

☼   ☼   ☼

Stones flew here and there in the early evening darkness, sometimes hitting an unfortunate street light or window. Dr. McNeece of the Health Board looked out the office window and was hit and badly cut. All of Montreal's 263 policemen were on duty. "Posses" of them used batons freely to keep crowds moving. The crowds in Cartier Square and on the Champ de Mars became thicker. By seven o'clock the air buzzed with rumours: the quarrymen were coming ... Hingston's house would be next ... no, someone else's.

The mayor looked pale and sick, but resolute. He pleaded with the crowd to disperse. He decided to send soldiers to protect the doctors' homes. As companies of the Prince of Wales Rifles and the Royal Scots emerged from their base in Bonsecours market and began passing City Hall, the throng murmured, jeered, hooted, tossed a few more stones. Were the soldiers going to march east to confront the people? Would this crowd, which at first seemed just curious but was now turning ugly, attack City Hall? What was that damned tooting in the background, somebody blowing on a fish-horn, now over by the courthouse, now on the Champ de Mars? Sounded like a ringleader trying to rally the anti-health forces to battle.

Rudolph Laflamme, a former minister of justice in the government of Canada, appeared on the scene to urge Beaugrand and Colonel A.A. ("Sandy") Stevenson, commander of the militia, to stay calm. "For God's sake, be careful. You don't know the feeling of the people, how they are worked up over this and the Riel business. Don't send out the troops unless it is necessary, because if you bring about a conflict between them and the citizens you may kindle a fire of rebellion which may be difficult to subdue."

"What do you advise then?"

"If you must send out a force, let it be an overwhelming one ... and counsel moderation."

"That is just what I propose doing," Beaugrand said. He thanked Laflamme and muttered that too many cooks often spoil the broth.

No East End rioters appeared. Joe Vincent, a boatman locally famous for his life-saving feats, slipped through the crowd towards the fish-horn. "Come along boys," Vincent heard the bugler say, "Pick up stones and we'll do for the damned police." Vincent collared the young man, silenced his horn—"I'll see how you can blow it in jail"—and with help muscled the captive to Central Station. Police dispersed gatherings around City Hall and along St. Denis Street. The Prince of Wales and Royal Scots, about 350 strong, marched into the West End to protect doctors' homes. In that part of the city onlookers offered nothing but cheers.

Out at the exhibition buildings, cavalry patrolled the perimeter while troops stood ready in the grounds. Nothing happened. There was much grumbling about a shortage of tobacco. At Bonsecours market the reserves held an impromptu concert. Some may have helped themselves to a stallkeeper's barrel of apples (newspapers worried the issue for days afterwards). Throughout the city police broke up every suspicious gathering; one mob was said to have been rousing itself to attack the Sisters of Providence convent. By ten o'clock the people had gone home, leaving the heart of town to police and soldiers. At 1:30 a.m. most of the volunteers were dismissed. One group of them struck up "God Save the Queen" as they passed the *Herald* building. Windows flew open and reporters and compositors joined in the anthem. The night ended with three cheers for the paper, three cheers for its editor.

o o o

The police were out in force every night, waiting at Central Station for the ringing of the telephone (a loud noise, still foreign to the ears) which would signify trouble. Militia units took turns guarding the exhibition grounds while Health Department workers began converting the buildings into a hospital. At the central health office armed sanitary policemen stood guard.

On Thursday afternoon placarders were driven off by an angry crowd at Maisonneuve and Mignonne, a block away from the boarded-up wreckage of the East End office. The sign-posters returned with Dr. Laberge, Chief Paradis, and ten constables. A man stood in one doorway with a plank, his wife in another with an ironing board, threatening to split the skulls of anyone who came near. Angry neighbours, some bearing sticks and clubs, watched the confrontation. The placards were posted out of ironing-board reach, and were torn down the moment the police turned their backs. A well-known French-Canadian physician was given a hearing by the mob as he spoke on the benefits of vaccination, and then ignored. Another disturbance was caused by a delirious patient, breaking from restraint and running into the streets shouting "Murder, murder!" Aided by their dog "Senecal," the police finally apprehended the wretch.

The Health Department insisted that it was not intimidated and would redouble its efforts. In fact, the vigour of isolation and vaccination efforts slowed noticeably. The official explanation was the realization that the first priority had to be the new hospital. Would the East End health office be immediately reopened? Not at this time, the board decided, for there would be no purpose to it. Such practicality outraged the tough-minded folk in the English community whose viewpoint was often expressed by the *Herald*. "MUST IT BE KING MOB?" the paper asked.

Is the city to be governed in a manner to suit the Mob, to please the least intelligent and most disorderly, the most vicious and violent, the rowdies, the loafers and low demagogues; or are the men who made Montreal what it is—the peaceably disposed, the law abiding, the thrifty, the industrious, the energetic and enterprising, the capitalists, the bankers, the manufacturers—to rule what they have created, to feel certain of the possession of what is their own, to retain their property of their own free will and not by the consent of an East End Mob? ... LET THE OFFICE BE KEPT OPEN IF IT TAKES EVERY SOLDIER IN MONTREAL TO DO IT.

One letter-writer suggested that a law-and-order mob might have to be formed, another that a special civilian police force should be enrolled. Some of the French papers, anxious to deny that the rioters represented the true feelings of French-Canadian Montreal, and aware of the shadowy presence of at least the one Frenchmen, Chappelier, during the disturbances, had suggested that the troubles might be the work of veterans of the Paris Commune of 1871, that is of communists. "In order to put the blame on the right shoulders and get the metaphorical nigger off the fence," the *Witness* sent a reporter to interview two respectable tradesmen known to be communist sympathizers. "Lay the riot to the Communists?" one told him. "Not at all.... Whenever anything is smashed here you cry 'Communist,' but you forget that we Communists are reasoning people; if we wanted to raise an insurrection we should go to work differently; we might make a barricade, but to start an anti-vaccination riot composed of little boys is a business that a Communist laughs at."

In any case, the other communist commented, they were not at all against vaccination: "We are in favor of it. I have done my utmost all along to persuade my French-Canadian customers to be vaccinated and they are now seeing the necessity of it. Loafers of all nationalities and bits of boys were what went to make up that mob. It was not Communists, certainly not.... You will not find us on any side but that of law and order. We have no grievances. I have been vaccinated of course."

That other radical reformer, A.M. Ross, was much less unhappy with the work of the mob. Not that anyone was going to tell Montreal what he felt about the disturbances, for the newspapers, all of them, had stopped publishing anything about or by him. "We will be heard!" Ross announced in the first number of *The Anti-Vaccinator and Advocate of Cleanliness*, a four-page broadsheet published on September 30. He denounced vaccination as "stamping in"

the smallpox, the newspapers for "out-Heroding Herod" in supporting vaccination, and Montreal's "medical Robespierres" for supporting a reign of terror. Vaccination was just a "fetish" and only one man
was brave enough to say so. Ross offered his "History of a Crime,"
written in very bad doggerel:

> Brokers, bankers, merchant tailors,
> Manufacturers, grocers, nailers,
> Priests & doctors met together
> And denounced the anti-vaccinator
> Who alone in all Mount Royal
> Would not bow down to the *fetish*
> Or acknowledge that the doctors
> Had the right to force the people!
> Force the people, French & English
> To receive into their bodies,
> And the bodies of their children,
> The foul *virus* of a beast.

Ross could not be prosecuted for crimes against medicine,
public health, or poetry. Some of the rioters were brought to justice. Alphonse Marois, shoemaker, and William Beulac, barber,
were told by Police Magistrate Dugas that in throwing stones and
inciting the mob to riot on Monday night they were behaving in a
disgraceful manner exactly when French Canadians should weigh
their actions to give no cause to be reproached by anyone. To set an
example, Dugas sentenced the miscreants to four months' hard
labour. Had they not pleaded guilty they would have had six. Elie
Champagne, the mayor's assailant, was arrested at his Maisonneuve
Street home on Wednesday night. He was a forty-three-year-old
carpenter who said he remembered very little about Monday night,
for he had been drinking heavily. Five witnesses testified that he
had been a ringleader of the mob and the man who struck down
Paradis. Police Magistrate Desnoyers gave him the maximum sentence: six months and a $100 fine, or no fine and twelve months.

Three men charged with loitering on Tuesday night were discharged; Beaugrand had urged leniency for them. The young man

with the horn, Joseph Germain, wept for mercy when he was arrested and wept again in court. His mother appeared in his defence, crying as well, and pleading that her son was her sole support. The city's prosecutor said he was not inclined to press for severity. Desnoyers sentenced Germain to four months at hard labour for vagrancy. He was taken out, "sobbing piteously."

* * *

Was there more trouble in store? No one knew. No one knew the temper of the poor people of Montreal, afflicted by the smallpox, afflicted by the demands of the vaccinators and the Health Department. "A spirit of evil seems to be abroad in Montreal," the *Star* despaired. A French-speaking journalist with Joseph Pulitzer's New York *World* was able to get closer to the wretched of the East End that troubled week than any Montreal outsider. One of the rioters from Monday night told him they would continue to fight the placarders and vaccinators. "If they force us to be poisoned by vaccination we will burn the city. À bas Maire Beaugrand!"

One hundred men of the Victoria Rifles, supported by cavalry, were on guard at the exhibition buildings on Saturday night. It was an intensely dark, rainy night, with no visibility. About 7.30 a rumour reached the troops that one hundred armed men from St-Henri were coming up to attack the buildings. The men were ordered to loosen their ammunition, just in case. One of the sentries, nineteen-year-old Private Rodden, thought he had been ordered to load his rifle and did so. Then he learned that they were not to load, but merely to prepare the cartridges in their ball bag. As Rodden tried to unload his rifle in the rain, his hand slipped, and the gun went off at half-cock. The ball ricocheted off a rock and struck Private John H. Samuel, age twenty-five. "My God, I am done, I am done," Samuel exclaimed as he fell to the ground. "My God, what have I done?" Rodden cried.

Samuel was rushed by ambulance wagon to the General Hospital. As it passed a grocery at the corner of St. Lawrence and Guilbault, a clerk pelted the vehicle with rotten apples and eggs.

Samuel arrived in great agony, for the ball had entered his lower back, shattering the hip joint, and lodged in his abdomen. Surgeons decided it could not be removed. Private Samuel died about three a.m. Nobody attacked the exhibition buildings.

John Samuel had been a popular young dentist, who lived and worked on Beaver Hall Hill. He was a member of the St. George's Snowshoe Club, Britannia Football Club, and Montreal Athletic Association. He had joined the "Vics" on the outbreak of the North-West rebellion, but of course this was the first time he had been on active service. The perfume of flowers filled the air at St. Paul's Church as crowds overflowed onto the streets to witness his funeral. The minister eulogized Samuel as "a martyr to lawlessness and riot, one of many victims of the lamentable ignorance and prejudice which have brought such disaster to our fair city.... May the city hear his voice, and, as it mourns his death, learn, as it has not learned from the living, to be wiser and more faithful in the keeping of God's law and health and order." Led by their sixty-piece band, the Royal Victoria Rifles conducted Private Samuel to his grave. He was the only victim of the smallpox epidemic who had a legal funeral.

PART III

PART III

God is deaf now-a-days and deigneth not hear us,
And prayers have no power the Plague to stay.

— William Langland, *Piers Ploughman*

CHAPTER 9
CARNIVAL OF
DEATH

S *aturday morning, October 10*

In partly cloudy weather a procession of carriages winds its way from City Hall to the exhibition grounds. The Board of Health have hired the vehicles for the official opening of the new Mount Royal Hospitals for smallpox patients. Scores of municipal politicians, clergy, doctors, journalists, and other prominent citizens make the pilgrimage to the suburban site. It is to be a grand show of civic unity. Entering the grounds, the elite visitors are saluted by the men of the Fifth Royal Scots, standing guard to protect the buildings from attack.

In the eleven days since the health authorities have seized the site, squads of carpenters have worked round the clock turning the frame shells of the exhibition pavilions into modern, winterized hospitals. Catholic and Protestant smallpox patients will be cared for in separate quarters, with separate nursing staffs (Grey Nuns on the one hand, the Episcopalian Sisters of St. Margaret on the other), and separate physicians. The Catholic hospital, soon to be named St. Camille's, can easily accommodate 350 patients; the Protestant quarters, St. Saviour's, will hold at least fifty. Both hospitals have up-to-date ventilating systems to draw off noxious air, hot water supplies for bathing (with drains into special cisterns), electric arc lamps in the hallways, Heap's Patent Earth Closets, brand new iron bedsteads featuring woven wire "mattresses," and rooms for private patients. To maintain public confidence, the Montreal Medico-Chirurgical Society will appoint outside "visitors" to inspect these civic institutions as thoroughly as other hospitals are scrutinized.

Louis Perrault, chairman of the board's hospital committee, guides the notables through the wards, giving descriptions in both English and French. The Roman Catholic and Anglican bishops bless the respective facilities. This is a rare, possibly unique, meeting of the city's Catholic and Protestant clergy in 1885. After the hospital inspection, visitors tour the laundry, where all linen will be steam-cleaned, and the incinerator that will reduce liquid and solid waste to ash. Mayor Beaugrand gives a short speech on the unity of citizens of both nationalities and all denominations in their determination to restore Montreal to its position as one of the continent's healthiest cities. He leads three cheers for Henry Gray and the Board of Health.

All of the visitors are urged to sign a testimonial testifying to the perfection of the arrangements at the new hospital. Here there will be constant medical attendance in clean and comfortable, virtually odour-free surroundings. Patients should be happy to accept "the duty of isolation." Only Alderman Jeannotte refuses to sign the testimonial. For the other dignitaries, above all for the members of the Board of Health, the opening marks a major step forward. The preparation of the new hospitals has had the highest priority in the aftermath of the rioting. Their excellence will surely restore confidence in the board and its policies, and create a new atmosphere in which the harried workers can press forward to save the city from the smallpox.

Sunday afternoon, October 11

Gorgeous autumn day. A much more massive procession. Thousands of faithful Catholics, chanting and praying, telling their rosaries. Led by a man in flaming scarlet robes. He is the beadle of Notre Dame Church, and serves as the ceremonial head of the pageant marking the annual Feast of the Rosary. This year it is dedicated to imploring the Virgin Mary to intercede with God to stay the smallpox epidemic. At the heart of the procession Bishop Fabre walks, crozier and mitre in hand, surrounded by black-robed clergy. In front of them twelve men carry a brass statue of the Virgin, resting on a large globe on a pedestal surrounded by rosary beads.

It is the Madonna of Bonsecours, brought to New France some two centuries ago and revered for generations in Bonsecours Church by ships' crews praying for successful voyages. During the cholera epidemic of 1848 Bishop Bourget had ordered the image to be carried through the streets to help ward off the wrathful visitation. Now the Madonna is again implored, by thousands of the faithful, to save Her Catholic city. The crimson-garbed beadle leads all of those who believe the Church's magic is more powerful than any of the physicians' rituals.*

o   o   o

The health authorities would have preferred that the Church not hold its procession. They thought it would stoke the smallpox further, as last June's big street ceremonies had almost certainly done. Were the clerics acting responsibly in bringing large crowds together at this time? Did they have a duty to protect the public health by postponing such gatherings? Some health experts and citizens thought the city should order the churches to close down completely until the epidemic had passed.

Churchmen were perplexed. They knew that some crowds were

---

* The beadle of Notre Dame Church was known to be an opponent of vaccination. In its major October 5 story about Montreal, the *New York World* reported that this belief had caused the beadle to be suspended. Newspapers often got facts like these wrong, and if there was a suspension we do not know its duration. So we do not know whether the crimson-garbed head of the throng praying for relief from the epidemic was an enemy of the one sure preventive, which would have made the symbolism excruciating.

a problem, but could not bring themselves to believe that *their* crowds could possibly make things worse. Father Sentenne spoke of the crowds gathering to ascend to the mountain park by the inclined elevator, the crowds clamouring to board excursion steamers, the crowds about to attend the reopened theatres. Smallpox might be propagated in secular gatherings, but surely not on occasions when the children of God gathered to seek His aid. Surely not. Why, look at all the demonstrations being held on behalf of Louis Riel, *Le Monde* noted. Could it possibly be that "Riel et ses adorateurs avaient plus d'immunités que les saints du paradis"? Surely not.

Surely prayers and processions had never been more needed. Was not the smallpox a sign of God's displeasure, His wrath, His scourging of the city? No Christian, certainly no Catholic Christian, could deny that the smallpox had been sent from God. All things came from God, in His infinite goodness. Only God could stay His hand and save the city. Only God could answer the people's prayers, and take away the smallpox.

Exactly why God had chosen to smite Montreal so severely at this time was difficult to comprehend. Some priests dared to attempt to explain the mystery anyway. Abbé Filiatrault had expressed the view that Montreal was being assessed the wages of sin as a result of God's displeasure at last winter's secular festivities, the Carnival. A severe thought, but not untypical of a French-Canadian priesthood some of whom were children of the puritanical jansenist traditions of the old Quebec Church, some believers in the new ultramontane fundamentalism, some who had married both traditions. To them Carnival had been a revelling in materialism, worldliness, even the promiscuity of the toboggan slides and skating rinks. Festivities utterly without thought of God, the Saviour, the Virgin, the Holy Catholic Church. Impiety, immorality, without restraint. So much of what was wrong with the modern world, turning its back on religion.

"UN CATHOLIQUE," identified as one of Montreal's most devout merchants, spelled out this world view in a remarkable letter published in *L'Etendard* on October 19 under the heading "La Picotte et le Carnival." These views would scandalize many "hommes de progrès," an editorial note suggested, but in fact represented what was being said in most of the city's churches:

> Everyone, wicked and righteous alike, knows that God is infinitely good. However for the last several months He has laid a heavy hand upon us, and sickness and death are the means He uses to chastise us. We, the work of His divine hands, suffer terrible evils today, but these evils cannot come to us without God's permission and for our greater good. God in His infinite goodness would not put us to the test this way any more than is necessary for us. Thus it is for us to make the most of this trial....
>
> We have sinned.... We have sacrificed morality to the god of money. We have sinned ourselves and we have invited others to come and sin with us....
>
> After all, what is the real basis of our carnival? Only a folly invented by the devil. Everyone remembers the throngs of lost souls who have come here seeking death in the pleasures of carnival. And what is there to say about these altars of the devil, raised up to the glory of their master at the four corners of our devoutly Catholic city! These accursed toboggan slides, the meeting place of depraved men and women! These altars where so many young girls have gone to dishonour themselves for life!
>
> Oh, the money we make at carnival costs us too dearly! ... We have trod a false path in choosing the revelry of carnival; we have taken a false way in building toboggan slides. We must no longer hesitate; we must make a full sacrifice; and this sacrifice must be made to a merciful God who cannot fail to end this plague, the fruit of the disorders of carnival.
>
> I dare to hope that the Catholic athletic clubs ... will take the axe to their toboggan slides, and that Catholics and Protestants alike will rise up as one to destroy for evermore these altars of the devil.

Less certain, less censorious Catholics knew that the ways of the Lord were not always revealed to sinful mortals. If the precise

nature of the people's transgressions and the reasons for this particular chastisement were difficult to understand (did it make any
sense that the little children of devout French Canadians should die
in punishment for sins committed mainly by English Protestants?*),
it was nevertheless certain that God had somehow to be appeased.
How to do it except through repentence, humility, prayer, prayer,
and more prayer? Pray to the Virgin to intercede with God. Pray to
the saints, who also inhabited the highest circles of the heavenly
court. Pray to St. Roch, to whom God seemed to listen in time of
plague. By October that holy man's picture was on sale in many
Montreal shops and on display in many homes as a symbol and a
reminder—and for some, perhaps, a shield.

When Protestant Christians thought about the epidemic, they
were much more inclined to unite theological and natural explanations. From the beginning Protestant ministers had talked about the
sin of ignoring the laws of good health, laid down by God for man's
benefit and discovered by science. Yes, God as creator was, in a theological sense, the cause of the plague. As the prophet Amos said,
"Shall there be evil in a city and the Lord hath not done it?" But it
was man's sin in ignoring the laws of health that had precipitated the
punishment. And just as there was a natural, God-created cause of
the troubles, so there was a natural, God-given remedy, vaccination.
From the beginning of the epidemic Protestants of all stripes had
preached vaccination. Some Protestant clergyman had actually taken
up the "points" and ministered to their people with vaccine. To Hugh
Graham's *Star*, "A Well Kept Sabbath" would be one in which parents took their children not to church, but to the vaccinator.

Most Protestants assumed that Catholic priests had nearly
total power over their flocks. If only the priests would insist on
vaccination, while perhaps de-emphasizing unhealthy processions

---

* The fundamentalist explanation seems to have been that Montreal Catholics were
guilty in not having been devout enough to put an end to the materialistic indul-
gences of the city's irreligious/Protestant element. With more attention to the
demands of the faith, the godless would either be won over or suppressed and
Montreal could take its appointed place as a holy Catholic city. While the scourge
of the smallpox on Catholics may have seemed unjust, it was light chastisement
compared with the eternal hellfire awaiting those unrepentent carnivallers.

and idolatry, all would be well. Smallpox raged in Montreal, this argument went, because the Catholic Church failed in its duty to advocate vaccination.

But this was not exactly true. The Church spoke repeatedly in favour of vaccination. And it complied with almost all of the requests made by the civic authorities. On the first Sunday after the riot, October 4, a special letter was read in all the churches from the Board of Health explaining its policies and emphasizing that no one would be forcibly vaccinated. At high mass in Notre Dame, Father Sentenne told the congregation to submit to the laws at once and be vaccinated. He warned them that no respectable French Canadian or true Catholic could have participated in the recent acts of lawlessness and thereby disgraced themselves and their nationality. On instructions from Bishop Fabre, priests in the other Catholic churches repeated their recommendations that people go to the doctors and be vaccinated. Abbé Filiatrault himself, exponent of the Carnival explanation of the plague, told his congregation that he had attended hundreds of cases but did not get the disease because he had been vaccinated.

Catholic sisters were visiting the sick and distributing relief and running St. Roch's hospital. They would staff St. Camille's ward of the new hospital, and we have seen Bishop Fabre give his blessing at the October 10 opening ceremony. In fact Fabre submitted to re-vaccination that week to set an example. So did the curé of Ste-Cunégonde Church and all his vicars. Catholic priests did believe it important not to cross the divide between ministering to men's souls and the doctor's work of curing their bodies. Priests did not offer vaccination or accompany vaccinators, and Bishop Fabre wrote privately to at least one curé advising that he not serve on a local board of health. Still, the Church at no time turned away from cooperation with the Board of Health. The sources do not contain a single example of a Montreal priest being in any way involved in anti-vaccination activities.

But there were always qualifications, catches, complications. If Catholic support of vaccination and other precautionary steps was proper, ungrudging, and increasingly explicit, it was also neither heartfelt nor uncompromising.

Some churchmen were uncomfortable with the thought that vaccination was a new kind of dogma, preached by men of science pretending to near-infallible certainty. Such assurance by the scientists was a bit puzzling, because until very recently doctors had often disagreed about vaccination, which made it difficult to know what science was saying. During the 1870s Bishop Bourget had taken the position that since learned men of science could not agree on vaccination he could not offer advice on the subject. This was not Fabre's position in 1885. But reactionary ultramontanes, Bourget's spiritual children, kept toying with the notion that there might be alternatives to vaccination. Whatever most of the doctors said, there were still some who dissented. At the very least, the believing mind was tempted by the thought that processions and prayers could stay the epidemic by themselves, as history claimed they had from time immemorial. The more uncritical your faith, the more you thought God controlled these events by direct, supernatural intervention. At one point *L'Etendard* suggested that the remains of bishops Bourget and Lartigue should be again paraded through the streets of Montreal to bring about Divine cleansing of the city.

More important, all Catholic churchmen insisted that their traditional rituals were an essential part of the war against the plague. All right, let the doctors prepare the body with vaccination. But it would be sacrilege to deny the vital role of the Church in cleansing the soul with prayer, confession, and atonement. The procession to celebrate the Feast of the Rosary was originally scheduled for October 4, but was delayed because of the weather and possibly because of Father Sentenne's doubts in the face of public concern and Bishop Fabre's absence. A week later, with the weather splendid and the bishop back in the city, it went ahead. Catholics with smallpox in their families were ordered to stay away from the procession, just as they had been excused from attending church. The vaccinators could not save the city without the help of the Virgin and her humble petitioners.

*　*　*

The outside world puts its trust in the vaccinators. We are heading south from Montreal. At Sutton Junction, near the border, an elderly, bespectacled, kindly-looking gentleman boards the train to check the passengers' status. He is Dr. Hamilton of Richford, Vermont, examining physician, working for the Marine Hospital Service of the United States government.

"Been vaccinated?"

The pretty, brown-eyed girl says she has.

"Got a certificate?"

Well, no. But "I would not lie to you, indeed I would not, sir. I have been vaccinated."

"Sorry, madam, but I can't help it; either let me see your certificate or your arm."

"It was but just a little while ago, indeed, it was doctor. I can't show you my arm here.... Can't you believe me?"

The modest lass with the tight-fitting sleeves finally has to tug her shirt waist down from the neck, baring her shoulder and her arm.

"When were you vaccinated?"

"Two years ago."

"Scar is not fresh enough."

Out comes his scarifier and his vaccine. A scratch and a scream. "There, that will do." The girl sinks back in her seat, rearranging her clothes.

Some of the travellers in the smoker are more manly. They will get off the train, some say, rather than submit to such arbitrary measures. That's fine, the doctor says, for you must leave if you will not be vaccinated, and he motions to a burly companion to stand guard. Most of the time the objector thinks the better and agrees to take the knife. Passengers crane forward to see the blusterer submit, "as sheepish as a whipped dog," the *Herald*'s reporter notes.

A young French Canadian, the son of a Liberal member of Parliament, shows the journalist his vaccination certificate. It bears an authentic Montreal doctor's signature, but in fact it is completely bogus. That doctor will give anyone a certificate for a dollar. It's good enough to fool old Doc Hamilton on this trip.

It probably won't bamboozle the tough young Ontario inspectors who ride all the westbound trains out of Montreal and stop the upbound boats at the locks at the Cornwall canal. These "vaccination sentries" decided early in the game not to trust most certificates. Passenger who don't have a pass given by one of the Ontarians stationed in Montreal will probably be asked to show their mark. If you won't bare your arm, you don't get into Ontario. *Bare* it, mind you: there was no mark under the handkerchief one passenger said was binding up a tender arm; the vaccination "scab" apparently visible beneath another person's undershirt turned out to be a button.

Sometimes it's hard to see anything on the dirty arms of the lumberjacks or the poor immigrants, especially at night in the dim light of the second-class cars, even when the doctor holds his lantern right to the skin. Sometimes people object and the doctors have to hold their ground, calling on sanitary police for help, bringing protestors before border town magistrates. On the Montreal-Ottawa trains J.E. Elliott has a number of passengers get off at Hull rather than be vaccinated. Elliott sees one of them hire a cab; on a hunch he gets off the train, hires his own cab, and follows the traveller across to Ottawa. Seeing he is about to be arrested, the man suddenly gallops back to Hull and goes home to Montreal.

Some people hide under seats or in the toilets. Sometimes people appear to be sick or have suspicious rashes on their face or cause other problems. Excerpts from the report of E.H. Williams, MD, who handles the Ottawa express:

> Thursday, September 10th—One man on 8 p.m. express did not look altogether well, but had been recently successfully vaccinated, so I did not stop him.
> Friday, September 11th—A very ugly eruption on the face of one of the passengers—train authorities wanted to stop her, but on examination determined it was a sore.
> Thursday, September 17—Had to compel three roughs to submit to vaccination at Ottawa.
> Friday, September 18th—Received some abuse from a cabinet minister while in performance of my duties.

If you come from an infected area of Montreal, the Ontario doctors might insist that your luggage be fumigated. It is taken from the train at a fumigation point, put into a closed boxcar, and subjected to six hours of burning sulphur, three pounds per thousand cubic feet. The smallpox-free bags then go out on the next train. At the international boundary, even out of Ontario, the ordeal is much worse, for the Americans insist on fumigating all baggage originating in Quebec province. Usually they unpack it and hang it up on clotheslines—undershirts, ladies' dainties, everything. On some of the lines south from Montreal Americans disinfect the whole train or require passengers to change cars at the border. The old smallpox cars stay in Canada.

The Ontario inspectors vaccinate about 150 people a day. Every day they turn several objectors back at the frontier. Both Canadian and American officials report that French Canadians supply most of the resistance. "They would as soon have the small-pox as be vaccinated, and I believe most of them who object, would rather," says old Dr. Hamilton. Objections to the inspection gradually diminish, as those who cannot pass avoid trains. Of course it is not difficult to slip across many borders on foot. The Maine state board of health asks the Marine Hospital Service to station special inspectors at Moose River, a major crossroads for French Canadians en route to the winter lumber camps. In both Maine and Michigan all of the camp operators are urged to be on the lookout for smallpox and require vaccination of all their hands.

*   *   *

The isolation of Montreal was only partly effective. People who were incubating smallpox got out of the city on foot or by carriage, or slipped through the inspection nets on the boats and trains. You might show a vaccination mark and be perfectly safe yourself. You might even be a doctor. But you could still be carrying smallpox on your clothes, literally in your pocket. The epidemic was like a great pinwheel, centred in Montreal, hurling sparks far and wide. They landed in villages, towns, and cities throughout Quebec and the northeast. Beginning with its own suburbs, Montreal infected the Quebec countryside, Ontario towns, Ottawa, Toronto, Quebec City, communities in Atlantic Canada, and several French-Canadian communities in the United States. Smallpox was found on transatlantic steamers out of Montreal and lake boats as far west as Chicago.

Smallpox was in all of the villages around Montreal by August and September. Early in October it broke out hundreds of miles away in settlements on the north shore of the St. Lawrence below Quebec City. The germs had travelled there from Montreal along the Intercolonial Railroad's main line. The village of Cap St-Ignace, where there had been no vaccination, suffered 107 cases and twenty-two deaths. At the other end of the province, in the poor Ottawa River village of Montebello, a Montreal child brought smallpox into a local store, from which it spread to a hotel. One of the hotelkeeper's children died. A local physician obligingly listed a different cause of death. The child was given a full funeral at the parish church. The first Montebello board of health was headed by a doctrinaire anti-vaccinationist.

The Provincial Board of Health had not existed until early September. Its headquarters and most of its attention was centred in Montreal. Its full-time staff consisted of detective Cinq Mars. Hingston's board was akin to a handful of volunteer firemen ordered to protect every building in the province. It took weeks, months, to establish local boards of health, even to find out what was happening in Quebec's hundreds of villages and towns. Cinq Mars travelled from town to town, mostly near Montreal, looking into what were said to be bad situations and doing what he could. Clerks and secretaries were added to mail out copies of the board's regulations. They were put up in train stations, council chambers, and on church doors. Until late in the epidemic there were no controls on train travel in Quebec.

No one knew what was happening in the province. For a time the most detailed public information on smallpox in Quebec was provided by Maine's state board of health, issuing compilations made from newspaper reports. The Quebec Provincial Board periodically announced that scores of municipalities had established boards of health under its jurisdiction, but it clearly knew almost nothing about their activities.

The most effective local boards of health were in the heavily English areas of the province's Eastern Townships. Sherbrooke,

Knowlton, Sutton, Coaticook, and other township communities carried out extensive vaccination campaigns and had no smallpox. In poor, rural areas of the province many villages did nothing or went through the motions of appointing a board of health that did nothing. In one village people were said to "inveigh against the expense of a sanitary organization and protest that it can do no good, since if people must die of smallpox they will do so, no matter what expense and what labor their neighbors may be put to." Native Canadians who lived on the large Caughnawagha reservation near Montreal were happy to accept vaccination provided by the government of Canada. A minor outbreak there was quickly contained.

In most areas the smallpox infected one or two families, took a few lives, and burned out. The greatest danger of a second major outbreak was in the provincial capital, Quebec City, with a population of about 63,000, including many very poor residents in the Lower Town. But there was less resistance to vaccination there and a determination not to be infected by the raw metropolis upriver. Quebec's health officers managed to hospitalize the first few cases that arrived from Montreal and in early October they began inspecting incoming trains and boats for evidence of vaccination. When smallpox kept getting through anyway, alarm and confusion led to the establishment of two city boards of health, one appointed by council, one by the province. Fortunately there was no major outbreak in the city to turn the comedy black.

In Ontario and the United States the merest rumours of smallpox caused instant alarm and drastic action. Wherever they saw smallpox, public health agencies rushed to stamp it out. Victims were isolated at home or in emergency hospitals, contacts quarantined, buildings fumigated, belongings disinfected, thousands vaccinated, sometimes in response to a single case.

Ontario's zealous Provincial Board of Health intervened wherever local people seemed apathetic or incompetent—sometimes the case in Franco-Ontarian villages near the Quebec border. The public usually supported strong measures and there was no massive resistance to vaccination. All churches, Protestant and Catholic, supported vaccination. Terrified of seeing another Montreal-like situation develop, Ontario newspapers went out of their way to report cases of smallpox. If the reporting was sometimes exaggerated, if people became a bit panicky and took needless precautions, what was the harm? There was probably more fear of smallpox in Toronto in 1885 than there was in Montreal. There were five separate outbreaks in the Ontario city, and each was contained. Toronto had a total of twenty-seven cases of smallpox, with no deaths. Ontario had a total of 146 cases in 1885, with sixteen deaths.

Wherever smallpox slipped through the Americans' border screening system it was quickly stamped out. French families from Montreal caused minor outbreaks as far afield as Wisconsin. In Massachusetts there were a total of thirty-two cases, mostly in Boston, Lowell, and Fall River. Twenty-four of the victims were Canadians. Eleven died. Maine had only one or two scattered cases. Michigan's controls were so effective, and vaccination so widespread, that no smallpox got into the state from Canada. Nor was smallpox a problem in Chicago in 1885, the city from which it had come to Montreal. American health authorities' reports for that year were redolent with thinly-veiled contempt for Montreal's handling of its plague. "We have had carried on for us by the anti-vaccinationists an experiment on a gigantic scale, to show whether small-pox is still the same implacable foe to human life that it used to be," the secretary of the Maine State Board of Health wrote. "Such a cruel spectacle of the slaughter of the innocents they might have spared us...."

At an early stage in Montreal's epidemic, the province of Prince Edward Island asked the government of Canada to quarantine all ships entering Charlottetown from Quebec. The request was turned down because quarantine did not apply to interprovincial shipping. In early November smallpox broke out in a hotel-worker's family in a poor area of Charlottetown. Many Prince Edward Islanders were unvaccinated. Some thought the province's lovely climate protected them from smallpox, others saw it as a "French disease." Dozens of cases a day began appearing in the island city.

As in Montreal, a citizens' committee was formed to pressure Charlottetown's City Council into drastic action. As in Montreal, citizen pressure was instrumental in the decision to seize a provincial building, in this case the old lunatic asylum, for a smallpox hospital.

As in Montreal, there were problems with hospital staff hired by the city, and the secular power had to ask for help from the convents. Trains and mail leaving Charlottetown were fumigated. Ships from the island were quarantined, even by other provinces. Farmers stopped coming into town.

Then Charlottetown got tough. The city closed its churches and its schools, banned all public meetings, and instituted compulsory house-to-house vaccination. Most of the population was vaccinated. The epidemic lasted just over six weeks, killing fifty-three people. It was the worst Canadian outbreak outside of Quebec that year.

❂ ❂ ❂

The outside world's isolation of Montreal threatened it with economic disaster and immense human misery. Every product made in Montreal was suspect. When the scare erupted in August, buyers everywhere stopped placing orders for Montreal goods. Some competitors were not unhappy to draw customers' attention to Montreal's plight. Cigar advertisement in a Toronto newspaper:

SMALLPOX RAGING

Over sixty deaths in a day in Montreal among the cigarmakers and others. Caution is necessary in using goods manufactured in Montreal. Cigars manufactured in Montreal are particularly dangerous on account of the susceptibility of the mucus membrane of the mouth, as the part put in the mouth is finished in the fingers, and may leave virus on the head of the cigars.

It was absolutely essential to restore confidence in Montreal's products. Ontario took the lead in banning the importation of rags and requiring special clearance of all other Montreal-made goods. From headquarters in the St. Lawrence Hall, Ontario's Dr. T.S. Covernton and his assistant provided certificates to companies able to demonstrate that their employees and their families had all been vaccinated. Some eighty Montreal firms made use of the certification process; more than twenty thousand certificates would eventually be issued for individual shipments. The system was so useful that authorities in Nova Scotia, Prince Edward Island, Manitoba, and Quebec itself accepted and sometimes required the Ontario certificates. Neither Montreal's Health Board nor the Quebec Provincial Board of Health was involved in the process.

Montreal merchants rushed to comply with outsiders' requirements. Particularly in the aftermath of the riots, employers renewed their insistence that every worker supply proof of vaccination. Many offered free vaccination, on the factory floor or at home. Many pledged openly to dismiss anyone who refused to cooperate and to blacklist the unvaccinated. Some employers, including W.C. McDonald, the tobacco man, set an example by lining up with their operatives to be vaccinated. The *Star*, which was most enthusiastic about the employers' movement, published the names of cooperating firms.

Concerted employer action, amounting to coercion, led to more vaccinations than the Health Board's off-again, on-again, not-quite-compulsory policies. A few instances of worker resistance led to firings or brief walk-outs, but there were no major strikes and no one seriously objected to the idea of compulsory vaccination in the private sector. The Montreal journalist most sympathetic to the problems of the working class, Jules Helbronner (author of a weekly column in *La Presse* as "Jean-Baptiste Gagnepetit"), did not personally believe in the principle of compulsory vaccination. He received many letters from readers complaining of the tyranny of employers in the matter, he wrote, but in this case he had no sympathy. Helbronner thought it perfectly within a boss's right as a private citizen to insist that the people he associate with be vaccinated. "Je dis que les patrons usent de leurs droits quand ils ne veulent employer que des ouvriers vaccinés." People who did not want to be vaccinated were free to find some other employer. There were many parallels between using the workplace to attack smallpox in the 1880s and using the workplace to attack smoking a century later.

o o o

Smallpox streets were quiet streets. Children had stopped playing outside. People were not socializing. It was no use watching for the black-and-yellow warning signs, for some of the worst-infected areas had the fewest placards. Look at the blinds instead. The nuns were urging the families of the sick to keep the blinds drawn, even if they would not accept placards. The sufferers were learning that it was not becoming to display their stigmata.

Everyone knew that the smallpox was playing havoc with the French population of Montreal, especially their unvaccinated children. Fifty deaths a day from the pestilence, day upon day, through dismal October rains and then the soft sunshine and flaming colour of the beautiful Canadian autumn. Fifty acknowledged deaths. Everyone knew that the plague was worse than the Health Department said, worse than anything Montreal, or most other North American cities, had gone through since the cholera onslaught of 1832. There were hundreds, possibly thousands of hidden cases. Some said that the English were no more eager to be placarded than the French, and that they did their share of concealing too. Which was no doubt true in some instances—*so much better to keep the child at home where she can be isolated and given loving care*—but no one denied the racial/religious imbalance. King Picotte ruled a French and Catholic domain.

Up on the hill there was hardly any smallpox. At the end of October a Scots-Canadian physician who had been in active practice all year long still had not seen a single case. Everyone was vaccinated. No one had friends who were sick. After Sir Francis's unfortunate death, no other socially or politically prominent English-speaking Montrealer was carried off. If you were vaccinated you really had nothing to fear, at work, play, or worship. The letters and histories of English Montreal for 1885 are virtually silent on the subject of an epidemic that for most of them was a very long way away. Read the biographies of the railway barons, driving to finish the Canadian Pacific that autumn, and you know nothing of the smallpox. Listen to the heroic William Van Horne, interviewed as he leaves for the West where the last spike will soon be driven: "The danger from smallpox in Montreal is enormously exaggerated outside. In the business part and in the English sections there is no excitement about smallpox, and no particular danger. There seems no danger about the hotels. The fuss is all made outside."

Not exactly true. The two Montreals were not so completely separate. The city's sporting life and its saloons and churches and cultural places were fairly thoroughly self-segregated; so there was little danger, for example, in allowing the theatres, which were exclusively English, to reopen. But the downtown commercial districts and the handsome avenues and squares and the long shopping streets and the old train station and the bustling markets touched upon mean and crowded residential areas around every corner. Travellers could see smallpox placards from the train as they came into Bonaventure Station. There was smallpox within a stone's throw of the Windsor Hotel and Dominion Square and a lot closer than that to City Hall.

Montrealers kept their eyes pealed for the sight of scabbed, scarred faces. Did you doubt the story of the girl who was seized and had her cheek rubbed against that of a smallpox victim? Newspaper exaggeration? Possibly. But on October 3 the *Herald* reported that the two small boys of Mr. T.S. Vipond had met two girls badly marked with smallpox on Durocher Street, near their home. One of the girls ran after the boys, caught the youngest and rubbed her cheek against his, calling out "Picotte, picotte!" On October 21 the *Witness* noted that a fifteen-year-old young lady on Notre Dame had been approached by a man with a badly marked face who said to her "Will you accept the small-pox from me, miss?" On October 28 the *Gazette* reported: "A man with his face covered with smallpox was observed while on Commissioners street yesterday afternoon, in an intoxicated condition, to pick up a little child and rub its face against his."

Perhaps it was all exaggeration, the product of the heightened fear of smallpox. The disease personified by those who wear the masque. Several papers on October 13-14 carried a note about the niece of a well-known drygoods merchant. She was quietly promenading on Sherbrooke Street when she saw the smallpox van rolling along beside her. When she quickened her steps, the driver kept up. Then she seized her skirts, pulled them over her head, and started running. When she peered back she saw the van, keeping pace, and the patients in its window, staring. Then she ran away in terror down a side street.

Stories like these kept people off the streets and away from Montreal. It was by no means a deserted city—empty streets are a common exaggeration during a time of plague—but it was dull and quiet and reeked of disinfectants. Commerce was slow. Hardly any tourists were in town. The hotels were half-empty, relying on their permanent guests and a few business travellers. Comparatively few people walked the main streets, almost no ladies. There were fewer reports of crime, street gatherings, after-closing brawls, even of Salvation Army parades and music. One of Montreal's American "characters," the ex-parson William Henry Harrison ("Adirondack") Murray, closed his oyster bar, the Snow-Shoe Café, for want of business. He left town, taking with him the female companion who had been such a worry to the elders of Boston's Park Street Church. Down at Joe Beef's famous canteen, on the other hand, the sailors and wharf-rats and down-and-outs seem to have carried on unfazed. Probably most of Joe's clientele spoke English and was vaccinated. Or maybe the stench from the bears and the buffalo Joe kept helped to ward off the smallpox.

Nobody came to town to help fight the pestilence. No parsons from outside, no social workers, no politicians representing the province of Quebec or the government of Canada. It was a local problem, the responsibility of the local authorities. Governments each minded their own business in these far-off times. The ubiquity of politicians today has something to do with fifty years of big government, a lot to do with the ubiquity of television cameras.

Even the greatest physician of the era, Dr. William Osler himself, a former worker in the smallpox wing of the General during the 1870s, apparently paid no attention to the epidemic when he came to Montreal for the opening of McGill College's new medical building on October 22. Osler and his colleagues, among the medical elite of North America, orated about medical education past, present, and future, toasted old McGill and her brilliant prospects, and dined sumptuously at the Windsor Hotel. They said nothing about the smallpox that was holding high carnival among the children of French Montreal behind the drawn blinds so few streets away.

And John said, "Master, we saw one casting out devils in thy name; and we forbade him, because he followeth not with us." And Jesus said unto him, "Forbid him not; for he that is not against us is for us."

— *Luke* 9, 49-50

CHAPTER 10

GOD'S JUDGMENTS

BY THE AUTUMN OF 1885 EVERY Montrealer who had had any reasonable acquaintance with smallpox and the facts of the epidemic should have known enough to be vaccinated. All but a few of the doctors were saying so, all of the newspapers were saying so, the priests and the nuns were saying so, if not quite as emphatically as the Protestants, and the bosses were too. There was no longer any evidence that rumours and complaints about the quality of Montreal's vaccine had any foundation. The only people now who failed to get vaccinated were the deluded, the misguided, the ignorant, the irrationally fearful. The tragedy of 1885 for Montreal was that there were still so many of them in the city—so many of them the illiterate poor, virtually unreachable by education or propaganda at such short notice in a city rent by racial and religious division. As in Camus' classic novel, "la peste" was as much an epidemic of the mind as a disease of the body.

What was wrong in Montreal? Protestant North America thought the problem was mostly the Church's fault. Confident, progressive rationalists—the "hommes de progrès"—in outside places, could not believe the backwardness of people who said that winter carnivals caused smallpox and who fought the epidemic by carrying statues of the Virgin through the streets. *The New York Times'* early coverage, for example, burned with voltairean anger at "the French Canadian piety that forbids a man to try secular means for dodging providences." It condemned Filiatrault's sermon connecting smallpox and carnival as "blasphemous" in its superstitious ignorance. "The existence of a man capable of talking this drivel from the pulpit," the Americans wrote, "implies the existence of a considerable number of persons in the pews more ignorant and more superstitious than the preacher.... However difficult it may be, the administration of carnal vaccination and secular soap and water should be persisted in by the Canadian authorities upon both priests and people." The September rioting convinced the *Times* that "the wildest freaks of stupidity and superstition in Spain and Italy have been reproduced in Canada. The Spanish and Italian mobs assaulting the doctors and exhibiting relics of saints to check the ravages of cholera are repeated in the mob of Montreal." Montreal had to prevent "superstitious fools" from spreading the pestilence.

Other outsiders had a racial explanation for the plague. Too much French power. According to the Toronto *News* (editor Sheppard fresh from his near horse-whipping in Montreal), the September 28 violence was "the legitimate outcome of the way in which French domination has been tolerated and pandered to by the English-speaking people.... Concession after concession to the ignorance, prejudice and intolerance of the French-Canadian element has only served to render them more arbitrary and domineering, to intensify their race prejudices and to confirm them in their obstinate and headstrong determination to ... either control or defy the law." They had ruined and plundered the enterprising members of other races in Quebec, and now they had made Montreal a menace to the whole continent:

> Owing to the prejudice of these ignorant creatures against vaccination, which is largely due to race antagonism, Montreal has been suffered to become a plague spot, and though the

fell ravages of the disease sweep away hundreds every week the deluded and fanatical masses still cling to their absurd and unreasoning hostility to the only remedy that will meet the case, because it is an "English notion." ... They would sooner die in their filth and squalor than put faith in the remedy which runs counter to their traditional opinions....

We hope that this demonstration will be a lesson to the English speaking people of Canada as to the mistake of concessions and compromises in dealing with these cowardly and irreconcilable foes to nineteenth century progress, liberty, order and good government.

Overheard on a Grand Trunk train:

Frenchman: "I am sure you are not one of those brutal Englishmen who would vaccinate us by force."

Englishman: "You are perfectly right. I am one of those who would prefer that you should all have the smallpox."

The New York *World*'s French-speaking reporter came to Montreal in early October with a fairly open mind. He found "a city laid low with shame, grief and suffering." Inside it, the French formed "as distinct a people as if they lived under another Government from that of their English fellow citizens." The phrase "je suis Américain" literally opened doors closed to Montreal journalists. He saw clean, neat dwellings where children lay on their beds in suppurating wretchedness and delirium. He saw mothers with hideously marked, dying babies in their arms, about to get on with their work as laundresses. He saw the healthy and the sick playing and sharing beds together, saw placards torn down as fast as they were erected, and was driven away from one mean hovel by an axe-wielding, screaming mother.

Their faith comforted some mothers with dying children, the reporter observed. If death was God's will, the infants' souls would be safe. The Virgin would look after them. Most children would probably recover, and when they did they would be "purified" and perhaps healthier than ever (the smallpox having caused the body to expel so much poison). Prayer and the care prescribed by their own

French-Canadian doctors—to those who could afford doctors—might see them through.

"Why in the name of all that is good don't you have that child vaccinated?"

"Ah! Non, non." Snatching the infant up, away from even the friendly journalist.

Reporters, the health officers, physicians, all agreed that many of the people feared vaccination more than they feared smallpox. Everyone knew that large numbers of French Canadians had not accepted vaccination for themselves or their children. It was not a matter of religious impulses, or racial inferiority, but of unrelieved fear and ignorance and fatalism.

The more we learn about the history of vaccination, the more we find that it was widely resisted. People did not take naturally to the new procedure. Who would want to be inoculated with a pox virus, even the benign germs of cowpox? At the best of times, vaccination occasionally caused severe reactions. In the nineteenth century, and particularly in the early era of arm-to-arm vaccination, the dangers of bacterial contamination were very high. Vaccination sometimes meant moderate rashes, sometimes meant erysipelas, sometimes (almost always, according to vaccinophobes who liked to relate small pox to great pox) meant syphilis. The vaccinators said it meant protection from smallpox, but none of them could explain exactly how or why the operation worked. And they were proven flatly wrong when they said it meant lifetime protection. Most of the time smallpox was not that great a menace anyway, for there was a lot less of it around than there used to be. So what good was vaccination?

In many countries it took decades to convince most people to accept vaccination as a matter of course, and there were always large numbers who did not normally have their children vaccinated. It seems that the earlier vaccination was introduced, the earlier and harder that public health authorities pushed for mass vaccination, the sooner most of the resistance was broken down. The acceptance of vaccination by Roman Catholic Irish in Ireland, pressured by the governing English, seems to be a case in point. In Quebec, by contrast, and in most of the rest of Canada, there was no tradition of routine vaccination of children. Governments had never made the concerted effort, had never enforced the compulsory vaccination legislation of 1861. Even supposedly expert physicians, like W.H. Hingston, had their doubts about vaccination under the wrong climatic and constitutional conditions. Generally, people resorted to vaccination only when they felt menaced by smallpox. After the menace had been removed from Montreal in 1880-81, for example, very few French Canadians, and probably not many of the English, had their children vaccinated. In the absence of smallpox the Health Department had not exerted itself on behalf of vaccination.

When the menace returned, enlightened people rushed to be vaccinated. Those imprisoned in fear and ignorance and fatalism did not. Sadly, this group of Montrealers had its prejudices pandered to by men who should have known better, the anti-vaccinationists.

During the smallpox years of the 1870s in Montreal, Dr. Coderre and his followers had enjoyed considerable success reinforcing popular doubts about vaccination, even causing churchmen to lapse into neutrality while doctors argued. In those years supporters of vaccination hurled blame and abuse at the anti-vaccinationists for poisoning the people's minds about an operation that could save their lives. Coderre and company were condemned as cranks and obscurantists, but were all too influential in their crankiness and backwardness.

As Coderre liked to point out to his critics, the leaders in the world-wide movement against vaccination, which was gathering strength in the 1870s and 1880s, were English. Doctrinaire vaccinophobia in Montreal was not a matter of Roman Catholic or French-Canadian ignorance. Rather, it was a Canadian manifestation of an international coalescence of sanitarian, sectarian, and libertarian criticisms of mainstream medicine and public health.

The old-fashioned sanitarians could not bring themselves to believe that inoculating people with the foul pox of beasts was a surer preventative of smallpox than cleanliness. Sectarian doctors—hydropaths, homeopaths, natural healers—tended to identify vaccination with the old-fashioned, and thoroughly discredited, heroic cures of regular or "allopathic" medicine, such as bleeding and blistering. Libertarians simply said it was a man's inalienable right to make up his own mind about what he would put in his or his children's bodies, including the germs of the cowpox. The state and its doctors had no right to force any specific treatment on anyone.

Coderre's English-speaking Montreal ally, Alexander Milton Ross, was about as pure a representative of "orthodox" anti-vaccinationism as you could find. A spokesman for radical medicine, Ross championed sanitarian ideas, clean living, and food reform. His correspondence shows that he was part of the international network of anti-vaccinationists, doctors and laymen who saw themselves as progressive reformers, fighting what to them was an unscientific, barbarous, tyrannical establishment of medicos and their political and journalistic dupes. They would not be silenced. In 1885 their movement was growing in America, England, Europe, and now, Ross and Coderre thought, in Canada too. They believed that the Montreal epidemic, which had not gotten fully out of control until the authorities started vaccinating completely promiscuously, spreading the poison all over the city, would further their cause.

The anti-vaccinationists, in Montreal, England, America, everywhere, were wrong. Their understanding of smallpox was wrong, their understanding of vaccination was wrong. Their case studies were based sometimes on misunderstandings, sometimes on exaggerations, sometimes on statistical fallacies, sometimes on deliberate distortions. The vaccinophobes were ideologues, not empirical scientists. Like a parallel British-born sectarian movement, anti-vivisectionism, the anti-vaccinationist crusade attracted increased attention just as its scientific credibility declined. By the 1870s vaccination was so well established as an empirically effective procedure that reputable doctors took it for granted. In those years the vast majority of Montreal's physicians, English and French, had endorsed the need for widespread vaccination. By 1885 the feeling was even stronger. Especially in the midst of a ghastly epidemic, serious physicians simply dismissed anti-vaccinationism as malefic quackery.

They had properly dismissed A.M. Ross at their September meeting. As a physician this pompous old reformer was a semi-trained illiterate. Along with Coderre, another old radical whose training was suspect, Ross had an understanding of smallpox and immunization that, in its way, was as half-baked as the ideas of the poorest French-Canadian tenement-dweller. Ross and Coderre stood valiantly for liberty, for freedom to persist in ignorance and fear at any cost. Like anti-vaccinationists everywhere, the radical doctors and their followers stood against the claims of the interventionist state, against the desire of the Board of Health to break down the barrier of ignorance, fear, and fatalism that was taking the lives of Montreal's poor French-Canadian children.

There were so few anti-vaccinationists in the city by 1885 and the epidemic was so frightening that they ought to have been overcome or bypassed, swept into the dust-bin of history. They might have been, and Montreal might have been spared its awful calamity, had it not been for Bessey's use of contaminated vaccine that spring. It was the worst possible disaster at a time of staggering peril. It played perfectly into the hands of the anti-vaccinationists, reviving the 1870s tradition in the East End, giving Ross's absurd, scurrilous broadsheets a superficial credibility they would never otherwise have enjoyed, perpetuating and reinforcing the ignorance and fear of those who knew no better.

William Bessey's unilingualism and arrogance may have helped tilt French-Canadian resistance to vaccination in the peculiar nationalist direction noticed by some of their harsh critics. Then Louis Riel and the North-West rebellion helped raise French-Canadian self-consciousness to a higher level. Finally, PRO BONO PUBLICO and the other Anglos who blamed the smallpox on French filthiness further alienated the people who somehow had to be educated. Vaccinophobia got reinforced by anglophobia until for some lower-class French Canadians hatred of the English and hatred of vaccination seemed to go together. You resisted the oppressors and all their works.

Montreal's Board of Health was more often part of the problem than the instrument of its solution. Henry Gray and his staff had misjudged the epidemic at almost every turn. They had always reacted to events, usually too late. Their vaccine had been bad, their officers were disliked and unpopular and overworked, their resort to compulsion an apparent embrace of oppressive force. Gray, a tolerant and not a foolish man, knew how important it was to have the confidence of the citizens he was trying to help. The tragedy of his organization was that it had lost that confidence (if ever it had it) very early in the game. It never won it back.

Could confidence in vaccination have been quickly restored if the Health Department or the province had taken the vaccine situation in hand during the early summer and supervised the production of a reliable supply of impeccably pure vaccine? Easier said than done, for the most experienced vaccine supplier in Quebec, William Bessey, had left for Ontario in disgrace. Apart from the lingering suspicion, too, that many of those said to be waiting for pure vaccine would only resume the operation "quand les poules [hens] aient des dents [teeth]." Or, in another colloquialism, "chat échaudé craint l'eau froide [burned cats fear cold water]."

If fear of vaccination in May had a certain justification, there was no longer any excuse in these black days of October. The city was well supplied with good lymph from the United States. Public vaccination was widely and freely available. Rational people could no longer pretend that this was a light epidemic or that children would benefit from some mild exposure. Family after family, street after street, were being ravaged by the horrible plague. Intelligent people would not now resist preventive measures. Intelligent people had become horrified of smallpox.

But still there was resistance.

Some of the apparently shocking carelessness was misunderstood, being simply the confidence of immune adults and children who knew the disease could not hurt them. Some of the resistance, such as the actions of those who hid cases of smallpox for fear of losing their livelihood, was narrowly, grimly rational. It was understandable, too, that people living five or ten to a room would scoff at the idea of weeks of enforced isolation. Nor did it probably do the sick children much good to carry them away to St. Roch's in the black wagon. And loving mothers normally do not stand by calmly when their children are taken from them.

But the resistance to public health measures had darker overtones: They say that it was really vaccination that killed Sir Francis Hincks, and people have gone to Alderman Jeannotte to tell him that seventeen-year-old Albert Bélec had died after being vaccinated, and did you hear about the poor vacciné whose arm had to be amputated by a butcher? Did you read this tract by A.M. Ross, translated by Dr. Coderre? Stir rumour and more fear into the plight of the already frightened and helpless, and the broth only gets thicker.

Many of the poor people had probably not been "medicalized" in the sense of ever seeing physicians. They endured smallpox as a fact of life and death. Their priests and nuns were starting to tell them that this fatalism was not necessary, that science had given them a way to escape their prison. But at the same time the Church accommodated itself to fear and fatalism, offering comforting, consoling ideas and practices for people who chose to live in a world that the nineteenth century was passing by.

*　*　*

In that hard, poor world, if you tried to fight smallpox at all, the first resort to medication would not be vaccination. It would be to the folk cures and household remedies, passed on by word of mouth, and then to whatever you could buy for a few cents in some store. Those mothers who deliberately exposed children to smallpox were acting as their mothers and grandmothers before them. As the epidemic deepened, that practice was abandoned. Rumours that old-fashioned inoculation with smallpox was widespread in Montreal seem to have had no substance. Nor were there any reports of the use of red lights or garments as sympathetic anti-smallpox magic.

The most common home remedies seem to have been cooling draughts of cream of tartar, and the ointments derived from sarracenia or pitcher plant. Other soothing lotions or distracting counter-irritants were widely available. So were aromatics, such as the "sachet rose" available from M. Joule, "Docteur," or the "Pastilles Du Semail"—"pour perfumer les appartements contre le Choléra et la picotte"—available from T. Gauthier, 38 St. Laurent. "La picotte diminue tous les jours dans les quartiers où l'on fait usage de l'eau minérale de St-Léon," the people read in *Le Monde* and other papers. If clean food and clean water were preventives against the loathsome disease, then J.B. Richer offered several excellent anti-smallpox products for sale, including Labatt's India Pale Ale and Treble X Stout. These came complete with a testimonial (dated 1879) by Mr. Henry R. Gray, chemist, as being "perfectly sound and desirable articles to be used in cases where Malt and hop beverages are prescribed by physicians."

Perhaps the crying, feverish baby would be helped by another dose of "Sirop des Enfants du Dr. Coderre," widely advertised in the French press. No claims to prevent smallpox, mind you, but all the magic of Coderre's name. By 1885 no reputable Montreal physician had his name on bottles of patent medicine.

On October 13 the *Gazette* carried a story about a well-known anti-vaccination doctor who had a man enter his office, his face covered with pustules. "Look at me!" the victim exclaimed, grabbing the doctor by the shoulders. "This is what you and your pet theory has brought hundreds like me to. Curse you!"

◦ ◦ ◦

A stroke of luck. Alexander Milton Ross has to leave Montreal for Ontario. He later says it is to be at the bedside of a dying friend. Ross takes the train, the Grand Trunk's Western Express, at nine o'clock on the night of October 12. He must know he is heading for trouble, for his enemies are everywhere:

> All the railroads, steamboats, cross-roads,
> Leading from the doomed city,
> Guarded are by vaccinators.
> Vaccinators on the right,
> Vaccinators on the left,
> Vaccinators in front—
> None can 'scape the vaccinators ...
> Cutting off the hope of freedom ...

Dr. Theodore Covernton, chief of the Ontario inspection staff, rides in the same Pullman car, apparently having learned of Ross's trip in advance. An officer of the Illinois Board of Health is also on board.

Rolling west from Montreal, John Crombie Burt, MD, medical inspector for Ontario ("... a seedy doctor,/ With weazened face and rattish eyes/ Head crowned with a threadbare stove-pipe hat,/ Trembling, quaking with cowardly fear") begins to work his way through the car. Ross gives him his card and says he is going to Toronto.

"Have you been vaccinated?"

"I have."

"When?"

According to Burt, Ross replied, "Recently."

"How recently?"

"Within a year."

"Have you a certificate to that effect?"

"No, I have not; but surely that is not necessary. Among professional men a practitioner's word should be sufficient."

Burt shakes his head. Ross appeals to him. Burt refuses. "I could not do it. The Board is no respecter of persons. You must either show your arm or produce a satisfactory certificate of vaccination, or go back to Montreal."

"You are making a special case against me," Ross protests.

Burt says he is only doing his duty. Ross agrees to show Burt his arm in private. They go to the closed compartment at the front of the car. Ross bares his arm.

In Ross's version,

> Then the cowardly vaccinators,
> With their press—hireling press, of Montreal
> Bound themselves by vaccine contract,
> That between them they would make,
> Make up such a damning story
> That the Anti-Vaccinator
> Would be ruined for evermore.

"EXPOSED" is the head on the Montreal *Star*'s story. "The Great Anti-Vaccinationist Humbug Shown Up—He Bares His Arm and

Displays Three Vaccination Marks—One of Them a Recent One."

There it is. Vaccinated in infancy, vaccinated as a boy, vaccinated very recently. The hypocrite caught out. "The doctor has been playing his hand with a vaccination card up his sleeve," comments the *Herald*. "How many more anti-vaccination doctors are there in Montreal with three good marks on their arm?" asks the *Star*. How many slaves did A.M. Ross keep while he was an abolitionist? A mercenary quack, a fraud, a ridiculous man:

SING HEY! THE PORTLY DOCTOR AND THE SCAR

Kind doctor, I'm opposed to vaccination!
(Sing hey the Health Inspector, that you are)
And I won't be bull-dosed by a Corporation!
But step in here and I will show the scar.
It's very, very recent.
Yes, very, very recent.
A very, very recent, vac-cine scar.
Yes, Doctor, I'm opposed to vaccination
(Sing hey the Health Inspector that you are)
Now won't you please accept my explanation
And take away your vaccine—I've a scar?
Sing hey the portly Doctor.
The very portly Doctor.
The portly, portly Doctor, *with* a scar.

Ross is appalled. He takes an oath before the mayor of Toronto, claiming that he was vaccinated only once in his life, fifty-one years ago. Three Toronto doctors supply affadavits saying he has only one mark; two say it appears to be an old one. Ross dashes off furious letters to the editor denouncing the "malicious lie," the "stab of an assassin." He offers to go before any number of physicians and show he has only one old mark. If he is proven wrong he will serve for six months as a menial assistant in the smallpox hospital.

What happened on the train? Ross claims that when Burt looked at his arm he said the mark was pronounced and looked fresh, not more than twelve months old. "I made no reply. If he had asked I would have told him, but he did not ask."

In a sworn affadavit, Burt says that Ross twice said he had been vaccinated within a year. Covernton, Rauch of Illinois, the conductor, and another passenger, endorse Burt's testimony. To his critics it doesn't matter whether Ross has one, two, or three vaccination marks, or how he got them. The great crusading idealist, champion of truth and justice, has, at the very least, been caught lying to the medical inspector.

"A baser, meaner plot has never been concocted since the plot to betray the Man of Nazareth," Ross cries out. "When I began my warfare against vaccination I expected obloquy, slander, lies and persecution. I have not been disappointed.... My offence—for advocating cleanliness in place of vaccination, health in place of disease, purity in place of filth, sanitation in place of uncleanliness, science in place of superstition, common sense in place of fetishness, and liberty in place of medical tyranny—I have been subjected to the vilest and most scandalous personal abuse. Surely a day of retribution will come."

✻　✻　✻

After September's alarms and violence, October was a month of grim, quiet struggle. Confidence had to be restored; all extreme solutions were discredited. The new hospitals were opened on the 10th. The Board of Health continued to try to placard infected dwellings, and on October 5 carefully recommenced its program of house-to-house vaccination. Taking the names of those who refused to cooperate, canvassers began in West End neighbourhoods where they were most likely to be welcomed—and unneeded. The board obtained more ambulances, contracted with undertakers, hired more sanitary policemen and special isolation constables, and, after bitter debate pitting Graham against Gray, improved its office routine. The sanitary police increased their inspections of yards, lanes, privvies, and drains, and kept the scavengers and dead animal contractors hard at work (from September through November the corpses of 105 horses, 25 cows, and 302 smaller animals were removed from Montreal streets). William Mann's incinerators worked at full blast destroying night soil. Mayor Beaugrand was insisting, finally, that all civic employees supply proof of vaccination. Many could not.

The militia still stood guard round the clock as the exhibition buildings were transformed into hospitals. The English soldiers were not popular in the East End, and neither they nor the magistrates who served with them liked the duty. On October 6 a detachment of volunteers was jeered in St-Jean Baptiste as it marched by an outdoor meeting held by the Dry Goods Clerks' Early Closing Association. After the meeting, a group went over to the exhibition grounds, singing and tossing a few stones. The guards at the gates beat a retreat, the cavalry came out onto Mount Royal Avenue, formed "a thin black line," and dispersed the visitors. No one could agree afterwards on the size of the crowd, its temper (one newspaper's "howling" was another reporter's good-humoured singing), or the reasons for its appearance. Were banners inscribed "À bas la tyrannie" and "La liberté est douce" aimed at the soldiers and the Board or Health, or were they carry-overs from the early closing meeting?

The suburban villages certainly resented the tyranny of a city which had forced its way, with squads of armed and mounted soldiers, onto land outside of its boundaries to build its pest-house. Officials from the municipalities of St-Louis du Mile End, St-Jean Baptiste, and Côte St-Louis tried every recourse to have the appropriation declared illegal and the hospitals closed. The more arrogant of the Montrealers trumpeted that possession was nine-tenths of the law, and even Beaugrand told Council that he had taken the buildings "and meant to keep them." More important, the city carefully obtained formal provincial consent, some of it after the fact, to the use of the buildings. Montreal's possession was upheld in court. After the formal opening of the new hospitals, the militia units were withdrawn and discharged. A squad of forty Montreal policemen replaced them.

People continued to resist the Health Board's work and revile its officers. Placarders were threatened by mobs, one had red pepper thrown in his face, sanitary constables were beaten up or driven away at pistol-point. Dr. McNeece, in charge of the board's activities in the West End, was evicted from his lodgings and had to sleep at the health offices. There was a spate of accusations that board employees were drunk, disorderly, unsanitary, and in other ways offensive. In October it was being said that Laberge himself, Montreal's chief medical officer, was doing shocking things in houses he visited—taking the pulse of young ladies, insisting on examining them intimately for marks of smallpox, making outrageous suggestions. Tearful women complained to their priests.

Laberge realized that someone must be impersonating him. On close questioning, he learned that the imposter was missing two fingers on one hand. The board had one such employee, F.-X. Daoust, its chief placarder. Laberge went to Daoust's home and accused him. When Daoust denied the charge Laberge said they would go together to confront the complainants. Daoust refused. Laberge grabbed the man's badge and ripped it from his shirt. The chief placarder of the Montreal Board of Health was charged with indecent assault.

After cooling off for a few days in the wake of the riot, the more extreme English newspapers, the *Herald* and *Witness,* resumed attacking the board and Council for past failures, present inadequacies, and unconcern about the city's blighted future. Hints about horrible conditions at St. Roch's leaked into their columns, and hints that a lot more could be said. It was said that Council and the board were bowing to mob rule in backing away from compulsion. Gray was incompetent. It was wrong to compare aldermen to Spanish dogs; they were more like jackasses. Newspapers that called for only constructive criticism of the health authorites were exhibiting moral cowardice. When would the East End health office be reopened? The world's contempt for Montreal was intolerable. And so on.

Offended aldermen decided to withdraw city advertising from and subscriptions to the *Herald.* This called forth more ridicule, sermons on the freedom of the press, and more satirical verse.

So they boycott THE HERALD, did Gray and his friend,
And they closed up the Health Office in the East End.
"And now, King Picotte, you can have your own way,
"For I'll never stop you, says Alderman Gray."
Singing-Tooral-ri-looral-etc, etc.

Now there's to the health of Jeannotte and Picotte,
And down with vaccine points, for they are all rot,
Three cheers for the Français—ils sont picottés,
Dr. Alex M. Ross and Alderman Gray.

On October 15 the board began moving patients from St. Roch's hospital to St. Camille's and St. Saviour's. Compulsory removals from dwelling-places to the hospitals were to begin on October 23. Every victim over fifteen would have to go to hospital, as would every child who could not be thoroughly isolated. Mothers could accompany their children. Special constables would stand on guard at houses that were being isolated. The city, through the Sisters of Providence, would supply relief in kind to the inmates. Magistrates P.E. Normandeau and J.H. Isaacson had agreed to preside at a special sanitary court where offences against the health laws could be dealt with quickly. Masses of literature were being distributed, including a broadsheet entitled *L'Ami du Peuple*, to counter anti-vaccinationist fear-mongering. The house-to-house vaccination campaign would go forward.

On October 20 the *Gazette* argued that the Board of Health had done all that could reasonably be expected to cope with the epidemic in the face of obstruction from all quarters. Why not reduce coverage of the epidemic; why not stop hounding the gentlemen (including the *Gazette*'s publisher) who were giving their time to serving the city? "What good has been accomplished, we ask, by the course of abuse of the Health board, of the civic authorities, of all who have not seen eye to eye with those who have set themselves up as Sir Oracles, or by the persistent parading in the columns of newspapers of sensational head lines and needlessly alarming statistics of the death rate?"

The death count, the ghastly, relentless record of burials, was the critics' damning justification. Day after day. Plague out of control. Carnival of death. Every week the *Herald* published the names, ages, and addresses of the dead. It was the only newspaper that recorded their names. That was the closest anyone came to reckoning their lives.

From October 1 through 16 there were 624 smallpox deaths in the city, 55 in St-Jean Baptiste, 46 in Ste-Cunégonde, 34 in St-Henri, 43 in Côte St-Louis, 15 in St. Gabriel and 1 in Point St. Charles. "818!" proclaimed the *Herald.* Macabre vindication. No decline in the death rate. No end in sight.

❖   ❖   ❖

On the morning of October 20 the Health Board decided it had to consider asking the Provincial Board of Health to authorize the closing of all places where crowds might gather, including the churches. One of the French-Canadian members of the board urged continued reliance on voluntarism. Alderman Roy replied that every day's delay meant sacrificing more lives to the smallpox. Hugh Graham spoke strongly in favour of closing the churches. "It is beyond question that the churches are to-day so many centres for disseminating smallpox," his paper said. Drastic steps could only improve Montreal's image in the eyes the world, because the city was already painted as black as could be. The Montreal board asked the Provincial board to close the churches.

Some Protestant clergymen were said to be agreeable to shutting down for a few weeks until the epidemic abated. The logic of the thought that vaccination was salvation, sent from God, suggested that the other forms of worship were expendable, at least for a time. Other Protestants thought this would be going too far. The *Witness*, an evangelically Christian newspaper, had been uneasy about attacks on religious people, even Catholics, for putting so much faith in prayer and God during epidemics. Plagues *were* related to sin, it argued, and they should be fought with both spiritual devotions and carnal safeguards. The newspaper was furious that the Board of Health, responsible for the carnal side of things, and such a manifest failure, would now try to suppress institutions whose activities could hardly be criticized. How dare it attempt to bring on "such an unprecedented revolution as the suppression of public religion at a time of calamity."

Catholics were appalled. It seemed monstrous, insane, to want to close the houses of God at a time when God had the community under judgment. Close the houses of amusement and sin, if you must—the theatres, the dance-halls, the saloons—give dispensations for the sick to stay at home, but never, never close places of worship. Never stop the processions, the prayers, the sacraments. Did not history teach Catholics of how devotion and processions had brought on miracles in the past, saving Rome and so many other cities from the plague? Without the vessels of its faith, Montreal would surely be lost, godforsaken.

Some of the godless had wanted this all along, hadn't they? Here it was, all unfolding. First materialism and carnival, then free thought, Freemasonry, Beaugrand, then smallpox and an all-powerful Board of Health. Governments already prone to meddle in education and the running of lunatic asylums. Now the absolute triumph of the secular. Salvation offered only by the doctors. The "billets de vaccination" were worth more than the priests' "billets de confession." Just try to leave Montreal by train and you would see. Now the final step. Suppress the Church altogether.

To the ultramontanes at *L'Etendard,* a newspaper popular with the religious community, the proposal to close the churches was another manifestation of the real plague menacing Montreal. It was a moral pestilence, worse than the smallpox. The disease of secularism, unbelief. Through God's judgment, Montreal's impiety had probably brought on the smallpox, as well. Close the churches! Never!

The bishop of Montreal laid down the law. At high mass at the cathedral (sponsored by the merchants of Notre Dame Street between McGill Street and Chaboillez Square, to give thanks for the disappearance of the epidemic in their area) Fabre reiterated that plagues were sent by God "as a warning from His infinite goodness." Vaccination was also a gift from God, but spiritual acts were absolutely necessary, for the essential good that came from epidemics was repentance:

To close the churches would simply be to laugh at God, to go against His wishes and to call for a continuation of the epidemic.

The putting into practice of such a scheme is absurd. No; let the churches be opened and flock into them, as numerous as possible, for common and united prayer is always more powerful than that of each isolated individual.... I repeat: Come to church and implore the Lord. To prayer you will again add mortification, especially abstaining yourselves from forbidden pleasures, such as licentious theatres, etc. With such means and the Christian faith ... I have full confidence that the Lord will have mercy on us and deliver us from the terrible epidemic.

Dr. Hingston, a Catholic, was one of several members of the Provincial Board of Health who would not support the Montreal board's request to close the churches. Not only would it be a delicate matter to interfere with freedom of worship, he argued, but it would be disastrous to alienate religious men and women at this crucial time. In any case, crowd control was now less important than vaccination and hospitalization. Eventually vaccination and the smallpox would have to meet. "The unvaccinated," Hingston said, "must go to the wall."

The Provincial board reminded the Montreal board that people with smallpox in their families had already been banned from church and all other public gatherings. This was as far as it would go. The churches would stay open. The battle would be fought on both fronts, secular and spiritual.

Armed with its hospitals, its sanitary police, its health court, and virtually a blank cheque from the city, the Health Department was ready to start removing smallpox patients from contact with the community. The Roman Catholic Church readied itself for a month of special services throughout November, beginning with All Saints' Day. In the Catholic calendar November was the Month of the Dead, a time to commemorate and pray for the souls of the departed. The month would start with a special pilgrimage to the tomb of Bishop Bourget. Through prayer, his followers would beseech his intercession with God to lift the plague.

His thoughts dwelt upon the image of the desolate and calamitous city, and he was giddy with fugitive, mad, unreasoning hopes and visions of a monstrous sweetness.

— Thomas Mann, *Death in Venice*

CHAPTER 11

THE MONTH OF THE DEAD

T*uesday, October 27*

Cold, grey. The lower West End, between Dow's brewery and the canal.

The stench from the rear of the shack at 65 Young Street repels bystanders fifty feet away. Three ambulance vans are lined up in the laneway. Doctor Laberge rushes out of the house, complaining that the filth and smell are unbearable. His men are still inside, where a woman begins to shriek. Pleas to Heaven above. Fervent beseeching—*spare her, spare my only child.* Screams from the heart. Cries of wrath.

A sanitary policeman emerges, carrying a baby wrapped in a blanket. The frantic mother is at his heels, trying to drag the child away. The baby is laid in the ambulance van. The mother runs about the yard, shrieking and gesturing. She falls prostrate at her door, gasping for breath, begging them to give her back her child. Laberge and some neighbours tell her that she can go to the hospital with her infant; she seems too distraught to listen.

The vans move on. Nothing at 188 Murray—must have been a false report. At

19 Rolland Lane, a rickety tenement over an archway, there is a confirmed case. But both the front and rear doors are locked, and no one answers when the constables knock. A warrant will be issued against the tenant, one Elie Gagnon, for refusing admittance to the health authorities. Another case at 17 Rolland, another warrant. Wherever the vans stop a crowd of bare-footed children and ragged adults gathers. At 185 Barré five members of the Gravel family—two little girls, two babies, and the mother, all with smallpox—are taken away in two vans while the police hold back the crowd. At 365 Richmond there are three cases in the lower flat, four above. A young girl has just died. The vans will have to come back for another load.

Wednesday, October 28

East End. Abraham Cloutier of the isolation unit is standing guard outside 278 Maisonneuve. A knot of people gathers across the street. Somebody throws something. Cloutier is pelted with eggs, potatoes, tomatoes, stones. He holds his ground, and threatens to arrest one of the men who approaches the house. He is set upon, beaten, kicked, left bleeding in the street. A passing hackman finds him and takes him to shelter.

Six sanitary constables are sent to stand guard. One is assaulted in the small hours of the 29th. One of the gang is heard to say that if the damned policemen are about tomorrow night they'll get a bullet in the head.

* * *

The vans began the removals on Friday, October 23. They started with the tenements closest to City Hall and then fanned out to the worst-infected neighbourhoods east and west. Crowds gathered on the streets and at windows wherever they stopped. Most of the people were hostile; squads of sanitary police kept them back. Whenever someone came out the onlookers would surge forward. There might be a glimpse of a hideous face or pitted hands clutching a miserable blanket.

Wherever isolation could be enforced as an alternative to removal, the board left men from its isolation squad on twenty-four-hour guard. They soon found that by sealing exits one man could watch several dwellings. Where there was more than token resistance, the officials backed off, got a warrant, and returned. The first case in health court was that of Joseph Trepanier, a carter at 64 St. Martin Street. He had barricaded his house with neighbours' help and said they would get his child over his dead body. With their warrant the sanitary police persuaded him to come quietly and eventually took him to St. Camille's to see the care his child was getting. In court he apologized, saying the hospital was better than Hôtel-Dieu itself. Because Trepanier was contrite, he was only fined $5 and costs.

The excellence of the St. Camille's and St. Saviour's wings of the Mount Royal hospitals was the board's best talking-point in overcoming resistance to removals. The wards were spacious and clean and well-provided with good food and good nursing. The care was as good as you'd get at the Windsor Hotel, a visitor commented. There were not even foul odours. A person could not even detect the sickly fumes of smallpox unless he actually bent over a victim. Mothers could stay there and care for their children. No one entered or left without passing through a fumigation chamber.

From the pulpit the priests urged people to cooperate. People who were too frightened or ignorant, or too hateful of the maudit Bureau de Santé, were overcome by the show of force and the use of the law. There was not nearly the resistance there would have been a few weeks earlier. The smallpox had taken so many.

A grim and thankless job, nevertheless, going into the poorest, vilest sections of the city, taking away the sick, sometimes literally fighting with their families, being cursed and screamed at by ugly crowds and sometimes being attacked. Dealing with the dregs and despised of the city, sufferers from a wretched, putrid disease. Tending to the sick in their houses and in the hospital could not have been easy or attractive for the Sisters of Providence and the Grey Nuns. But the good sisters were usually revered, or at least respected by the people. Most of the board's employees became wretched pariahs, shunned as though they had the smallpox itself, hated as enemies of the people. Nobody would give isolation guards a roof over their head at night. They could not even stay at police stations. The Health Board's employees were not very high quality; many of them turned to drink to get through the days and nights.

Respectable Montrealers held their noses, literally and figuratively, and shunned everything to do with the smallpox. The citizen appointees to the Health Board all did yeoman work, most of them being more active than any of the aldermen except Gray. But they got little by way of support from other citizens. The Citizens' Committee, kept going by a small rump of activists headed by Hollis Shorey, hired professional detectives to uncover inadequacies in the city's efforts and used their reports as the basis for carping criticism. Partly to shame some of his critics into real sacrifices, Hugh Graham had his isolation committee issue a call for volunteers to help with the work. Two people volunteered.

Montreal's medical establishment was not much better. Physicians did not like treating smallpox, partly because of the washing and disinfection of their clothes necessary before seeing any other patients. Doctors did not like having to report cases. They offered practically nothing but criticism of the work of the health authorities. Only a few public-spirited medical men, such as Hingston and Mount, along with the board's paid vaccinators, had been useful. "No help whatever has been given the Health Board by the doctors of this city," Gray stated bitterly in mid-October.

Just as the board got the hospitals in tip-top condition, just as the removals and isolation began to bite, just as public confidence seemed to be rising, the newspapers attacked again. Now it was the horrors of St. Roch. Day after day the *Witness* and the *Herald* printed testimony by former patients about the filth, the hideous attendants, the lack of care, the deaths, and the nightmares of the old hospital, which in fact was still being used. Stories that blackened the reputation of the board, its staff, even the Catholic sisters who had taken over in mid-September and whose upgrading of the care was not clearly evident from these stories in English Protestant newspapers.

Recriminations, denials, calls for investigation, calls for resignation, new revelations, more denials. Intense anger. A relative of a patient who had died in St. Roch wrote this:

> This wholesale slaughter of the helpless ... must stand through all future time as the blackest stain on the name of our proud city, and for years to come orphan children and childless parents will curse the management of an institution which has slain their loved ones. We have shuddered over the horrors of the "Black Hole of Calcutta," but that was mercy compared to this.... "The Horrors of St. Roch's" will be the by-word for misery for generations to come. No wonder the patron saint of pestilence and plague has turned a deaf ear to the cries of those who pray to him. No wonder appeals to the "Blessed Virgin" elicit no response. It would sour the sympathy of an angel towards those who can perpetrate such horrors....
>
> We trusted ... and now it is revealed to us that our people were shamefully neglected, that all their cries fell upon ears dead to human sympathy, and noble men and women were allowed to die ... words utterly fail.

Angry aldermen and Health Board members blamed the newspapers for sabotaging their work. The past is history. Why rehash the fate of the dead? Is it to destroy confidence in those who are fighting for the living? The once-crusading *Star* and the always cautious *Gazette* condemned the *Herald* and the *Witness* for sensationalism and money-grubbing. The muckrakers claimed their only interest was to witness for righteousness and humanity against evil. Was there ever such evil in the history of Montreal as had infected St. Roch's hospital?

No one could rightly say. The most extreme charges were flatly denied by Dr. Nolin and former patients who came forward to say that conditions were not nearly as bad as portrayed. The complainants were mainly Protestant and English, and some of their testimony was probably the product of bias and/or delirium. Beaugrand argued that people had gone to hospital with absurd expectations. "When they got there they expected champagne, jams, jellies, and the like; they did not get it and then they raised a

231

row afterwards." Henry Gray more accurately thought it was a case of people used to better things in life, people who were never expected to go to a place like St. Roch's, being disgusted at conditions the lower classes took for granted.

In fact it had been a grim clash of standards. Our picture of St. Roch's is based on parts of the evidence that were not seriously contested. Until the nuns took over, the hospital was a horrible place, a traditional or pre-modern institution, a lazzaretto in which brutal and slovenly staff offered a place for the poor to die in misery. To those who knew no better it was not bad. After the management was changed it became much better, though still overcrowded and under-staffed. Smallpox hospitals were bound to be unhappy places because the disease was so ghastly and untreatable and the mortality so high. With the construction of the Mount Royal hospitals the Health Board made tremendous progress, shooting up from the lowest to the highest standard in hospital care. A spectacular, even a revolutionary improvement, much too late.

Monday, November 2

The October death count is made public: 1,284 people are known to have died of smallpox last month in the city, 85 in St-Jean Baptiste, 81 in Ste-Cunégonde, 55 in St-Henri, 115 in Côte St-Louis, at least 12 in St-Gabriel and Côte St-Paul. Grand total for October: 1,632. Grand total for the epidemic (counting the suburbs for this month only): 2,641! The mortality has been almost tripling every month. Will it be five thousand in November? Smallpox traditionally does well in Montreal winters.

The disease has to burn itself out sometime, but when? How many more will have to die? The Health Board says there are twenty-five hundred cases presently in the city; the Citizens' Committee, which is probably better informed, says five thousand. Plans are afoot to add eight hundred more beds to the hospitals on the exhibition grounds by converting the Crystal Palace. Montreal's imitation of the world-famous symbol of Victorian progress is slated to become a pest-house.

This day should mark another great step forward in the city's and Canada's progress. In a pouring rainstorm early in the afternoon the first Canadian Pacific Railway through train for Manitoba and the Rocky Mountains pulls out of the city: five cars, fifty-nine through passengers, three cheers, and deafening shrieks from the engine's whistle. Will the westerners really want to see the Montrealers? "Greatly as the people of Manitoba are delighted with the prospect of the Canadian Pacific railway being opened through from Montreal," says a gloomy *Herald* editorial, "their first thought is to erect a barricade against smallpox reaching them from the eastern provinces."

In its lead editorial on this landmark day for Montreal, the newspaper argues that the smallpox is still out of control, the health authorities have had no more success than someone trying to keep back the ocean with a mop, and the city is a menace to the world. "A great crisis is upon the country. The Board of Health of Montreal has practically broken down. The Provincial Boards have not succeeded.... The powers of the General Government, extending over all the Provinces and covering all our relations, whether internal or external, can alone meet the grave emergency." The government of Canada should step in to save Montreal and the nation.

At eight o'clock in the evening the big bell of Notre Dame and the bells of the other Catholic churches toll a special call to prayer for the souls of the dead in purgatory. The bells will sound at eight every night during this month of the dead. Yesterday the cold and rain prevented the planned procession to Bishop Bourget's tomb. But a very large number of persons went and prayed over his remains.

❀   ❀   ❀

The idea of calling on the government of Canada to intervene in Montreal got short shrift. So did talk of calling in outsider experts, from Britain or the United States. So did the *Witness*'s idea that City Council appoint a "sanitary dictator." Montreal had all the resident experts on smallpox that it needed. The government of Canada had no organized public health service, and would have been perceived by East End Montrealers, already suspicious enough of their fellow citizens, as a foreign power. There was no point in changing horses in mid-stream, the Health Board's supporters argued. The job was to get on with the grim work. Vaccinate, isolate, remove.

Tuesday, November 3

19 Rolland Lane. The tenement-dweller Gagnon, known to have smallpox in his family, will now be dealt with.

The first time that Sanitary Officer Beaudoin went back with a warrant, Gagnon met him in his doorway, loaded revolvers in each hand. Said he'd put a bullet through his brain if he crossed the threshold. Beaudoin backed off, got a second warrant to arrest Gagnon for threatening. Yesterday Beaudoin and Constable Beauchamp returned to get their man. Gagnon and wife, both armed with revolvers, said they'd put daylight through the intruders if they didn't clear out. Come again, Gagnon said, and you'll suffer for it.

Tonight at 6:30 a squad of six armed sanitary police, led by sergeants Moran and Carpenter, surrounds the wooden tenement. A crowd starts to form. Police climb the back stairs, enter the rear door to the main corridor, and knock on the inside door to the Gagnon flat. Without opening it, Gagnon threatens to to shoot the first man who advances. He says he will give himself up when his children are better, but will never leave while they are ill. Outside, constable Quinn is climbing the steps to the rear entrance when someone fires two shots at him from the Gagnon window. Another shot is fired out the front window. No one is hit. The crowd is yelling, threatening the city's men. They form a line, promise to shoot the first man who disputes their passage, and clear out.

Wednesday, November 4

As chief magistrate of Montreal, Mayor Beaugrand has determined to enforce the law. He has ordered Chief Paradis to support the Board of Health. At noon a posse of about twenty city policemen, led by Sub-chief Maher, joins the sanitary police at Number 6 Police Station. Gray and Beaugrand are also present. Beaugrand orders the police to serve the warrant on Gagnon, at any cost, and remove the smallpox patients to Mount Royal Hospital. He will bear the responsibility.

Two city detectives enter Rolland Lane first, probably hoping to do the job cleanly and quickly. Gagnon, a burly, powerful-looking man, leans out his window and demands their business. They say they have come for him. He says he will dress and go with them. Just wait. As they wait, the crowd gathers.

The main force arrives, led by Beaugrand, who orders the police to clear the lane. Every window is filled; people are on roofs, watching.

Gagnon finally comes out onto the landing. He will go with the police, but they must not take his children. What is the ambulance doing in the lane? He won't go. A struggle, and half a dozen police wrestle the man down the stairs and into one of their vans. As the crowd hoots and jeers, he is taken away.

The police are now ready to get the children. The squad clamber up the stairs, kick in the door, and head into the corridor. A young man leans out one of the Gagnon windows, points a revolver at a constable, and fires. He misses.

The inside door is barricaded. Beaugrand orders the police to advance and to defend themselves if fired upon. They cover the outside windows with drawn guns and prepare to smash through the inside door. As they splinter it with an axe three more shots are fired. Using the broken outer door as a shield, the police force their way into the Gagnon apartment. Eugene "Jimmy" Gagnon is waiting for them armed with a fowling rifle. His mother wields her rolling pin. In a wild mêlée the police finally subdue the resisters. Young Gagnon is dragged outside struggling violently. Captors and captive wrestle in the mud. They finally get him into a police cab. From their windows women scream at the crowd to rescue Gagnon. Surging hands reach for the spokes of the wheels. The driver lashes his horses forward and forces his way out of Rolland Lane.

At last, anticlimactically, the ambulance wagon is backed up to the tenement. Two little children and one young girl, all with bad cases of smallpox, are carried off to the smallpox hospital. Their mother goes with them. The police lock up the battle-scarred tenement, and go away.

◦　◦　◦

PLAGUE: A STORY OF SMALLPOX IN MONTREAL

This was public health? Using armed policemen to take sick children to hospitals. Breaking down barricades. Fathers and mothers and sons defending their sick families at gunpoint. Had it come to this in Montreal? Were people going to be killed in the struggle to save the lives of the children?

Afterwards at City Hall Elie Gagnon told reporters that he had resisted the police because their first appearance, days earlier, terrified his sick son. "Papa, papa, la police m'emmène!" Fear had made the boy sicker, and then he had died. Gagnon had gone to a lawyer who had told him the Board of Health had no right to take away his children and he could use force to defend his family. So he had. He was a law-abiding, honest workman, never before in trouble, and very poor. He regretted everything, and knew that his family would be well cared for by the sisters at the hospital. Henry Gray gave the poor man a dollar to buy some food.

The affair seemed to have ended. But the next day, *Le Monde* published this editorial:

HIS HONOUR, THE MAYOR

The scenes of violence and barbarism which took place yesterday in Rolland Lane between you, Mr. Mayor, your gendarmes and the brave Gagnon family are the shame and dishonor of the Municipal authorities of Montreal.

You have thrown into prison the Gagnons, father and son, because they defended their humble and poor homestead against your gendarmes.

You have violently taken away from a father's and children's affections a frightened mother and wife. What you have done is a crime. Force does not triumph over right. Every man is master in his own home. You seem astonished at Gagnon's faithful guard over his hearth and the cradle of his children.

If you have no heart, you have not got the right to maltreat those who have the honor of having one. Your inhuman and barbarous conduct caused the death of the brave Gagnon's child.

You are responsible for this death. Yesterday you triumphed over the poor and courageous Gagnon, from whom you took his children and his wife, and whom you have thrown in prison with one of his children.

You are victorious, but your injustices, your cruelties, your barbarisms already crush you and cover you with shame and dishonor.

Montreal has smallpox; it is a scourge. The reign of Mayor Beaugrand is another.

The worst is not the one which it is generally believed to be.

Outraged, the mayor announced that he would sue *Le Monde* for criminal libel. The newspaper replied editorially:

... If the coward who presides at the City Hall, surrounded by soldiers and gendarmes, thinks he is going to frighten us he is mistaken.

We laugh at his threats....

We have accused the violator of the domestic hearth.

We have avenged paternal authority cruelly outraged by the tyranny of the Mayor....

The courage of Gagnon is admirable; the patience of the crowd who witnessed the perpetration of the crime is astonishing....

The Mayor of Montreal, the First Magistrate of the free city of Montreal, who orders to fire on a woman, on a mother defending her children!

Mr. Mayor, you are a coward! ...

Liberty is too dear to the citizens of Montreal to suffer in silence his cowardly oppression.

The Mayor is not above the law.

The reign of terror will no longer be maintained in the midst of our city.

Return us our liberty, or we will tear it from you.

Peace or war.

It is for you to choose.

In the window of its office *Le Monde* displayed a bullet said to have been fired by the police at the Gagnons. From its office a handbill was distributed, entitled "The Reign of Terror," which was as violent as the editorials.

Le Monde was trying to tap the wellsprings of French Montreal's dislike of the Board of Health. It was playing not only to the mob, but to conservatives' fears of the implications of drastic use of state power in the name of public health. Did the state have the right literally to break into the family and take children away from their parents? Did it know the childrens' welfare better than their parents did? Was the state so infallible, compared with, say, the Church? Why didn't it use gentle persuasion, as good-souled churchmen would certainly have done? Why didn't it clean up the dirt in the poor areas of Montreal which probably was the true cause of smallpox?

Here were events that seemed to justify what ultramontane Catholics had always feared about secular, free-thinking Liberals. These revolutionaries, led by Beaugrand dit Champagne, were out to elevate the authority of the state over even the sanctity of the family. Tearing children from their mothers' arms! Echoes of the Great Terror in the days of the French Revolution. Beaugrand's Reign of Terror. The pestilence of the all-powerful, tyrannical state, as barbaric and hideous as the smallpox itself.

Montreal did not buy the argument. *La Minerve* was the only newspaper that echoed *Le Monde*'s line. The truly arch-conservative journal, *L'Etendard*, understood all the principles at stake but would not countenance disobeying the law or inciting civil disobedience. The absurdity of blaming Beaugrand for the Gagnon child's dying of smallpox was patent. None of the accounts of the incident, including *Le Monde*'s original story, claimed that the police fired any shots. Father Sentenne advocated calm, respect for the authorities, obedience to the law, and recognition that here, as in fighting fires, it was necessary to take drastic protective measures. Prominent Montrealers, English and French, condemned the incendiary editorials. Even former mayor Beaudry disassociated himself from *Le Monde*.

Le Monde's consistency and timing were suspect. Until now the paper had always grudgingly encouraged obedience to the law. The ferocity of its attack on Beaugrand and its incendiary language, was very much out of character. Did all of this have something to do with the impending execution of Louis Riel out in Regina, now scheduled for November 10?

If Riel died, it was expected that a tremendous outburst of French-Canadian wrath would be directed at the Conservative government of Canada. *Le Monde* was controlled by one of the most prominent Quebec Conservative cabinet ministers, Sir Hector Langevin, and was editorially writhing on the spikes of the Riel affair. The Gagnon affair might be a fine counter-pétard on which to hoist the Liberals. It would take the war into the enemy's camp, for Beaugrand was a prominent Rouge and his newspaper was a champion of Riel's cause. "If your wrath must have vent," *La Patrie* warned, "keep it for those who have wrought you an injury, keep it for the day when your brother Riel is hanged."

Beaugrand brought charges of personal libel and incitement to sedition against *Le Monde*'s editors. He was again receiving threats on his life. He publicly appealed to Langevin to stop his journalists from advocating rebellion and bloodshed. Sir Hector denied any responsibility. At City Council on November 9 Beaugrand explained his actions in Rolland Lane and asked for support. "In these hard times of epidemic," the mayor concluded, "when the whole press of America from Labrador down to the Gulf of Mexico and even across the Atlantic have represented the people of Montreal as wild Indians, it is the duty of every good citizen to try and throw oil on the troubled waters.... What we have done we have done for the good of Montreal.... The only question which arose in the case the other day was whether the police were to be shot down or whether the laws for the protection of Montreal and its citizens were to be enforced." Most aldermen applauded.

Jeannotte attacked Beaugrand at length, claiming that all these problems were the fault of the Citizens' Committee, and that he, Jeannotte, had the support of 90 per cent of French Canadians in attacking the harsh measures of the sanitary authorities. Nobody else supported Jeannotte. Jacques Grenier moved a resolution of censure against *Le Monde* and *La Minerve*. Henry Gray offered his most eloquent defence of the Health Department's stewardship and its resort to forceful measures:

Does a surgeon hesitate to use the knife to amputate a limb when a question of human life is involved? Must not we resort to a disagreeable measure to save ourselves and our fellow citizens from death, and must not every citizen of Montreal make up his mind to make some sacrifice to rid the country of the foul destroyer, smallpox? (Applause).

We had, sir, week after week 300 children dying in our midst from the disease, and are we, intelligent men with some humanity left in our breasts, to stand with folded arms and say, "Let them die"? No, we shall not do this. The Board of Health loves those little ones, and why should we not? Who are these children? They are the rising generation of the honest working-men in Montreal. (Applause) ... The working man of my own country, the country which I come from, is much lower in the social scale than the honest, industrious ouvrier of the Quebec suburbs. (Applause) ...

We take the children from the loathsome, infected houses to save not only the afflicted from death but the other members of the household. I ask, is this not a work of charity? Is it not a godly work to take them from the centre of disease and place them under the care of the good Grey Nuns of this city? (Applause) ... We take them to rescue them from death and give them to the tender, loving care of religious ladies....

If it be an unjust law, let the fact go forth from this council ... and then our power to stop the epidemic is over, and we of the Board of Health will tomorrow resign our positions.... The contagion, now checked, will spread its deadly grasp over the city, and the children of the people who revile us today will be in the tomb to-morrow. (Loud applause) ...

Gagnon was misled by educated men who knew better.... The mean scoundrels counsel a poor man, without a cent in his house, to disobey the law, to spread contagion, and perhaps to murder the rest of his children. Such men, who would thus advise an ignorant fellow man, have something to answer for before God. (Loud applause).

The motion to support the mayor and censure his opponents was passed with one dissenting vote. *Le Monde's* editors were committed for trial at the next assizes. So were the Gagnons, father and son. *Le Monde* gradually calmed down. Riel's execution was again postponed. The removals to hospital continued, as did incidents of resistance. One night a crowd formed outside Beaugrand's house, gave him three cheers and dispersed. At City Hall the health workers were thrown into panic by a noisy mob in Gosford Street: some fled through a back window; the others doused the lights, drew their guns, and prepared to fight for their lives. The mob of McGill medical students, letting off steam, passed them by.

        o   o   o

The day of the Gagnon removal, Dr. McNeece told the press he thought the smallpox was declining. Probably he was not believed, for the health officers had been nothing but wrong in their predictions. But the board's isolation committee said much the same the next day, in reporting that their men seemed to be outrunning the disease. Isolations and removals far outnumbered new cases. The count for the first week of November was 208 lives taken, compared to 273 the week before. Maybe a turning point.

Thursday, November 12 was the Thanksgiving Day holiday in Canada. At special church services some ministers suggested that good would come out of the evil of the plague if Montreal learned to respect sanitary laws. One Presbyterian divine offered thanks to God that the plague had not been worse, that it was now declining, and that death had no sting anyway because of the promise of life everlasting. Students and professors from the Montreal School of Medicine and Surgery marched in a body to the Church of the Gésu for a special requiem mass for the repose of the soul of Bishop Bourget. Afterwards they made a pilgrimage to Bourget's tomb at the cathedral.

Le Monde, Friday, November 13:

MGR BOURGET
UN MIRACLE RAPPORTE

It is reported that a young child, blinded a few days ago as a consequence of smallpox, was miraculously cured yesterday afternoon through the intercession of Monseigneur Bourget.

Apparently the mother led the young sufferer to the tomb of the venerable and holy bishop. Her ardent prayer was answered when her child completely recovered her vision. Until confirmation by competent authorities, we pass this on simply as a rumour.

❂   ❂   ❂

Monday, November 16

Millions of words had been written about his fate in the six months that Louis Riel had been a prisoner. Judged to be of sound mind, he had been convicted of treason and sentenced to death. Most French Canadians thought he would not hang. If he had not been insane during the rebellion, he had surely lost his mind since. Or he was not really guilty because the government of Canada was at least partly at fault. Or he would surely be given clemency in this modern, enlightened age, the way that rebels like Jefferson Davis and Robert E. Lee had been treated after the American Civil War. Or enlightened Canadians would not repeat the mistake of the Americans in hanging the poor lunatic Guiteau who had assassinated President Garfield. Or the political muscle of French Canadians in Ottawa would at least win some kind of reprieve from the gallows. Riel would not die.

His fate would be a harbinger of their own destiny as a people, many French Canadians had come to believe. Riel had become a symbol of their insecurities and aspirations. Canada's determination to execute him seemed a sign of anti-French prejudice, an attack on the whole French nationality in the country. Riel was the rally-ing-point for a surge of French-Canadian nationalism. If they would kill Riel, it was said, they could never be trusted; all French Canadians would have to stand together and find new political strategies to combat the enemies of the race. But they would not kill him.

The gallows was erected in the jailyard in Regina, North West Territories, some two thousand miles from Montreal. There had been months of appeals, reprieves, reconsiderations, postpone-ments. Now the government of Canada, convinced that its prisoner was a sane man who had knowingly incited bloody, murderous rebel-lion, wished justice to take its course. Riel went to his fate calmly in the early morning. At eight o'clock he stood on the scaffold, the rope around his neck, reciting the Lord's Prayer. At the line "deliver us from evil," the trap door opened. Riel died.

Word of the execution flashed across the continent by telegraph. Montreal's City Council abandoned its regular business that after-noon to consider Riel's fate. Before a packed gallery aldermen voted nineteen to four to protest this "odious violation of the laws of jus-tice and humanity." The onlookers cheered, and councillors adjourned to join other politicians and the crowd in Cartier Square for more speech-making. The tricolour of republican France was hoisted over City Hall. It flew at half mast.

Thousands paraded in the streets and packed the Champ de Mars that night to protest the execution. Effigies of the prime min-ister and his leading French-Canadian ministers, Chapleau, Caron, and Langevin, were burned. The elegantly clothed, beaver-hatted Macdonald figure was hung from the statue of the Queen in Victoria Square before being set to the torch. Marching demonstra-tors groaned and hissed as they passed English institutions as diverse as the YMCA and the Salvation Army barracks. Police looked on nervously.

Street demonstrations continued nightly for most of the week. The protests reached a kind of crescendo on Sunday afternoon in the largest political meeting Quebec had ever seen. More than twenty thousand people packed the Champ de Mars, standing ankle-deep in mud and cold, as politicians from all parties, speaking simultaneously from three stands, each platform draped with the flags of France, Britain, and the United States, condemned the government of Canada for the murder of Riel and called for unity and vengeance.

There were thousands and thousands of words of oratory that day, but not one recorded word about the smallpox or its victims. Tens of thousands of marching men and women that week, no rioting or violence. Observers commented on the good humour and orderliness of the crowds. No ugliness, a lot of singing (most often the "Marseillaise"); the rage would come later at the ballot box. The *Gazette* thought the show was almost "refreshing" after three months of dullness in the city. In a way French Canadians and their politicians had a cause they could feel good about, one that did not embarrass them. Perhaps it was something of a catharsis, like the lancing of a boil.

Riel and the smallpox epidemic were the two phenomena that drove English- and French-speaking Montrealers apart that year. In some important ways they did not reinforce each other. Riel's cause brought together French Canadians who had been bitterly divided about the smallpox, forging a remarkable alliance between secular nationalists such as Honoré Beaugrand and his Rouge friends on the one hand, and ultramontane xenophobes, such as F.-X. Trudel of *L'Etendard* on the other. Riel also divided the English along unfamiliar lines. Both of the newspapers that had been most critical of French Canadians' response to the smallpox, the *Witness* and the *Herald*, opposed the execution of Riel.

Here was the hated *Herald*, publisher of the PRO BONO PUBLICO letter, offically banished by City Hall for its poisonous attacks, reviled among French Canadians as a fanatical enemy of their race, making common cause with Catholic ultramontanes and the people of East End Montreal. Such odd bedfellows. When the *Herald's* staff came to their windows to watch the Victoria Square demonstration on the night of the 16th, the crowd did not know whether to hiss or cheer. It apparently did both. When Beaugrand, fiery champion of Riel, tyrannical enforcer of vaccination and removal, appeared before the crowd that night, some voices cried "Picotte" and "Old Smallpox"; others called for a speech.

These were the smallpox deaths in Montreal on the day of Louis Riel's execution in Regina:

Diane Cadotte	1 yr 6 mo	160 1/2 Maisonneuve
Malvina ___	7 yrs, 6 mo	64 Desery
H. Charbonneau	3 yrs	347 Amherst
Marie Tessier	1 yr 11 mos	276 Panet
Oscar Sigouin	1 yr 3 m0s	203 St. Elizabeth
E. ___enard	3 yrs 6 mo	362 Maisonneuve
Amanda Leroux	3 yrs 3 mo	_____
Arthur Fréjeau	4 yrs	_____
Marie Riel	3 yrs	27 Gosford
Marie Brisebois	6 yrs 7 mos	1205 St. James
A. Laporte	1 yr 1 mo	131 St. Urbain
Michael Brabant	21 yrs	245 Jacques Cartier
O. Massicotte	7 yrs	1135 St. Catherine
Henri Chevalier	9 yrs	190 St. Denis
Marie Gascon	7 mos	375 Maisonneuve
A. Laflamme	5 yrs	135 Dufresne
Fanny Lynch	3 yrs	88 Beaudry
Jos. Beaudoin	7 yrs	206 Champlain
Obidon Gascon	3 yrs 9 mo	306 Maisonneuve
J. Bte. Laurier	9 yrs 6 mos	210 German

Riel got all the attention, the children got none. Louis Riel, ultramontane ascetic, enemy of liberalism everywhere, would have shared the Catholic fundamentalists' belief that Montreal's carnivals of secularism had caused God to send the plague and take these lives. Riel himself had lit the fires of rebellion in western Canada, insanely, to create a haven from the decadence of societies plagued by modernism.

Of Montreal's newspapers only the most independent one, Hugh Graham's *Star*, commented on the absurdity of it all:

The indignation at the death of Riel of the demagogues who are in the City Council, and of the demagogues who are outside but would like to get in too, becomes ridiculous in an almost ghastly way, when it is compared with their action in the case of the smallpox epidemic, which we are slowly mastering. For three months after the scourge attacked us there was heard no sound from the City Council. The body which was so solicitous yesterday for the life of one man at Regina was content for months to sleep while the lives of hundreds were being sacrificed in Montreal. While a disease was progressing here which was imperilling all life and property in this great city, the councillors made no move; but yesterday this body, so criminally supine at home, ventured to reprimand the Goverment of the dominion for allowing law to take its course in the North-West territories. What a spectacle this for gods and men!

The Riel demonstrations in Montreal ended with the mass meeting on the 22nd. Poor Riel had hinted about a return from the grave, but no stone was rolled away. It was left to politicians and historians and those who prayed for his soul to keep Louis Riel's memory alive. Under the auspices of the St-Jean Baptiste Society preparations went forward for a special mass for the repose of his spirit. It attracted a very large congregation at Notre Dame Church early in December. By then the Month of the Dead had ended, and the bells had stopped tolling nightly for those who had been taken.

The malignity of the distemper was spent, the contagion was exhausted, and also the winter weather came on apace, and the air was clear and cold, with sharp frosts; and this increasing still, most of those that had fallen sick recovered, and the health of the city began to return.

— Defoe, *A Journal of the Plague Year*

CHAPTER 12

AND WINTER CAME

NOVEMBER ENDED WITH A MAJOR snowfall and then cold, clean air and clear blue sky that drove away memories of the mud and mists of late autumn. Montrealers had their sleighs out before the end of the month. Navigation closed on the St. Lawrence for the ice season. The harbour police were paid off and disbanded. The city laid in its supply of stones for the poor to break up during the winter. Honoré Beaugrand left Montreal for the south, to try to recover from asthma and nervous strain. The sporting classes got out their blanket suits, their winter furs, their snowshoes and toboggans and skates. Father Auclaire of St-Jean Baptiste Church denounced skating rinks, snowshoeing, and tobogganing as dangerous to the morals of young ladies. Women were forbidden to wear tuques at Catholic church services.

Seasonal thoughts turned to carnival. But only briefly. The moment you thought about a winter carnival, you realized it was impossible. Because of the smallpox no one would come.

◦　◦　◦

Most signs were good: only seventy-seven deaths in the last week of November, only 633 all that month, compared with 1,391 in October. Smallpox seemed to have been driven out of most Montreal neighbourhoods, and was making a last stand only in benighted lanes and alleys on the fringes of the city and in some of the poorest suburbs. Would it flare up again? Had it been rekindled by the Riel demonstrations, which packed so many thousands together in the streets and on the Champ de Mars? Would it be brought back to Montreal from outside, from one of the suburbs or one of the Quebec villages the city had infected months ago? Did carters' buffalo and bearskin robes, which had been in storage or in pawn all summer, still contain last spring's smallpox germs? Would they infect the sleigh-riding public?

The Health Board reduced its staff and redoubled its efforts. In the health court, magistrates Normandeau and Isaacson heard eight or ten cases a day of people charged with tearing down placards, breaking the isolation rules, refusing the removal of their children to hospital. Most were fined a few dollars. Those who complied with the law immediately after sentencing were let off, as were those whose families had been punished dreadfully by the smallpox. Dr. McNeece of the Health Board had also been punished by the small-pox—assaulted, stoned, evicted from his lodgings. There were rumours that he was drinking heavily. In mid-November he was arrested for drawing a gun on a boy during an altercation, and lost his job.

Taking the war into Africa, the Health Board had charged Dr. Coderre with failing to report a case of smallpox. A crowd of his medical students accompanied him to health court on November 24, only to be ejected. They marched to the Health Department and made a silent demonstration. The case bogged down in legal wrangling. The anti-vaccinationists struck back by persuading Elie Gagnon that his children were being kept too long at the smallpox hospital. Gagnon applied for a writ of *habeas corpus* to force the release of his daughters, Eveline and Rosanna, from St. Camille's. Drs. Coderre and J.O. Roy (another vaccinophobe, also recently charged in health court) had examined the girls and pronounced them cured. The hospital doctors said they were still covered with smallpox and were contagious and they were acting within the law. The court upheld the board. A few days more of convalescence and the Gagnon girls were liberated.

In mid-December the board began to charge people who had refused to be vaccinated after call-backs by the house-to-house canvassers. The court gave them the choice of paying a fine or being vaccinated on the spot. Violent resistance had not totally subsided. An isolation constable was attacked. Mr. Quinn, a poster-paster who had contracted to do the board's placarding, had to whip his horse into a gallop to narrowly escape an angry mob. Madame Alphonse Duquette barricaded her door against the removers, who broke it down and brought her into court. When the magistrate released her to get money to pay her fine, the health authorities said she would only put up the barricade again. She and her lawyer were chased down Notre Dame, captured at St. Lambert Hill, hauled back to court, and finally released.

Slick outsiders moved in to exploit fear in these last days. Towards the end of November Montreal's newspapers suddenly spouted new columns about smallpox:

IS SMALLPOX SPREADING?
VIGOROUS MEASURES TAKEN TO PREVENT THE SCOURGE FROM
SPREADING THROUGHOUT THE DOMINION AND FROM ONE END
OF THE UNITED STATES TO THE OTHER
WHAT IS TO BE DONE IN THIS CRISIS?

The headlines changed every few days, but in all cases what was to be done was to take Dr. Morley's Standard English Remedy for Smallpox and Fevers, made by the Standard Drug and Chemical Company of Boston. If you had smallpox it would break it up in twelve hours. If you didn't you should keep a supply on hand. "Smallpox is continually cropping up in the small villages and towns throughout the provinces, and will be likely to prevail through the winter. Every one liable to exposure should keep a package of the medicine in the house, and a vial in the pocket, and if a suspicion exists of having been exposed take a dose of it, and thus ward off this loathsome and disfiguring disease." A column entitled "Vaccination:

Some of its Dangers and the Method of Avoiding Them," advised readers that the practice was normally safe, but could occasionally disturb the kidneys. Best to get vaccinated *and* take Warner's Safe Cure to ward off the side effects.

If you are bored with smallpox, there's a man in town from Regina exhibiting pieces of the rope that hanged Louis Riel. How about that affair of the poisoning at the Metropolitan Club? Eight people severely ill from arsenic in their soup. The cook and a female servant arrested. "Death in the Pot!" the *Herald* calls it. People living with ongoing facial problems left by smallpox can send $2.50 to Geo. W. Shaw, 219 Tremont Street, Boston and he will mail back the patented and world-renowned "OBLITERATOR," made by Leon & Company of London, Perfumers to H.M. the Queen. Guaranteed to remove Small Pox Marks of long standing.

        ❂   ❂   ❂

In the darkest days of the year, parallel lines finally meet. The plague and madness come together. There is smallpox in the insane asylum at Longue Pointe. Smallpox among the lunatics.

If there was a God watching over Montreal in 1885, the proof might lie in the good fortune of the city's big institutions. After Hôtel-Dieu's misfortunes, the regular hospitals suffered no significant outbreaks. Nor did boarding schools, orphanages, prisons, homes for the destitute or aged or unwed mothers. Vaccination was widespread in some cases, but usually not until the autumn months. Most establishments protected themselves, effectively, by banning visitors for the duration. But now in December there are rumours about the largest and most vulnerable of all the shelters.

The Asile St-Jean de Dieu at Longue Pointe is an immense stone warehouse for the mentally ill of the Montreal region. Built by the Sisters of Providence, it is operated by them on contract to the government of Quebec. For $100 per patient per year, the nuns feed, clothe, and care for almost one thousand sick souls. It is the largest asylum for the mentally ill in Canada. According to Daniel Hack Tuke, the famous British alienist who toured Quebec institutions in

1883 and published his scathingly critical report the next year, it has been one of the worst run: overcrowded, neglectful, brutal, mismanaged, a blot on the nineteenth century.

Catholics have questioned every syllable of Tuke's report, dismissing him an ignorant Protestant fanatic. No insane asylum in the nineteenth century has many friends. Many people in Montreal hate and fear the lunatic home as much as they dreaded the old smallpox hospital. Militant Protestants have claimed that innocent people have been held there against their will, partly because the contracting system gives the sisters a financial incentive to maximize the number of inmates.

Now a new scandal. On December 23 it is admitted that there have been eighteen cases of smallpox at the Longue Pointe asylum, with at least two deaths. Rumour says there have been twenty deaths. The asylum's medical superintendent, Dr. Henry Howard, reveals a shocking state of affairs. Back in early September he had given orders for the inmates to be vaccinated. Sister Thérèse-de-Jésus, the Mother Superior in charge of the Longue Pointe, had refused to allow his medical staff to do vaccinations. She insisted that vaccination would be carried out by house doctors hired by the Sisters of Providence.

Every inquiry Howard made about vaccination met a similar response. On December 2 he learned that smallpox was in the institution and doubled his efforts to ensure that the patients were protected. Sister Thérèse turned away his doctors. When Howard and his men returned, under instructions from the Provincial Board of Health, they were again denied permission to vaccinate. Of the 957 patients in the asylum, they learned, the house staff had only vaccinated 128. The government-appointed medical superintendent of the largest insane asylum in Canada had not been able to inspect the isolation facilities for the sick, did not know how many patients had died of smallpox, and now tells reporters it is all a "farce."

The deranged residents of Longue Pointe are pawns in the ongoing political struggle between the contracting nuns and the provincial government. Contentious for years, the question of medical supervision of the asylum has become even more muddled in the aftermath of the Tuke report. The Quebec government has created a board of medical supervisors, headed by Howard, that the contracting sisters refuse to recognize, claiming it is in violation of their contract. The nuns are in charge of the asylum. They will not allow Howard and his staff to carry out medical procedures in their building. Their own house doctors went ahead with vaccination insofar as circumstances permitted, the nuns claim. It is not easy, sometimes not possible, to vaccinate the insane. If people do not want to be vaccinated, sane or not, what can you do?

The Provincial Board orders the placarding and isolation of Longue Pointe and mass vaccination. Conservative newspapers rush to the defence of the sisters and their autonomy. Critics wonder how many helpless people are going to die from smallpox because the nuns have refused to obey the law of the land.

o   o   o

At the other smallpox institution, the Mount Royal Hospitals, Christmas was not an unhappy time. Throughout December, the hospitals gradually emptied out. The Crystal Palace addition to St. Camille's and St. Saviour's stood ready but unused. On December 23, the day the problems of the asylum became known, no new cases of smallpox were reported anywhere else in the city for the first time since June.

Montreal's churches were crowded for Christmas services, Sherbrooke Street blazed with lights, merriment, and winter promenaders, the rinks and toboggan slides were in full operation and were faster and better lit than ever. On Christmas eve the members of the isolation police had a party at which they presented their head, H.V. Maltby, with a complete smoking outfit. Members of the sanitary police waited on Sergeant Moran at his residence and presented him with a tea service. At hospitals "Noël Chez les Picotes" featured special services for the patients. Protestants had special decorations and an electrically lit Christmas tree, the Catholics had statues of Saint Joseph and the Holy Virgin and the Infant Jesus. Everyone in the Catholic wing took communion at midnight. Faces that were once beautiful were now scarred and seamed, but said to radiate fervour and piety.

Sister Thérèse opened the Longue Pointe asylum to reporters on the 26th. They toured the public and private wards, remarking on the neatness and order and cleanliness of the asylum, and the interests of some of the inmates in magnetism, spiritualism, and mind-reading. The smallpox patients were perfectly isolated, and vaccinators were now doing the last, most violent group of inmates. "Many of the poor creatures entertained an hallucination that the doctor was going to kill them," the *Gazette*'s man observed. "Some of them had to be held down firmly while the lance was being applied. Even after the operation had been performed the demented creatures had to be held to prevent them wiping off the vaccine."

"Don't come in here or you will get the smallpox," a patient cried out to the visitors. "The nuns are trying to keep it dark, but I know all about it." To prevent panic the sisters had tried to suppress knowledge of the epidemic. Word had spread anyway. Fortunately, their isolation procedures and now the mass vaccination contained the virus. There were four deaths and a total of twenty-three cases of smallpox at Longue Pointe. The struggle between state and church for control of the institution continued.

✹ ✹ ✹

Quarantine met quarantine. Some of the rules were gradually being relaxed, but the world was still inspecting Montrealers for signs of smallpox. In November Montreal began inspecting newcomers to the city to protect itself from re-infection. Thanks to Montreal, smallpox might now be lurking anywhere in Quebec. Few Quebec communities outside of Montreal had organizations capable of containing the sickness.

One of the least-equipped communities was one of the last fastnesses of smallpox. The village of Ste-Cunégonde, huddled right at Montreal's western boundary, was a swollen parish of several thousand poor labourers, mostly French Canadian, squatting on a few hectares of mean, low-lying land north of the canal running from the city limit to Atwater Street. It was completely absorbed by the city in everything but what counted most—government. Smallpox burned in the streets of Ste-Cunégonde, and nothing was being done about it. Except for the curé, the village's board of health did not believe in vaccination or isolation. Three of the five board members had smallpox in their own families. They would not allow placards on their houses. Ste-Cunégonde placards were so small, anyway, that they were hardly noticeable, and many were pasted indoors. The town paid Joseph Juneau, carriage-maker, a dollar a day to remove the bodies of the dead. He had a special express sleigh, painted black. He paid two boys twenty-five cents a body to do the work. Families provided their own coffins.

Montreal authorities who visited Ste-Cunégonde came away appalled. It was "a perfect pest hole" they reported, in "utter disregard of the laws of the country and of humanity" according to the Citizens' Committee. At the beginning of December the sanitary police recommended quarantining the village from the city by shutting off the streets. In the middle of the month Hollis Shorey led a Citizens' Committee delegation to plead with the curé and mayor. He got into a shouting match with the curé. Nothing was accomplished.

On December 24 Montreal sanitary police carried out one of the last of their removals, from 42 Fulford Street, very near the Ste-Cunégonde boundary. A menacing crowd of villagers assembled. Constable Louis Cyr of the village police had recovered from his injuries, but had resigned from the force to become a touring strong man. Thirty Montreal police were called out to drive off the toughs if they crossed the line. Trouble was averted. "Why not bring matters to a crisis?" a disgusted doctor wrote about Ste-Cunégonde in the *Canada Medical Record*. "If every one there *must* have the smallpox why not have a grand mass-meeting for the purpose of contracting it—so get the agony over at once."

After Christmas the Provincial Board of Health served warrants on all the members of the Ste-Cunégonde board of health, including the curé. The medical health officer, Dr. Cypihot, was charged in Health Court with failing to report cases of smallpox, and failing to carry out isolation and placarding. Upon his conviction, the Montreal Board of Health decided to physically quarantine Ste-Cunégonde by

barricading all the streets connecting the village to the city. They put
up the barriers on the last day of the year.

December 31, 1885

The year ends with cold rain. On St. James Street the police of
Montreal are fighting a pitched battle with the people of Ste-
Cunégonde. Snowballs, stones, curses, bricks, gunshots, cries of
"Sacré Bureau de Santé!"

Carpenters were at work all afternoon erecting twelve-foot-high
wooden fences across Coursol and Workman, St. Antoine, and St.
Joseph streets. All the members of the isolation squad and the sanitary police have been on hand to defend the barricades. Ste-
Cunégonders have been gathering all afternoon, threatening to tear
down all the obstacles, tossing snowballs, making off with every
unguarded piece of wood. Detective Cinq Mars has already seized
one rabble-rousing orator and made off with him in a hail of stones,
coal, and empty bottles.

At 7:30 p.m. at the corner of Dominion and St. James the mob
attacks the fence. They use battering rams and throw bottles,
turnips, potatoes, and bricks. From their windows villagers see over
the Montrealers' wall and direct fire. The health police fall back, and
the barrier is destroyed.

Alderman Jeannotte had tried to withhold use of the city police,
but Paradis decides to authorize his men to come to the aid of the
smallpox-fighters. Thirty members of the regular force arrive and
charge the mob. More bricks and bottles and some gunshots. The
constables maintain "their uniform good temper," according to the
Gazette, as they scatter the mob. The *Star* says the dispersal is "to
the tune of a lusty skull and baton chorus." The fence is rebuilt
across St. James Street. Armed police spend their New Year's eve
guarding the smallpox shield.

Journalists find Ste-Cunégonde's police sitting around the stove
in their headquarters, smoking. The affair is none of their concern,
they say. Mayor Morin is in his store reading the newspapers, saying
he has nothing to do with it. An emissary from Montreal arrives to
negotiate a settlement. Fifteen minutes before the beginning of

1886 the city and its smallpox-infested suburb make their peace. Montreal agrees to postpone its quarantine so long as Ste-Cunégonde faithfully enforces the health laws.

At City Hall the first screech of the fire alarm in the new year sounds at 12:10 a.m. It is from the box 56, at the corner of Fulford and Coursol, near the scene of the fighting. A false alarm.

*　*　*

In the second week of January the ice-cold waters of the St. Lawrence rose up and flooded all the low-lying areas of the city, causing great hardship. The poor but vaccinated Irish labouring class in Point St. Charles and Griffintown suffered the worst flood damage. Fortunately the waters receded before a deep freeze set in. On January 20, for the first time in months, there were no deaths from smallpox in Montreal or any of its suburbs.

Sunday, January 31, was chosen by Protestant and Catholic clergy as a day of thanksgiving for the end of the epidemic. In Catholic churches there were special processions after mass, during which the *Te Deum* was chanted. Bishop Fabre issued a circular letter offering a plenary indulgence to all who confessed their sins and took communion and prayed for the pope. "We will hope that all will understand their duty, and that they will press in crowds to the churches, and there to the feet of the altars all will come to thank the Lord, to entreat Him to turn away His wrath from our heads, and seek His aid and protection for the future of Montreal."

While Catholics confessed and chanted and entreated, Protestant ministers sermonized about the year's events. Most said the plague had something to do with breaking God's health laws and hoped that good would come of it. "The smallpox epidemic, though a severe chastisement, had a blessing wrapped up in it," the Reverend Norton told the congregation in Christ Church Anglican Cathedral:

An epidemic of this kind points out some public sin, some neglect or disorder in the community. It may be want of care for the poor. If we allow masses of the population to crowd

256

together in squalid habitations, without pure water laid on, without proper drainage, without the enforcement of vaccination and other rules of health; and if we allow dust heaps to be piled up for months against the windows of poor dwellings, will not God visit us for these things? We shall have smallpox again, and we shall deserve it.

Many ministers urged their people to give thanks for the splendid men and women, English and French, Protestant and Catholic, that God had raised up to do His work in fighting the epidemic. Several Protestant ministers thanked God for giving Montreal Mayor Beaugrand. At St. Martin's Church, Rector J.S. Stone reminded his people that the service for the dead included "an anthem of joy," in which the burdened soul exclaims: "I heard a voice from heaven saying unto me, from henceforth blessed are the dead which die in the Lord; even so saith the spirit; for they rest from their labors."

It was too late to organize a carnival. But on Saturday, February 5, in the clean, cold of winter, while the blessed little children of Montreal rested from their labours in Notre Dame des Neiges and Mount Royal cemeteries, the skaters at the Victoria ice rink enjoyed their first masque of 1886.

It now becomes too manifest to admit of controversy, that the annihilation of the Small Pox, the most dreadful scourge of the human species, must be the final result of this practice.

— Edward Jenner, 1801

EPILOGUE

THERE WERE SEVENTY DEATHS IN THE 1886 embers of the epidemic. Ontario ended its border inspections in February, the United States in mid-March. The last cases in the Montreal hospitals were two children brought from St-Jean Baptiste Ward (the village was annexed on January 1) on May 21. In the fifteen months since George Longley had entered Montreal, officials counted 9,600 cases of smallpox in the city, a further 10,305 in the rest of the province. Most of the latter were in St-Jean Baptiste, Ste-Cunégonde, and other nearby villages. All the evidence suggests that the real number of smallpox cases was much higher than this total of 19,905. In the thirteen months since Pélagie Robichaud's death, the epidemic had taken, by official count, 3,234 lives in the city of Montreal. Of the 3,164 who died in 1885, 2,887 or 91.2 per cent were French Canadians. Two hundred and seventy-seven others died. In all, 2,717 or 85.9 per cent of all victims in 1885 were children under the age of ten; 2,036 or 66.5 per cent were under five.

The city of Montreal in 1885 lost 1.89 per cent of its population to smallpox; 3.08

per cent of the city's French Canadians were killed. The death rate from smallpox in the English-speaking community was 0.38 per cent. French Canadians died from smallpox at more than eight times the rate of other Montrealers. In Ste-Marie Ward in the East End of the city 4.5 per cent of the people died of smallpox.

The Provincial Board of Health later reported a total of 2,605 smallpox deaths outside the city (as well as a further twenty-five in Montreal), nearly all of which would have been French. King Picotte's total Quebec harvest in 1885–86: 5,864 souls.

The financial cost of fighting the epidemic in 1885 totalled $142,835.40, including $81.80 for revolvers and $25 for the funeral of volunteer Samuels. In 1886 accounts were settled for a further $34,334.42, making a total municipal expenditure on smallpox of $177,169.82 (perhaps $10 to 15 million in 1990s purchasing power). In 1886 Montreal built a new, fully-equipped, 130-bed smallpox hospital in the eastern ward of Hochelaga. St. Roch's was destroyed.

The Board of Health appointed a subcommittee consisting of Hugh Graham and Adolphe Lévêque to investigate the cause of the epidemic. Their report was published verbatim in several newspapers on January 9-10, 1886. It gave the full story of George Longley, Drs. Rodger and Hingston, Hôtel-Dieu, and the Robichaud sisters. Given the lack of vaccination in previous years, Graham and Lévêque concluded, "the great mistake was to allow an outside case of smallpox to enter our city and one of our largest charitable institutions, which was officially declared such ONLY AFTER THE CONVALESCENCE of the party attacked." In future the city should have a contagious diseases hospital always ready. If even St. Roch's had been open to receive Longley on that February night, "a great public misfortune would probably have been avoided."

In future outbreaks, they concluded, it should be realized that isolation could not work without compulsory removals. And while there was still resistance in the city, the effectiveness of vaccination was not in doubt. It should be "compulsory as much as possible." This could only happen if there was compulsory registration of births—which the subcommittee knew, but did not say, the Church opposed.

Dr. Hingston, who had been too busy to answer inquiries from the investigators, published his own version of events a few days later. He severely criticized Dr. Rodger for misleading him, implied that Hôtel-Dieu had fallen down on the job, and exonerated himself from any blame for admitting the case of smallpox that began the epidemic. That case, George Longley, was alive and well, back on his job, and a frequent visitor to Montreal. He joined the newspaper discussion, challenging Hingston's statement that he had not required medical attendance during his stay at the hospital: "I required no medical attendance! ... Perhaps Dr. Hingston will kindly tell me what I went to the Hotel Dieu for. Was it just for the fun of the thing?"

Hingston did not fully cover his tracks. In the broadest, most general sense, smallpox ran riot in Montreal in 1885 because fear and ignorance and apathy led to the creation of a very large population of unvaccinated children. This was the underlying but not a sufficient cause. The precipitating events that set the fire going were the series of blunders in February, March, and April, in which Hingston had played a major role.

Longley should never have been admitted to Hôtel-Dieu. Instead he should have been isolated in his Pullman in a quarantined area of the railway yards. Once in the hospital, he should have been isolated with the most extreme care. The decision to close Hôtel-Dieu in April was catastrophic and stupid; in his famous textbook Osler called it "a negligence absolutely criminal." The suspension of vaccination in May may have made sense for a week or two. Nothing excused the three-month delay in resumption. These events, all of which Hingston had the power to alter, if he had had the will, spread the smallpox in the city. William Bessey's problems with his vaccine contributed significantly to the ignition, and the street crowds in June were a kind of piling on of fuel. Fostered by human failure and bad luck, the ingredients all came together.

By mid-summer the health authorities had probably lost all chance of controlling the epidemic. That autumn they were in the position of a few score of workers trying to stamp out a forest fire. It was not until the flames burned very low in November and December—that is, until the smallpox ran out of unvaccinated hosts—that the containment strategy appeared to be effective. In the meantime, more than three thousand people, most of them children who never had the opportunity to help themselves, died. Every one of these deaths could have been prevented.

◊   ◊   ◊

Honoré Beaugrand's enemies finally scrabbled up an opponent to contest the 1886 mayoralty election. Many prominent French Canadians had refused to stand, and acclamation was a real possibility. Georges Decary was an unknown, who stood against compulsory vaccination and criticized the mayor for having ordered troops to fire on the Gagnons. If Beaugrand was re-elected, Decary's people said, he would probably order every Montrealer vaccinated again. To English Montreal the election was a question of whether "the picotte party" would gain control of Council. "Let Us Not Forget," the *Star* warned, that the ongoing activities of the anti-vaccinationists amounted to "the cruel murder of the infants of ignorant and misguided parents."

At the last meeting of the Health Board before the elections, Henry Gray thanked the citizen appointees, whose term of service now expired. Beaugrand and Grenier were on hand to thank Gray. The pharmacist told his fellows that Montreal had been his home for twenty-seven years, was where his children had been born, and where he would probably die. "Whatever may be said against Montreal, I wish to die in no better place." The board's last act was to vote $100 for each of the Catholic sisters who had nursed patients in the hospital—not as a reward, Gray said, because they looked on high for their rewards—but as some compensation for their hardships.

On March 1, 1886, Honoré Beaugrand was re-elected by 5,095 votes to 3,141 for Decary, an increased majority on an increased turnout. In the East End ward of Ste-Marie, Alderman Roy, who had supported compulsory vaccination, was defeated. Henry Gray was re-elected by acclamation and was unopposed in another term as chairman of the Health Committee. At the end of

1885 the anti-vaccinationists had formed the Canadian Anti-Vaccination League, Dr. A.M. Ross president, to continue their fight. Founding members included Dr. Coderre and William Robertson, the Adventist minister who had been so alarmed at indifference to the epidemic in August. Nobody in Montreal paid much attention to the Anti-Vaccination League. As well as building the new smallpox hospital that year, the Health Committee made arrangements with William Mann, whose incineration of Montreal's night soil had been a great success, to burn all the city's garbage. From now on Montreal would enjoy, as Henry Gray put it, "the immediate and total extinction of its refuse by fire."

London's great plague of 1665 had been followed by the great fire of 1666. On Sunday, April 18, Montreal was visited by its second flood of 1886. The waters rose faster and higher than ever before, pouring into streets and cellars never previously touched. St. Antoine/Craig Street was flooded as far east as St. Urbain. Victoria Square was a lake. One quarter of Montreal, in which about fifty thousand people lived, became a sea of rafts and boats. The waters held their carnival for a few days, and then subsided.

o   o   o

Montreal's ordeal did not create an instant revolution in attitudes towards vaccination or public health in Canada. In 1886, as a direct result of the epidemic, the Quebec legislature created its Provincial Board of Health on a permanent basis. But lobbying from anti-vaccinationists and rural municipalities frustrated an attempt to introduce compulsory vaccination, and the board was given only advisory powers. Distaste for vaccination remained in Montreal, Quebec, and many other parts of Canada, and sometimes flared into bitter controversy.

The international anti-vaccinationist movement, which interpreted the Montreal epidemic as having been caused by vaccination, continued its propaganda and lobbying and reached a pinnacle of success in Great Britain in 1898 when "conscientious objectors" (apparently the first recognition of this concept in law) were allowed exemption from compulsory vaccination. Few governments any-where seem to have been able to coerce people into total accep-tance of vaccination. Vaccination was widely neglected in Quebec even after the events of 1885.

But King Picotte's brutal reign in Montreal did increase fear of the disease and the willingness of many people to take precautions. When smallpox reappeared in the province in 1888, boards of health were more alert and the public more willing to be vaccinated and isolated. Each little importation was contained. The creation of a new flock of unvaccinated children made the 1891 visitation particu-larly ominous. Across Quebec there were 151 cases, with thirty-two deaths. A sailor on the S.S. *Brazilian* brought smallpox to Montreal that year, the first case since the epidemic, but there was no out-break in the city. The Provincial Board of Health's ability to contain smallpox rested heavily, it reported, on the goodwill of the popula-tion and the zeal of local authorities. In 1897-98, with still more kin-dling at hand, a virulent strain of smallpox reappeared in Montreal and killed sixteen of the thirty-five people it attacked in the city and the suburbs. Containment involved more than forty-two thousand vaccinations.

Montreal never again endured anything like the 1885 epidemic. Its experience that year entered world literature, especially Sir William Osler's classic textbook, *The Principles and Practice of Medicine*, as a ghastly object lesson. While anti-vaccinationists continued to make noise, win major victories such as the 1898 "conscientious objector" clause, and attract attention (as their movement still does from medical historians), the real march of his-tory was the slow, halting progress of intelligent medicine and public health. Fear and ignorance and superstition about vaccina-tion were overcome. Fear and knowledge of smallpox grew. Cities in Britain, the United States, and some European countries paid a horrible toll from time to time for backwardness in smallpox con-trol (two of the worst outbreaks were in Milwaukee, Wisconsin, in 1894-95, during which there was violent resistance to the Board of Health, and Gloucester, England, near Jenner's home, in 1895-96), but with each decade the outbreaks were fewer, the death counts smaller. After 1885 it does not appear that any city in the North

Atlantic countries was as desperately, uncontrollably stricken by smallpox as Montreal. It was the last uncontained holocaust of smallpox in a modern city.

A new strain of the virus, apparently from the Caribbean, appeared in Pensacola, Florida, in 1896. It moved northwards in epidemic proportions and reached Quebec in 1899-1900. There were 813 reported cases in the province that year, of which eighty-three were in Montreal. But there were only eleven deaths, eight in Montreal. This was a much less virulent form of smallpox; cases were milder, less prolonged, much less disfiguring, and killed many fewer people. It came to be called "variola minor"; classic smallpox was now "variola major." The more benign form of smallpox became dominant in the twentieth century, causing the vast majority of reported cases. The mortality rate from variola minor was 0.1-0.2 per cent.

Variola minor created new problems for public health authorities in being harder to diagnose than the major strain, less likely to be reported, and somewhat less loathsome (lacking the foetid stench, for example). By this time, however, most people knew that they were not necessarily fated to endure even mild plagues of smallpox. Vaccination may never have become universal, but it gradually became routine in developed countries.

The breakdown of civilization in the Great War of 1914-18 allowed smallpox one last fling in most western nations. In Canada totals of one to two thousand cases of smallpox were reported yearly during the 1920s. The worst Canadian epidemic after Montreal's in 1885 was an outbreak of variola major in Windsor, Ontario, in 1924 which killed thirty-two people. Citizens were so eager to be vaccinated that there was no need to consider compulsion.

Montreal suffered only one death from smallpox after 1918. In the 1930s smallpox practically disappeared from most European countries and from Canada. No Canadian cases were reported in 1944. Because of re-infections from Mexico, the United States was not able to stop the disease until 1951.

❍   ❍   ❍

Honoré Beaugrand declined to stand for a third term as mayor of Montreal in 1887, saying that his health was too precarious. In 1890 he was defeated as a candidate for the Quebec legislature. He sold his newspaper, *La Patrie*, in 1897 to enter semi-retirement at age forty-nine. A restless traveller and productive man of letters, Beaugrand published several books of essays, and developed a particular interest in Quebec folklore, including goblin tales. He was never a good Catholic. He was said to have made his peace with the Church during his final illness in 1906, but by then he was addicted to morphine and may not have been rational. In his will he directed that his body be cremated, a practice abhorrent to the Church. After "les funérailles de feu," Beaugrand's ashes were refused Catholic burial. So they were interred in Mount Royal Cemetery.

The leading anti-vaccinationists played no more role in public life. J.E. Coderre died in 1888, the same year that Alexander Milton Ross moved to Toronto. Ross billed himself as the "Medical Director" of the Toronto Anti-Compulsory Vaccination League, but aside from a squabble when Upper Canada College refused to allow his unvaccinated son to register, Ross seems to have subsided. He published his self-promoting *Memoirs of a Reformer* in 1892 and died in Detroit in 1897.

Many Montrealers urged Henry Gray to stand for mayor to succeed Beaugrand. But he pleaded the needs of his business and left city politics. For the rest of his life he was a governor of the Montreal General Hospital and Notre Dame Hospital, as well as a member of Quebec's Provincial Board of Health. As he had predicted, he died in the adopted city he had done his best to serve, in 1908. Dr. Hingston continued to be honoured for his scholarship and public services by scientific bodies, medical associations, and governments. In 1895 he was knighted by Queen Victoria and in 1896 appointed to the Senate of Canada. Senator Sir William Hales Hingston died in 1907, his role in Montreal's smallpox epidemic long forgotten or obscured.

Hugh Graham stayed out of politics and continued to build the circulation of the Montreal *Star*. By 1891 it had become the largest and one of the richest newspapers in Canada, specializing in being close to the people and supporting good causes. Graham became a major Canadian philanthropist, particularly interested in good government and public health. At one time he offered a $100,000 prize to the first college graduate who could produce a medicinal cure for cancer. There were many claimants, no cures. In 1917 Graham was given one of the last hereditary titles awarded to a Canadian, becoming Baron Atholstan. He died in 1937 at age ninety-five. Because he had no male heirs the title lapsed. In 1979 the *Star* realized it was beaten by the *Gazette* in competition for the loyalty of Montreal's shrinking English community, and went out of business.

The Roman Catholic Church in Quebec also flourished through the first half of the century. In the 1960s it began to suffer drastically from a crisis of unbelief which shows no sign of diminishing. Bishop Bourget still lies in his tomb in his Montreal temple, now named Mary Mother of the World Cathedral, surrounded by the remains of other Quebec prelates. The mortuary chapel was locked the day we visited the church.

Anglophones gradually lost much of their power and position in Montreal and Quebec, but the ghost of Louis Riel still haunts Canadian politics, as does the state of French-English relations in the country as a whole. As the last chapter of this book was being written in the summer of 1990 the people of the constituency of Laurier-St. Marie, which covers most of what was the East End of Montreal in 1885, voted in a by-election to elect an avowed Quebec separatist to Canada's House of Commons. No one knew how long Canada would remain intact as a nation. By the same token, Québecois were uneasy about their nationality's ability to survive as a small minority, now with a very low birth rate, in North America.

Former constable Louis Cyr was proclaimed the world's champion weight-lifter after winning a competition in Quebec City in the spring of 1886. He embarked on a two-year world's tour, winning global fame as the strongest man in the world. Later he was billed as the strongest man who ever lived, and in the 1890s he sometimes toured with Barnum's circus. Between tours he kept a tavern on Notre Dame Street in Montreal. Cyr died of Bright's disease in 1912 at age forty-nine. His funeral was one of the largest in the city's history.

Spectacular winter carnivals were held in Montreal in 1887 and

1889. But they were expensive, difficult to organize, and seemed to produce diminishing returns. The city's winter carnival tradition ended in 1889. Quebec City revived the idea in 1954, and still holds an annual festival of ice sculpture, happy snowmen, and boozy conviviality.

◦   ◦   ◦

By the early 1950s smallpox had been eliminated in Europe, the Soviet Union, and North America. It had become a Third World disease, still plaguing millions in Africa, South America, and Asia, still occasionally exported by travellers to the West. In 1958 the Soviet Union proposed that the World Health Organization organize a campaign to eradicate smallpox through mass vaccination.

The idea was officially adopted at the World Health Assembly of 1959, but with little enthusiasm about its feasibility. Earlier campaigns to eradicate yellow fever and hookworm had failed, and a well-publicized, massive attempt to rid the world of malaria was beginning to founder. Experts now doubted the practicality of this grandiose public health utopianism, seeing it as a naive carry-over of nineteenth-century optimism. "Even if genuine eradication of a pathogen ... on a worldwide scale were theoretically and practically possible," the distinguished French microbiologist René Dubos wrote in 1965, "the enormous effort required for reaching the goal would probably make the attempt economically and humanly unwise.

> Social considerations, in fact, make it probably useless to discuss the theoretical flaws and technical difficulties of eradication programs.... Certain unpleasant but universal human traits will put impassable stumbling blocks on the road to eradication. For example, it is easy to write laws for compulsory vaccination against smallpox, but in most parts of the world people would much rather buy the vaccination certificate than take the vaccine.... Public health administrators, like social planners, have to compromise with the limitations of human nature.

More or less to their surprise, the WHO administrators found that their poorly funded, erratic, and incomplete campaign, building on an ever-increasing base of national vaccination programs, was helping to drive smallpox out of more countries every year. Technological improvements in vaccine production and vaccinating devices were encouraging. In 1966 the WHO decided to increase its commitment and launched its Intensified Smallpox Eradication Program.

By then smallpox was becoming an evil memory in rich countries like Canada. The last case of smallpox in the Dominion appeared in 1962 when a fourteen-year-old Brazilian boy entered Toronto by train from New York just as he was becoming sick. He was isolated until he had completely recovered, all his contacts were vaccinated and watched, nobody else broke out with smallpox. During the 1960s anti-vaccinationist ideas had a respectable resurgence. Except for those travelling to infected countries, the risk of side effects from vaccination was now greater than its benefits in smallpox-free countries. The routine vaccination of children came to an end in North America and Europe. This author's oldest child, like his parents, bears a vaccination scar. The younger two do not.

As they zeroed in on the last fortresses of smallpox, in Africa and on the Indian subcontinent, the WHO campaigners realized that mass vaccination was neither sufficient nor necessary to stamp out the virus. They relearned some of the nineteenth century's lessons about the virtues of surveillance, isolation, and rigorous containment. Instead of trying to fireproof all combustibles, the strategy was to put out all the sparks. The obstacles to the effort included apathy, ignorance about smallpox (by ordinary people, governments, doctors, and the WHO itself), and appalling natural and man-made conditions. By the 1970s smallpox control was being attempted in famine- and war-ravaged jungles and desert villages in the far corners of the planet.

In sagas of authentically uplifting drama, which were the greatest, most satisfying events of their lives for many of the people involved, the WHO's smallpox fighters tracked down, cornered, and stamped out the disease village by village, province by province, country by country. National legislation supporting their efforts usually went unenforced or turned out to be counter-productive. As in the Montreal story, compulsion was useful only in limited situations at the end of the struggle and when all else failed. People not far from stone-age cultures would normally volunteer to be vaccinated at mass assemblies where there was, as the official history of the campaign puts it, a "carnival type of atmosphere."

Smallpox was driven from South America in 1970, Indonesia in 1972, India and Bangladesh in 1975. Its last hideout was in Ethiopia's Ogaden desert, one of the world's most godforsaken places, now made even less accessible by perpetual civil war. WHO workers in the region endured kidnappings, the destruction of trucks and helicopters, and the indifference or hostility of governments trying to grapple with problems much worse than smallpox. By the summer of 1976 the teams had contained the last Ethiopian outbreak. For seven weeks no cases of smallpox were reported anywhere in the world. The war seemed to have been won.

An epidemic suddenly flared up in Somalia, which had been supporting guerilla war against Ethiopia in the Ogaden and whose authorities had lied in claiming their country was smallpox-free. When the Somalis were finally persuaded to cooperate, the last battle commenced. On October 12, 1977, a vehicle containing two smallpox patients from a nomad's camp stopped at the hospital in the city of Merca, Somalia, to ask the way to the isolation hospital. Ali Maow Maalin, a twenty-three-year-old hospital worker, volunteered to show them the way. On October 22 he became sick, and eight days later was diagnosed as having smallpox. Here is the official history of what followed:

> The hospital was immediately closed to new admissions, all patients were vaccinated and quarantined at the hospital, all health staff were vaccinated, warning signs were placed around the compound, and a 24-hour police guard was posted. Vaccination teams, consisting of 2 smallpox eradication staff, a policeman and a local political leader, listed by name and vaccinated everyone in the 50 houses surrounding Mr. Maalin's home and later in the 792 houses comprising the ward in which he lived. Teams then undertook a search of the entire town each week during the succeeding 6 weeks. With police

assistance, a check-point was established on the road into Merca and 3 check-points were set up on footpaths also leading into it so that all persons leaving or entering the town could be stopped and vaccinated. In all 54,777 persons were vaccinated during the 2-week period from 31 October to 4 November. Meanwhile, meetings were held throughout Merca to inform the general public of the outbreak and to stress the need to report cases with rash and fever. The reward of 200 Somali shillings for reporting a case was widely publicized.

Ali Maalin recovered from his mild case of smallpox. No new cases were found. His was the last natural occurrence of smallpox in history. Except for supplies maintained in research laboratories, the virus had been destroyed.

Ten months later, Mrs. Janet Parker, a forty-year-old medical photographer in the anatomy department of the faculty of medicine at the University of Birmingham, England, became ill with fever, headache, and muscular pains. Then she developed a rash. On September 11, 1978, she died of smallpox, a case of variola major. Janet Parker had worked near a laboratory in which smallpox virus was being studied. Investigators concluded that she had been infected with that virus, either by contact with a laboratory worker or through the ventilation system. Mrs. Parker's seventy-year-old mother also developed a mild case of smallpox, from which she recovered. The accidental release of the virus took a second life when the director of the laboratory, Professor Henry S. Bedson, committed suicide.

After intense scrutiny, the World Health Organization announced the global eradication of smallpox on December 9, 1979. During the 1980s nations stopped requiring the vaccination of travellers. In 1988 the WHO published *Smallpox and Its Eradiction*, a 1,460-page obituary of the disease and official history of the campaign that destroyed it. This is a unique book in the history of disease in being written almost entirely in the past tense. Oddly, its historical section neglects to mention the Montreal epidemic of 1885.

Bubonic plague, cholera, yellow fever, malaria, and all of history's other pestilences are still with us. Smallpox was destroyed so easily because there were no animal reservoirs, because it could not survive without constant human fuel, because in the 175 years since Edward Jenner's great discovery physicians and public health workers had learned to conquer it with vaccination and containment, and because fear, ignorance, and fatalism had been overcome.

During the 1980s most laboratory stocks of variola virus were destroyed. The last two supplies, in Atlanta, Georgia, and in Moscow, were kept in the most secure conditions. Some people questioned the wisdom, even the morality, of deliberately extinguishing the last strains of a life form; others questioned the wisdom and morality of allowing the smallpox virus to survive. In 1990 Dr. Donald A. Henderson, who had served as chief of the Smallpox Eradication unit in the WHO, told me that he expected the virus to be annihilated after further research on its genetic structure. The destruction was scheduled for 1993.

Novelists take note. There is one last possibility of smallpox recurring. The virus might still exist in the bodies of people who died of smallpox and were buried in graves hacked out of permafrost. Despite its winters, Montreal is many hundreds of miles south of the permafrost line, and there is no danger there. But smallpox may live in suspended animation in frozen corpses in the Arctic. If the disease survives at all, it is entombed by ice in the clean silence of the north.

Otherwise the story is over. Millions of us have our vaccination scars, and thousands still live with the marks of the plague. These too will pass. For smallpox, history has come to an end.

APPENDIX

THE DEATH COUNT

The most authoritative estimates of Montreal's population in 1885 and its mortality during the epidemic seem to be those in the Health Committee's annual publication, *Report of the Sanitary State of the City of Montreal for the Year 1885*. This report does not estimate the suburban death toll, and therefore the weekly figures below do not agree with those in the text, which are taken from press reports that sometimes count the near suburbs and other times do not. As well, there are minor discrepancies in the board's own totals. Ward-by-ward figures, as well as other breakdowns of mortality in the city may also be consulted in the *Report*. The gender breakdown is taken from the Montreal Mortuary Returns for 1885, published in the Canadian House of Commons, *Sessional Papers, 1886* (No. 10). This return also contains lower estimates of Montreal's population in 1885 (157,000) and a slightly higher smallpox death count (3193).

I have not been able to locate any precise record of smallpox deaths in the suburbs and other Quebec municipalities. The figure of 2,605 Quebec deaths outside of Montreal, taken from an unpublished report, is found in the Quebec *Sessional Papers, 1898*, "Fourth Annual Report of the Board of Health of the Province of Quebec", p. 35n. Given the state of record-keeping in the 1880s, as well as the fear of smallpox, it is evident that no one will ever know how many people were killed in the epidemic.

Population

Total:	167,501
French Canadians:	93,641
Other Catholics:	29,627
Protestants:	44,233

I. Smallpox Deaths by Weeks (City Only)

Week of:

April 4:	2	July 4:	14	October 3:	283
April 11:	1	July 11:	10	October 10:	280
April 18:	0	July 18:	12	October 17:	303
April 25:	3	July 25:	10	October 24:	253
				October 31:	274
May 2:	3	August 1:	9	November 7:	239
May 9:	1	August 8:	36	November 14:	175
May 16:	1	August 15:	42	November 21:	142
May 23:	3	August 22:	56	November 28:	77
May 30:	2	August 29:	96		
June 6:	0	September 5:	102	December 5:	61
June 13:	9	September 12:	128	December 12:	66
June 20:	1	September 19:	184	December 19:	20
June 27:	3	September 26:	245	December 26:	18

Apr–July:	**75**
Aug–Nov:	**292**
Dec:	**165**
1886:	**70**
Total:	**3234**

II. Smallpox Deaths by Age, Religion

Age	French-Cdns.	Other Catholics	Protestants	Totals
Under 6 mos	191	13	6	210
6 mos to 1 yr	298	13	10	321
1 to 5 yrs	1417	68	20	1505
5 to 10 yrs	641	26	14	681
10 to 15 yrs	112	5	4	121
15 to 20 yrs	73	14	11	98
20 to 30 yrs	104	28	19	151
30 to 40 yrs	27	4	5	36
40 to 50 yrs	13	4	5	22
60 and over	5	0	1	6
Unknown	3	3	0	6
Totals	2884	178	95	3157

III. Smallpox Deaths By Gender

Male: 1662
Female: 1511

ENDNOTES

The sources of most facts and quotations are evident from the text. While the minutes of City Council and its committees may be consulted in the City of Montreal Archives, these were often simply clipped from newspaper accounts. The four English-language dailies, the *Gazette*, *Star*, *Herald*, and *Witness*, gave their readers the most detailed coverage of civic events. Reporters appear to have been trained to take shorthand, which helps to explain their frequent use of dialogue. Unless indicated in the text or below, material is drawn from the English newspapers, usually in the above order, on or about the dates mentioned. Any errors or confusions in the identification of sources should be drawn to my attention at the University of Toronto.

Foreword

p 27   "DES COCK-TAIL": *Journal d'Hygiène Populaire*, I, 17, 15 janvier 1885, p. 207.

p 28   LONGLEY, SHATTUCK, ROBICHAUD CASES: See Longley above.

p 29n   WOMAN AND PULLMAN: *Star*, Sept. 10; *Gazette*, May 29

p 36   HOTEL-DIEU MEASURES: See Longley above.

p 37   TERRIBLE MISTAKE: See *Canada Medical Record*, Jan. 1886, p. 383: "Had the management of the Hospital put their heads together to determine in what way they could most expeditiously and most thoroughly spread variola throughout this city, they could hardly have hit upon a more effective plan."

Chapter Three: Two Wars

p 39   SMALLPOX HISTORY: See Dixon, Hopkins, Fenner.

p 42   "INDIAN PLAGUE": Abbott, p. 61.

p 43   BLACK ROBES INFECTED: Hopkins, p. 236.

p 43   "BURNING FEVER": Heagerty

p 43   "LOVE AND SMALLPOX": Hopkins, 32.

p 43   Lincoln: Hopkins, 277-81.

p 43   ROYALTY: Hopkins, esp. 71-2 for death of Louis XV, quoting Cabanes, *The Secret Cabinet of History*, Paris, 1897.

p 44   SIXTY MILLION: Darmon, 56.

p 44   "BUYING THE POX"; INOCULATION: Miller.

p 45   MATHER: Hopkins, p. 250.

p 45   HISTORIANS DISAGREE: See Baxby, Razzell, and Fenner.

p 45   PLAGUE SYPHILLIS: Darmon, p. 13.

p 46   VOLTAIRE: Quoted in Hopkins, p. 51.

p 47   JEFFERSON: Quoted in Chase, p. 60.

p 47   "VACCINOFF": Darmon, p. 186.

p 47   CLINCH: See Heagerty, 84-5; also Roberts.

p 47   POPE: Hopkins, p. 83.

p 48   FIVE NATIONS: Heagerty, 49.

p 48n   COWPOX VIRUS LOST: Fenner, p. 278.

p 49   THROWING CHILDREN: Hopkins, p. 87.

p 50   500,000 ESTIMATE: Hopkins.

p 50   1870s DEATHS, MONTREAL: *Rapport de L'Etat Sanitaire, 1883*, p. 19.

p 50   INOCULATION & VACCINATION IN QUEBEC: See the articles by Tunis. The history of vaccination in Quebec needs much more study. In "De la Repugnance A La Vaccine Dans La Ville de Montréal, *Journal D'Hygiène Populaire*, II, 12, 1 novembre 1885,

Dr. L. Dagon-Richer argued that vaccination had been widely accepted in Montreal until the anti-vaccinationists began their agitation in the late 1860s.

p 51   FIGHTING SMALLPOX, 1870s: See the annual Board of Health reports on the Sanitary State of Montreal.

p 52   ONTARIO EPIDEMIC. See Ontario: "Special Report on the Hungerford Outbreak"; and Craig, "State Medicine ...".

p 54   "MOUNTAINS OF ASHES": *Herald*, April 16.

p 55   RADFORD REPORT: Health Committee, April 18.

p 57   BESSEY, "GOOD LYMPH": *Gazette*, May 7.

p 58   "NOUVEAU FLEAU": *Le Monde, L'Etendard*, 5 mai.

p 58   ASILE BETHLEHEM: *La Patrie*, 13 mai.

p 58   FAFARD, NO CONFIDENCE: *JHP*, II, 1, 15 mai.

p 58   LAROCQUE SICKNESS: *Witness*, October 21.

p 58   HINGSTON RECOMMENDATIONS: *Gazette*, May 13.

p 59   ROSS BIOGRAPHY: See A.M. Ross, *Memoirs of a Reformer*; quotes from pp 119, 143; see also Ross entry in *DCB* v. XII.

p 61   NORTH-WEST CASUALTIES. Estimate by Professor Desmond Morton, personal communication.

p 65   "ASSEZ CURIEUSE": *La Presse*, 23 mai.

p 65   ROSS LETTER: *Herald*, May 23.

Chapter Four: **Smallpox en Fête**

p 68   BOURGET BIOGRAPHY: See *DCB*, vol XI.

p 69   "DEVOTIONAL REVOLUTION": See Danylewycz, ch. 1; also Savard.

p 72   SIGHT RESTORED: reprinted in *L'Evenement*, 26 juin.

p 73   FORCIBLE VACCINATION: *Gazette*, June 23.

p 74   AUCLAIRE ASSIGNMENT: *Star*, Aug. 15; disaffection with hospital, *Star*, Sept. 7.

p 75   HOME REMEDIES: *La Minerve*, June 10; *Gazette*, June 8; *Herald*, June 16.

p 75   ROSS LETTER: *Herald*, June 10.

p 80   CODERRE BIOG: See *DCB*, v. XI, "Emery-Coderre"; his views on vaccination were expressed in many articles and letters in *L'Union Médicale du Canada* in the 1870s.

p 81   CODERRE LETTERS: *Le Monde*, 20, 25 juin.

p 82   DISTRUSTFUL FRENCH-CANADIAN DOCTORS: *Star*, Aug. 15.

p 83   "JE N'AI PAS PEUR": *La Presse*, 1 juillet.

p 85   TOSSING SKULLS: *Gazette*, July 7.

p 87   ERUPTIVE FEVERS: *Gazette*, July 10.
p 87   COOK'S TOURS: *Gazette*, July 8.
p 88   LAPRAIRIE BOAT: *Witness*, July 11; *Gazette*, July 14.
p 89   MISS O'CONNOR: *Witness*, July 30.
p 89   LABERGE DESPOTISM: *Witness*, July 15.
p 90   DESEVE INCIDENT: *Star*, Aug. 3.
p 91   CHANG POPULARITY: *Herald*, Aug. 1, 3.
p 91   RIEL JOKE: *La Minerve*, 13 août.
p 92   "TRAMPS AND LOAFERS": *Herald*, July 21.
p 92   REVIEW FIASCO: *Gazette, Herald*, July 27.
p 94   AYER'S AD: *L'Etendard*, 14 août.
p 94   "TEMPERATE ... LIVES". *Star*, Aug. 11.
p 94   *WITNESS* INTERVIEW: Aug. 13.
p 95   ROBERTSON/GRAY: *Witness*, Aug. 15.

Chapter Five: **"A State of Plague"**

p 102   "PEOPLE'S JOURNALISM": See Rutherford.
p 105   ROSS DISTRIBUTION: Ross Scrapbooks, vol 2.
p 107   HINCKS' ... SERVANT: *Gazette*, Aug. 26.
p 107   TORONTO ALARM: *Star*, Aug. 17; *Gazette*, Aug. 21.
p 112   "CITIZENS WALK": *Gazette*, Aug. 23.
p 113   FRENCH PAPERS, CHARACTERISTICS: See Rutherford, and De Bonville, *La Presse Québecoise.*
p 113   *LA MINERVE*: Aug. 24.
p 113   *LE MONDE*: Aug. 22, 25.
p 114   "ON REGISTERING FROM MONTREAL": *Gazette*, Sept. 3.
p 114   U.S. MARINE HOSPITAL SERVICE: Michigan, *Thirteenth Annual Report ... Board of Health*, pp 196ff.
p 115   BUFFALO BILL: *Ibid.*, p. 205.
p 116   *LA MINERVE*: Aug. 29.
p 116   *LA PRESSE*: Aug. 31.
p 117   "CARNIVAL OF DEATH": *Star*, Sept. 2.
p 117   VACCINATION TO REASSURE: *Witness*, Sept. 3.
p 118   NEW HAMPSHIRE LETTER: quoted in Michigan, ... *Board of Health*, p. 200.
p 118   *GAZETTE* FLIP-FLOP: Sept. 1.
p 118   "CITIZEN" LETTER: *Star*, Aug. 31.
p 120   "SMALLPOX AIR": *Gazette*, Sept. 2.
p 120   "YOU'VE GOT IT": *Star*, Sept. 7.

p 120   DEFOE QUOTE: *A Journal* ..., p. 167.
p 121   RUBBING PUSTULES: *Gazette*, Sept. 4.
p 121   GRAY TO MASSON: Quebec Legislative Assembly, *Sessional Papers*, 1886, No. 40 (unpublished), Gray to Masson, Aug 31.
P 121   *LA PRESSE, LA PATRIE*: 2 septembre.
p 122   *GAZETTE*: September 3.
p 125   CODERRE UNDERCUT: *Le Monde*, 3 septembre.
p 125   STEALING FRUIT: *Le Monde*, 11 septembre.
p 128   "DAYLIGHT THROUGH THE BUSH": *Star*, Sept. 5.

Chapter Six: **The Wages of Sin**

p 133   TUKE REPORT: See Francis; on Trudel, see Garon.
p 134   *NEWS* CAMPAIGN: See Rutherford.
p 134   *NEWS* EDITORIAL: April 20.
p 135   FUMIGATED VERSES: *Grip*, Sept. 12.
p 136   FRENCH COMMENT: *La Patrie*, 8 sept.; *La Presse*, 8 sept.; *Le Monde*, 4 sept.; *La Patrie*, 4 sept.; *L'Etendard*, 8 sept.
p 137   GENOCIDE, GERM WARFARE: *La Patrie, L'Etendard*, 5 sept.
p 138   "RACE SUPERIEURE": *La Minerve*, 7 sept.
p 138   "ORDURES ... BEAVER HALL": *La Presse*, 3 sept.
p 138   "YOU NOT ONLY WISHED ..." : *L'Etendard*, 8 sept.
p 138   *WITNESS*: Sept. 5.
p 139   *NEW YORK TIMES*: Sept. 15, 25, 30.
p 139   SENTENNE ARGUMENTS: *Star*, Sept. 7.
p 140   "NOBODY IS MORE TO BLAME": *Star*, Sept. 9.
p 142   ONTARIO ACTIONS: Ontario, Provincial Board, "Annual Report", 1885; Craig articles; Michigan ... *Board of Health*.
p 143   VOLUNTARY VACCINATION: *Star*, Sept. 14.
p 145   VACCINATING MATHIEU: *Star*, Sept. 17.
p 146   "CASES HIDDEN": Gray to Wendell Anderson, Sept. 19. NAC, MG10, series A1, reel M617.
p 147   CING MARS GOOD NERVE: *Gazette*, Nov. 19.
p 147   CATHOLIC SCHOOLS, *Star*, Sept. 14.

Chapter Seven: **Heart of Darkness**

p 149 ST. ROCH'S HOSPITAL, CONDITIONS: *Witness*, Oct 27, 28, 29, 30, Nov 2; *Herald*, Oct 8, 29.
p 153   "TEN TIMES WORSE": *Witness*, Sept. 21.

p 154   OUTREMENT HORROR: *Witness, Star, Gazette*, Sept. 22.
p 155   HOSPITAL IN A BALLOON: *Gazette*, Sept. 29.
p 156   CODERRE LETTER: *Le Monde*, 23 sept.
p 158n LECLAIRE QUOTE: *Star*, Sept. 23.

Chapter Eight: **East End Rebellion**

p 161   CYR BGD: *Gazette*, April 24; *Witness*, Sept. 22; Wise and Fisher, p 140-42.
p 163   "GIVE THEM REVOLVERS": *Witness*, Sept. 24.
p 163   "C'EST DU CIRQUE": *La Patrie*, 24 sept.
p 168   "YOU LOAFERS ...": *Star*, Sept. 29.
p 173   CHAMPAGNE ASSAULT: *Star*, Oct 2; *Witness*, Sept. 30.
p 173   WOMAN AND BABY: *La Presse*, 29 sept.
p 174   "HURRAH FOR THE FRENCH-CANADIANS": *Witness*, Sept. 29.
p 174   "A NUMBER OF MEN", *Ibid*.
p 177   65TH AND SMALLPOX: *La Presse*, 6 oct.
p 180   COMMUNIST INTERVIEW: *Witness*, Oct. 2.
p 180   ROSS, ANTI-VACCINATORS: Ross Scrapbooks, vol. 2.
p 182   "SPIRIT OF EVIL": *Star*, Oct. 3.
p 182   "A BAS ... BEAUGRAND": New York *World*, Oct. 5.

Chapter Nine: **Carnival of Death**

p 189   BEADLE AND VACCINATION. See *Star*, Aug. 15.
p 190   SENTENNE & CROWDS: *Star*, Oct. 1.
p 190   "RIEL ... IMMUNITES". *Le Monde*, 1 octobre.
p 192   AMOS SERMON: Star, Oct 5.
p 192   WELL-KEPT SABBATH: Star, Oct. 2.
p 193   FABRE & CURÉ: Fabre Corres., Fabre to J. Salmons, 6 nov. 1885.
p 194   BOURGET ON VACCINATION: See Coderre letter, *Journale D'Hygiène Populaire*, II, 14, 1 déc., pp. 162-3.
p 194   PARADING REMAINS: New York *Times*, Sept. 25.
p 195   INSPECTION INCIDENT: *Herald*, Oct. 12.
p 195   INSPECTION SYSTEMS AND DETAILS: Ontario *Sessional Papers*, 1886, N. 74, various reports, including the report of the Medical Inspectors on Trains, of Special Incidents Connected with their Work; U.S. Surgeon-General Report, 1886; Maine report, 1886; Michigan report, 1885; Craig.
p 198   CAP ST. IGNACE: *Herald*, Oct. 30.

p 198   MONTOBELLO: *Gazette*, Nov. 20; *Witness, Star*, Nov. 18.
p 199   "IF PEOPLE MUST DIE OF SMALLPOX": *Gazette*, Jan. 27, 1886.
p 199   CAUGHNAWAGHA: *Gazette*, Dec. 11, 14.
p 200   "CRUEL SPECTACLE": Maine Report, p. 58.
p 200   CHARLOTTETOWN EPIDEMIC: Charlottetown, *Annual Reports* (Board of Health), 1886; Baldwin.
p 201   CIGAR AD: *Gazette*, Oct. 21.
p 202   HELBRONNER, *La Presse*, 3 oct.
p 203   SCOTS-PHYSICIAN: *Gazette*, Nov. 9.
p 203   VAN HORNE: *Gazette*, Nov. 6.
p 205   ADIRONDACK MURRAY: New York *World*, Nov. 5.
p 205   JOE BEEF. See *Montreal by Gaslight; Herald*, Jan. 11, 1886.

Chapter Ten: **God's Judgments**

p 208   "FRENCH-CANADIAN PIETY": New York *Times*, Sept. 16.
p 208   "CARNAL VACCINATION": *Ibid.*, Sept. 15.
p 208   "WILDEST FREAKS": *Ibid.*, Sept. 30.
p 208   *NEWS* FULMINATIONS: Sept. 30.
p 209   OVERHEARD ON TRAIN: NY *Tribune*, reprinted in *Gazette*, Oct 1.
p 209   *WORLD* REPORTER: New York *World*, Oct 5; reprinted in *Herald*, Oct 6, 8.
p 210   ANTI-VACCINATION SENTIMENTS: See Darmon, Bator, Fraser, Huerkamp, Kaufman, Leavitt, Macleod arts., Porter, D.&R., "Politics of Prevention".
p 212   ROSS CORRESPONDENCE. Ross Scrapbooks, vol. 1.
p 214   "POULES", "CHATS", *Journal d'Hygiène Populaire*, 15 sept., p. 99-101.
p 215   REMEDIES: *La Presse*, 8 sept, 27 aout; *Le Monde*, 7 sept; *Star*, September 12.
p 216   ROSS ON TRAIN: *Herald*, Nov. 28; see papers Oct 14, affadavits and Ross's arguments, *Herald*, Nov. 27, 28; anti-Ross poems are in the *Herald* Oct 14, 20. also various papers Oct 13-14, 17, 19, 21. Ross scrapbooks, *The Anti-Vaccinator*, Oct. 1886 for the enlarged, revised version of Ross's poem, "History of a Crime".
p 220   "MEANT TO KEEP THEM": *Gazette*, Oct. 13.
p 221   DAOUST AFFAIR: *Witness*, Oct. 21.
p 222   *L'AMI DU PEUPLE*: Mentioned in Frith.
P 224   *L'ETENDARD*: Oct 24, 25; See also *La Minerve*, Oct 29.
p 224   FABRE: *Witness*, Oct. 22.
p 225   HINGSTON: *Herald*, Oct. 21.

Chapter Eleven: **The Month of the Dead**

p 227   OCT. 27 REMOVALS: *Witness*

p 228   CLOUTIER: *Herald*, Oct. 29.

p 229   LACK OF ODOURS: *Star*, Oct. 27.

p 230   DOCTORS NO HELP: *Gazette*, Oct. 14.

p 231   "WORDS UTTERLY FAIL": *Witness*, Nov. 4.

p 234   GAGNON AFFAIR: *Witness*, *Star*, Nov. 4.

Chapter Twelve: **And Winter Came**

p 248   HEALTH COURT POLICIES: *Report on the Sanitary State ... 1885.*

p 248   McNEECE: *Witness*, Nov. 14.

p 248   CODERRE CHARGED: *Gazette*, Nov. 25-26.

p 249   DUQUETTE: *Gazette*, Dec. 22.

p 250   RIEL ROPE: *Star*, Dec. 17.

p 250   "DEATH IN THE POT": *Herald*, Dec. 12.

p 254   *CANADA MEDICAL RECORD*: Nov. 85, p. 335.

Epilogue

p 259   POPULATION AND DEATHS: See Appendix.

p 260   COSTS: Reports on the Sanitary State ... 1885, 1886.

p 261   "NEGLIGENCE ABSOLUTELY CRIMINAL": Osler, *Principles and Practice*, p. 47.

p 262   "PICOTTE PARTY": *Star*, Feb. 27.

p 262   "LET US NOT FORGET". *Star*, Feb. 25.

p 262   "DIE IN NO BETTER PLACE": *Star*, Feb. 27.

p 263   ANTI-VACCINATION LEAGUE: *Star*, Dec. 29.

p 263   "EXTINCTION BY FIRE": *Report on the Sanitary State ...*, 1886, p 26.

p 263   DISTASTE FOR VACCCINATION: *Report of the Board of Health of the Province of Quebec*, 1895, p. 28: "Since the small-pox epidemic of 1885-86 vaccination has been, in general, but little practiced in the Province, unless perhaps during the slight epidemic of 1891, when in the infected localities and adjacent ones a slightly more pronounced movement was made in favor of vaccination. Outside of the few towns where the charter allows compulsory vaccination, very little is done. The population is still, as a rule, indifferent to this practice. It is only when small-pox ravages close at hand that it is had recourse to.

The reason of this apathy is that the population is not as yet sufficiently convinced of the protection which vaccination affords against small-pox and it is still slightly prejudiced against it on account of the campaign made against the practice by certain anti-vaccinators, perhaps, also, on account of the few bad results which followed vaccination during the epidemic of 1885-86, results due to insufficiently controlled vaccine, chosen with too little care of employed in a manner but little in conformity with the prescriptions of hygiene." See also Bator.

p 265   VARIOLA MINOR: See Fenner, p. 39-40.

p 265   CANADIAN CASES: *Ibid.*, p. 328.

p 265   WINDSOR OUTBREAK: Heagerty, vol I, p. 95.

p 265   MONTREAL LAST CASE: Copp, "Public Health."

p 266   BEAUGRAND: See Bance.

p 266   ROSS: Ross scrapbooks, *DCB*

p 266   GRAY & HINGSTON. See Atherton.

p 268   WHO ERADICATION CAMPAIGN: Fenner

p 268   DUBOS QUOTE: *Ibid.*, p. 388.

p 269   LAST CANADIAN CASE. See McLean, *et al.*

p 270   "CARNIVAL TYPE OF ATMOSPHERE": Fenner, 488.

p 270   MERCA OUTBREAK, *Ibid.*, 1062-3.

p 271   PARKER CASES: *Ibid.*

SOURCES

PRIMARY

i. Newspapers and Journals

Canada Medical Record
Canadian Medical and
  Surgical Journal
L'Etendard
L'Evenement (Quebec City)
The Gazette
Grip (Toronto)
Journal d'Hygiène Populaire
La Minerve

Le Monde
The Montreal Daily Witness
The Montreal Herald
The Montreal Star
New York Times
New York Daily World
La Patrie
La Presse
L'Union Médicale du Canada

ii. Manuscript

National Archives of Canada. Documents relating to the Recent Outbreak of Smallpox in Montreal. RG 6, vol. 60. Canada, Secretary of State Department.

Fabre Correspondence. Archives of the Archdiocese of Montreal.

Montreal, City Council. Minutes. City of Montreal Archives.

Montreal, City Council. Health Committee, Minutes. City of Montreal Archives.

Ross, A.M. Scrapbooks. University of Toronto Library.

United States government. Consular Reports, 1885. National Archives of Canada.

iii. Other

Bryce, Peter H. "Small-Pox in Canada, and the Methods of Dealing With it in the Different Provinces." *Proceedings of the Thirteenth Annual Meeting of the American Public Health Association* (1885): 166-181.

Canada. Abstracts of Return of Mortality Statistics. Parliament, *Sessional Papers* 1886.

Charlottetown, City. *Annual Reports.* 1886.

Dion, Ls. *Mémoire Sur La Vaccination.* Pamphlet, Québec, C. Darveau, 1887

Guyot, M. *A Brief History of the Small Pox Epidemic in Montreal, From 1871 to 1880 and the Late Outbreak of 1885.* Pamphlet, n.p., n.d., [1885 or 1886].

Hingston, W.H. *The Climate of Canada.* Montreal, 1885.

_____. *Remarks on Vaccination.* Pamphlet, Montreal, 1876.

Maine. *First Annual Report of the State Board of Health of the State of Maine.* Augusta, 1886.

Massachusetts. *Seventh Annual Report of the State Board of Health, Lunacy, and Charity of Massachusetts.* Boston, 1886.

Michigan. *Thirteenth Annual Report of the Secretary of the State Board of Health of the State of Michigan.* Lansing, 1886.

Morgan, Henry J., ed. *The Dominion Annual Register and Review,* 1884, 1885, 1886. Toronto.

Montreal. *Report of the Sanitary State of the City of Montreal.* Annual Report, Department/Board of Health, 1876-1886.

Ontario. *Ontario Sessional Papers.* Provincial Board of Health, Annual Reports, 1884-1901.

_____. "Special Report on the Hungerford Outbreak." *Ontario Sessional Papers, 1885.*

Quebec. *Annual Report of the Board of Health of the Province of Quebec.* Quebec *Sessional Papers,* 1896-1901.

United States Treasury Department, Marine Hospital Service. *Annual Report of the Supervising Surgeon-General of the Marine-Hospital Service of the United States for the Fiscal Year 1885.* Washington, 1885.

_____. *Annual Report . . . 1886.* Washington, 1886.

iv. Interview

Henderson, Dr. Donald A. August 16, 1990.

SECONDARY

Abbott, Maude E. *History of Medicine in the Province of Quebec.* Toronto: Macmillan, 1931.

Ackerknecht, E.K. "Anticontagionism between 1821 and 1867." *Bull Hist Med* 22 (1948): 562-93.

Ames, Herbert Brown. *The City Below the Hill.* Orig. pub. 1897. Reissue, Toronto: University of Toronto Press, 1972.

Ariès, Phillip. *The Hour of Our Death.* Translation of *L'Homme devant la mort,* Paris, 1977. New York, 1981.

Atherton, William H. *Montreal from 1535 to 1914.* 3 vols. Montreal, 1914.

Baldwin, Douglas O. "Smallpox Management on Prince Edward Island, 1820-1940: From neglect to fulfilment." *Canadian Bulletin of Medical History* 2 (no. 2, Winter 1985): 147-82.

_____ and Thomas Spira. *Gaslights, Epidemics and Vagabond Cows: Charlottetown in the Victorian Era.* Charlottetown: Ragweed Press, 1988.

Bance, Pierre. "Beaugrand et son temps." Ph.D. diss., University of Ottawa, 1964.

Bator, Paul A. "The Health Reformers versus the Common Canadian: The Controversy Over Compulsory Vaccination Against Smallpox in Toronto and Ontario, 1900-1920." *Ontario History* LXXV (no. 4, December, 1983): 348-73.

Baxby, Derrick. *Jenner's smallpox vaccine. The riddle of vaccinia virus and its origin.* London, 1981.

Beck, Ann, "Issues in the Anti-Vaccination Movement in England. *Medical History* 4 (October 1984): 310-21.

Behbehani, Abbas M. *The Smallpox Story in Words and Pictures.* Kansas City, 1988.

Bernier, Jacques. *La médicine au Québec: Naissance et évolution d'une profession.* Québec: Les Presses de l'Université Laval, 1989.

Bilson, Geoffrey. *A Darkened House: Cholera in Nineteenth-Century Canada.* Toronto: University of Toronto Press, 1980.

Boissonnault, Charles-Marie. "La Lutte Contre La Vaccination au XIXe Siècle." *Laval Médical* 32 (no. 2, September 1961): 178-84.

de Bonville, Jean. *Jean-Baptiste Gagnepetit: les travailleurs montréalais à la fin du Xixe siècle.* Montreal: L'Aurore, 1975.

_____. *La Presse Québécoise de 1884 à 1914: Genèse d'un média de masse.* Quebec: Les Presses de l'Université Laval, 1988.

Bradbury, Bettina. "The Family Economy and Work in an Industrialising City, Montreal, 1871." *Historical Papers.* Canadian Historical Association, 1979.

_____. "The Fragmented Family: Family Strategies in the Face of Death, Illness, and Poverty, Montreal, 1860-1885." In *Childhood and Family,* edited by Joy Parr, 109–128. Toronto: McClelland & Stewart, 1982.

_____. "Pigs, Cows, and Boarders: Non-Wage Forms of Survival among Montreal Families, 1861-91." *Labour/Le Travail* 14 (Fall 1984): 9-46.

Brown, John R., and Donald M. McLean. "Smallpox — A Retrospect." *Canadian Medical Association Journal* 87 (Oct. 6, 1962): 765-7.

Cadotte, Marcel. "Considérations médico-sociales des épidémies à Montréal au XIXe siècle." In *Montréal au XIXe Siècle: des gens, des idées, des arts, une ville,* 135-48. Leméac, 1990.

Camus, Albert. *The Plague.* Translation of *La Peste,* orig. pub. 1947. Penguin, 1948.

Chase, Alan. *Magic Shots: A Human and Scientific Account of the Long and Continuing Struggle to Eradicate Infectious Diseases by Vaccination.* New York: Morrow, 1982.

Collard, Edgar Andrew. *Montreal Yesterdays.* Toronto: Longmans, 1963.

Conrad, Joseph. *The Shadow-Line.* Orig. pub. 1917. Penguin, 1986.

Copp, Terry. *The Anatomy of Poverty: The Condition of the Working Class in Montreal 1897-1929.* Toronto: McClelland & Stewart, 1974.

_____. "Public Health in Montreal, 1870-1930." In *Medicine in Canadian Society: Historical Perspectives,* edited by S.E.D. Shortt, 395-416. McGill-Queen's University Press, 1981.

Corbin, Alain. *The Foul and the Fragrant: Odor and the French Social Imagination.* Translation of *Le miasme et la jonquille.* Harvard University Press, 1986.

Craig, Barbara L. "Smallpox in Ontario: Public and Professional Perceptions of Disease, 1884-85." In *Health Disease and Medicine, Essays in Canadian History,* edited by Charles G. Roland, 215-49. Toronto, 1982.

_____. "State Medicine in Transition: Battling Smallpox in Ontario, 1882-1885." *Ontario History* LXXV (no. 4, Dec. 1983): 319-47.

Crosby, Alfred W., Jr. "Virgin Soil Epidemics as a Factor in the Aboriginal Depopulation in America." *William & Mary Quarterly* 3 (ser. 33, April 1976): 289-99.

Cushing, Harvey. *The Life of Sir William Osler.* 2 vols. Oxford University Press, 1940.

Danylewycz, Marta. *Taking the Veil: An Alternative to Marriage, Motherhood and Spinsterhood in Quebec, 1840-1920.* Toronto: McClelland & Stewart, 1987.

Darmon, Pierre. *La Longue Traque de la Variole: Les pionniers de la médicine préventive.* Paris: Libraire Académique Perrin, 1986.

Deaux, George. *The Black Death, 1347.* London, 1967.

Dechêne, Louise, and Jean-Claude Robert, "Le choléra de 1832 dans le Bas-Canada: mesure des inégalités devant la mort." In *The Great Mortalities: Methodological Studies of Demographic Crises in the Past,* edited by Hubert Charbonneau & André Larose Liège, 229-55. 1979.

Defoe, Daniel. *A Journal of the Plague Year.* Orig. pub. 1722. Penguin, 1966.

Desjardins, Edouard. "La Grande Epidémie de 'Picote Noire.'" *L'Union Médicale du Canada* 99 (août, 1970): 1470-77.

Dixon, C.W. *Smallpox.* London: J. and A. Churchill, 1962.

Durey, Michael. *The Return of the Plague: British Society and the Cholera 1831-2.* Dublin, 1979.

Duffy, John. "School Vaccination: The Precursor to School Medical Inspection." *Journal of the History of Medicine* 33 (July 1978): 344-55.

Dufresne, Sylvie. "Le Carnaval d'hiver de Montréal, 1803-1889." *Urban History Review* XI (no. 3, Feb. 1983): 25-45.

_____. "Attractions, curiosités, carnaval d'hiver, expositions agricoles et industrielles: le loisir public à Montréal au XIXe siècle." In *Montréal au XIXe Siècle.* 233-67.

Eid, Nadia F. *Le Clerge et le pouvoir politique au Quebec. Une analyse de l'ideologie ultramontaine au milieue du xixe siécle.* Montreal: Hurtubise, 1978.

Emch-Dériaz, Antoinette. "L'inoculation justifiée . . . vraiment?" *Canadian Bulletin of Medical History* 2 (no. 2, Winter 1985): 237-264.

Evans, Richard J. *Death in Hamburg: Society and Politics in the Cholera Years 1830-1910.* Oxford: Clarendon Press, 1987.

Farley, Michael, Othmar Keel and Camille Limoges. "Les Commencements de l'Administration Montréalaise de la Santé Publique (1865-1885)." *HSTC Bulletin. Journal of History of Canadian Science, Technology and Medicine* 20 (1982): 24-46; vol. 21 (1982): 85-109.

Farley, Michael, Peter Keating and Othmar Keel. "La Vaccination à Montréal dans La Seconde Moitié du 19e Siècle: Pratiques, Obstacles et Résistances." In *Sciences et médecine au Québec: Perspectives sociohistoriques,* by M. Fournier, Y. Gingras and O. Keel, 87-119. Québec: Institut québécois de recherche sur la culture, 1987.

Federspiel, J.F. *The Ballad of Typhoid Mary.* Orig pub. Frankfurt, 1982. English ed., New York, 1985.

Fenner, F., D.A. Henderson, I. Arita, Z. Jezek and I.D. Ladnyi. *Smallpox and its Eradication.* Geneva: World Health Organization, 1988.

Firth, Donald C. "A Tale of Two Cities: Montreal and the Smallpox Epidemic of 1885." Master's thesis, University of Ottawa, 1983.

Fraser, Stuart M.F. "Leicester and Smallpox: The Leicester Method." *Medical History* 24 (1980): 315-32.

Frost, Richard H. "The Pueblo Indian Smallpox Epidemic in New Mexico, 1898-1899." *Bulletin of the History of Medicine* 64 (no. 3, Fall 1990): 417-445.

————. "American Isolation Hospitals and the Struggle Against Smallpox in the Late 19th Century." Paper delivered to the American Association for the History of Medicine, May 1991.

Garon, Louis. "Un homme politique ultramontain: François-Xavier-Anselme Trudel." In *Les Ultramontaines Canadiens Français,* edited by Nine Voisin and Jean Hamelin, 205-40. Montreal: Boréal Express, 1985.

Graham-Cumming, G. "Health of the Original Canadians, 1867-1967." *Medical Services Journal, Canada* (Feb. 1967): 115-166.

Hardy, Anne. "Smallpox in London: Factors in the Decline of the Disease in the Nineteenth Century." *Medical History:* 111-138.

Heagerty, John J. *Four Centuries of Medical History in Canada.* 2 vols. Toronto: Macmillan, 1928.

Hopkins, Donald R. *Princes and Peasants: Smallpox in History*. Chicago: University of Chicago Press, 1983.

Huerkamp, Claudia. "The History of Smallpox Vaccination in Germany: A First Step in the Medicalization of the General Public." *Journal of Contemporary History* 20 (1985): 617-35.

Kaufman, Martin. "The American Anti-Vaccinationists and Their Arguments." *Bulletin of the History of Medicine* 41 (no. 5, 1967): 463-78.

Kramer, Howard D. "The Germ Theory and the Early Public Health Program in the United States." *Bulletin of the History of Medicine* XXII (May-June 1948): 233-47.

Lalonde, Michèle. "L'épidémie de variole de 1885." In *Montréal, artisans, histoire, patrimoine*. Montreal: Fides, 1979.

Leavitt, Judith W. "Politics and Public Health: Smallpox in Milwaukee, 1894-95." *Bulletin of the History of Medicine* 50 (1976): 553-568.

Longmate, Norman. *King Cholera: The Biography of a Disease*. London: Hamish Hamilton, 1966.

MacDougall, Heather. *Activists and Advocates: Toronto's Health Department, 1883-1983*. Toronto: Dundurn Press, 1990.

_____. "'Health is Wealth': The Development of Public Health Activity in Toronto, 1834-1890." Ph.D. diss., University of Toronto, 1981.

McLean, Donald M., John R. Brown and J.S. Bell. "Smallpox in Toronto, 1962." *Canadian Medical Association Journal* 87 (Oct 6, 1962): 772-3.

Macleod, Roy M. "The Frustration of State Medicine, 1880-1899." *Medical History* (1967): 15-40.

_____. "Law, Medicine and Public Opinion: The Resistance to Compulsory Health Legislation, 1870-1907." *Public Law* (1967): 107-28; 189-211.

_____. "Medico-Legal Issues in Victorian Medical Care." *Medical History* (January 1966): 44-49.

McNeill, Wm. H. *Plagues and Peoples*. New York: Anchor, 1976.

Mann, Thomas. *Death in Venice and Seven Other Stories*. Orig. pub. 1930. Vintage, 1989.

Marsan, Jean-Claude. *Montreal in Evolution*. Translation of *Montréal en évolution*, orig. pub. 1972. Queen's-McGill University Press, 1981.

Metcalfe, Alan. "The Evolution of Organized Physical Recreation in Montreal, 1840-1895." *Histoire Social/Social History* (May 1978).

Miller, Genevieve. *The Adoption of Inoculation for Smallpox in England and France*. University of Pennsylvania Press, 1957.

Montreal by Gaslight. Montreal, 1889.

Moreau, Luc d'Iberville. *Lost Montreal*. Toronto: Oxford, 1975.

Morris, R.J. *Cholera 1832: The Social Response to an Epidemic*. London, 1976.

Nicolson, Murray W. "Peasants in an Urban Society: The Irish Catholics in Victorian Toronto." In *Gathering Place: Neighbourhoods of Toronto, 1834-1845*, edited by Robert Harney. Multicultural History Society of Ontario, 1985.

Osler, William. *The Principles and Practice of Medicine*. lst ed. New York: Appleton, 1892.

Paradis, André. "Un Bilan de L'évolution de l'intérêt des médecins Québecois pour les maladies infectieuses dans les périodiques médicaux (1826-1899)." *Révue d'Historie de l'Amérique Française* 43 (no. 1, été 1989): 63-91.

Pelling, Margaret. *Cholera, Fever and English Medicine, 1825-1865*. Oxford, 1978.

Porter, Dorothy and Roy Porter. "The Enforcement of Health: The British Debate." In *Aids: The Burden of History*, edited by Elizabeth Fee and Daniel M. Fox, 97-120. University of California Press, 1988.

_____. "The Politics of Prevention: Anti-Vaccinationism and Public Health in Nineteenth-Century England." *Medical History* (1988): 231-52.

Porter, Roy. "Plague and Panic." *New Society* (Dec 12, 1986): 7-9.

Powell, John Harvey. *Bring Out Your Dead: The Great Plague of Yellow Fever in Philadelphia in 1793*. New York: Arno Press, 1970.

Ray, Arthur, J. "Smallpox, The Epidemic of 1837-38." *The Beaver* (Autumn 1975): 8-13.

Razzell, Peter. *Edward Jenner's Cowpox Vaccine: The History of A Medical Myth*. Sussex: Caliban Books, 1977.

_____. *The Conquest of Smallpox: The Impact of Inoculation on Smallpox Mortality in Eighteenth Century Britain*. Sussex: Caliban Books, 1977.

Richardson, Ruth. *Death, Dissection and the Destitute*. London, 1988.

Risse, Guenter B. "Epidemics and History: Ecological Perspectives and Social Responses." In *Aids: The Burden of History*, edited by Elizabeth Fee and Daniel M. Fox, 33-66. University of California Press, 1988.

Robert, Jean-Claude. "The City of Wealth and Death: Urban Mortality in Montreal, 1821-1871." In *Essays in the History of Canadian Medicine*, edited by Wendy Mitchinson and Janice Dickin-McGinnis, 18-38. Toronto: McClelland & Stewart, 1988.

Roberts, K.B. "Smallpox: An Historic Disease." *Occasional Papers in Medical History*, #1. Memorial University of Newfoundland, 1978.

Rosenberg, Charles E. *The Cholera Years: The United States in 1832, 1849 and 1866*. Chicago: University of Chicago Press, 1962.

Rumilly, Robert. *Histoire de Montréal*. Tome 3. Montreal: Fides, 1972.

Rutherford, Paul. *A Victorian Authority: The Daily Press in Late Nineteenth-Century Canada*. Toronto: University of Toronto Press, 1982.

Savard, Pierre. "La Vie du Clergé Québécois Au XIXe Siécle." *Recherches Sociographiques* 8 (no. 3, sept-déc 1967): 259-72.

Shaw, Bernard. *The Doctor's Dilemma*. Orig. pub. 1906. Penguin, 1946.

Shilts, Randy. *And the Band Played On: Politics, People and the Aids Epidemic*. New York, 1987.

Smallpox and its Eradication. *See* Fenner.

Smith, F.B. *The People's Health, 1830-1910*. New York, 1979.

Sontag, Susan. *Illness as Metaphor*. New York, 1979.

Stevenson, Lloyd. "Science Down the Drain: On the Hostility of Certain Sanitarians to Animal Experimentation, Bacteriology, and Immunology." *Bulletin of the History of Medicine* 29 (1955): 1-26.

Spaulding, Wm. B. "The Ontario Vaccine Farm, 1885-1916." *Canadian Bulletin of Medical History* 6 (no. 1, Summer 1989): 45-56.

_____. "Smallpox Control in the Ontario Wilderness, 1880-1910." In *Health, Disease and Medicine: Essays in Canadian History*, edited by Charles B. Roland, 194-214. Toronto, 1982.

Temkin, Owsei. "An Historical Analysis of the Concept of Infection." In *The Double Face of Janus and Other Essays in the History of Medicine,* by Owsei Temkin, 456-71. Baltimore: John Hopkins, 1977.

Tétreault, Martin. "Les Maladies de la Misère: Aspects de la Santé Publique à Montréal 1880-1914." *Révue d'Historie de l'Amérique Française* 36 (no. 4, mars 1983): 507-526.

Thorpe, E.L.M. "The Social Histories of Smallpox and Tuberculosis in Canada (Culture, Evolution and Disease)." *Anthropology Papers*, (no. 30). Winnipeg: University of Manitoba, 1989.

Tuchman, Barbara W. *A Distant Mirror: The Calamitous 14th Century*. New York: Knopf, 1978.

Tunis, Barbara. "Inoculation for Smallpox in the Province of Quebec, a Re-appraisal." In *Health, Disease and Medicine: Essays in Canadian History*, edited by Charles G. Roland, 171-193. Hannah Institute, 1982.

_____. "Public Vaccination in Lower Canada, 1815-1823: Controversy and a Dilemma." *Historical Reflections* (1983): 265-78.

Viau, Robert. "Montréal, 1885: l'esclandre au suject des asiles d'aliénés." In *Montréal au XIXe Siécle,"* 45-64.

White, A.D. *A History of the Warfare of Science and Theology in Christendom*. Vol 2. New York, 1896.

Winslow, Charles-Edward Amory. *The Conquest of Epidemic Disease: A Chapter in the History of Ideas*. University of Wisconsin Press, 1943.

Wise, S.F. & Douglas Fisher. *Canada's Sporting Heroes*. Toronto, 1974.

Wohl, Anthony S. *Endangered Lives: Public Health in Victorian Britain*. London, 1983.

World Health Organization. *See* Fenner.

Ziegler, Philip. *The Black Death*. New York: John Day, 1969.

Zinsser, H. *Rats, Lice and History*. New York: Bantam, 1960.

INDEX

E

Eagle Hotel, 145
Early-closing movement, 84, 90, 220
Eastern Townships, 198-99
Elizabeth I, Queen, 43
Elliott, Dr. J.E., 196
Epidemics. *See* Cholera; Smallpox
Erysipelas, 58, 61, 210
Etendard, L', 16, 135-38, 164, 166, 190, 194, 224, 238, 244
Ethiopia, 270-71
Excrement, disposal of, 6-7

F

Fabre, Edouard, Bishop, 67, 73-74, 126-8, 146, 189, 192-93, 224-25, 256
Fafard, Dr. N., 58
Fairbairn, Alderman, 170
Fête-Dieu, 68, 69, 88, 143
Filiatrault, Abbé, 147-48, 190, 193, 208
Fletcher's Field, 31, 111
Floods: 1885, 55; 1886, 256, 263
France: inoculation in, 45-46; epidemics, 49; delegates in Montreal, 118
Fréchette, Louis, 16
Fumigation, 53, 196-97

G

Gagnon, Elie, and family, 228, 234-41, 248-49
Gazette: Spring outrage, 64; denies epidemic, 87; flip-flops, 118, 122; downplays coverage, 222, 231, 267
Germain, Joseph, 182
Gloucester, U.K., 264
God: responsibility of, 190-94
Graham, Hugh, 102, 116, 126, 145-46, 156, 163-64, 175, 219, 223, 230, 260; later life, 266-67
Grand Trunk Railway, 10ff, 29, 30, 87, 109, 114, 115, 138, 145, 216

Gray, Henry R.: *passim;* described, 19; spring resignation, 62, 64-65; failure, 213-14; eloquent defense, 239-240; later life, 266
Gray, James, 11
Grenier, Jacques, 62, 64, 76-77, 79, 109-10; blames "Toronto gold," 139-41, 162, 169-71, 174-75, 239, 262
Grey Nuns, 141, 146-47, 152, 165, 187, 229
Griffintown, 159, 256
Grip, 135
Grosse Isle, 20, 27

H

Hackman's Union, 9, 10, 84
Hague, George, 126
Hancock, James, 152
Hastings County, Ontario, 35, 52
Health Committee of City Council (Board of Health, Health Department), 6-8, 10; organized, 1885, 18-19; early history, 22-26; inadequacies, 105; reorganized, 144-47; assessed, 213-14
Health Court, 222, 248
Helbronner, Jules, 202
Herald: muckraking, 62-64; Pro Bono Publico letter, 119-20, 136, 138-39, 155; trashed, 172, 178; on mob rule, 179; attacks Council, 221-22; names dead, 223, 230-31; on federal intervention, 233; on Riel, 244
Higgins, William, 152
Hincks, Sir Francis, 106-8, 138, 203, 214
Hingston, William Hales: admits smallpox patient, 11-13, 18, 22, 23, 28-29, 36-37; mayoralty, 51; suspends vaccination, 58, 122-25, 141, 143, 158, 211, 225, 230; errors, 260-61; later life, 266
Hochelaga, ix, 155, 260

U

Ultramontanes, 16-18, 35-36, 69, 91, 132ff, 224, 238

United States, 45, 50; quarantine of Montreal, 114-15, 118, 120, 142-43, 194-202; end of smallpox in, 265

V

Vaccination: origin and spread, 46-49; in Quebec, 49ff; begins in Montreal, 53-54; suspended, 57-58, 73-75; resumption, 94-96, 108, 147; employers' campaign, 105-106, 108-109, 201-202; debate on compulsion, 157-58, 163-65, 169-70; explanations of resistance, 207-215; neglected afterwards, 263-64; ended, 269. *See also* Anti-vaccination

Van Horne, C. W., 203

Variola minor, 265

Variola. *See* Smallpox

Variolation. *See* Inoculation

Varioloid, 49

Vaudreuil, 88

Victoria Rifles. *See* Militia

Victoria Rink, 5, 6, 10, 84, 257

Vincent, Joe, 177

Vipond, T.S., 204

Voltaire, 46

W

Wallace, James, 152

Watters, Robert, 152

Westmount, xi

White, Richard, 145-46

White, Robert, 105-106

Whooping cough, x

Williams, Dr. E.H., 196

Wilson, Alderman, 170

Windsor Hotel, 9, 76, 103, 120, 204, 205, 229

Windsor, Ontario, 265

Witness: notices epidemic, 35; joins

crusade, 104, 138, 165; on riots, 176; interviews Communists, 180, 221; defends religion, 223; exposes St. Roch's, 230-31; wants "sanitary dictator," 233; on Riel, 244

Woodfit, George, 152

World Health Organization, 268-72

World, New York, 182, 189n, 209